The HIKING TRAILS OF NORTH GEORGIA

by
Tim Homan

PEACHTREE PUBLISHERS, LTD.

Ⓟ
PUBLISHED BY
Peachtree Publishers, Ltd.
494 Armour Circle, N.E.
Atlanta, Georgia 30324

Copyright © 1981, 1986, 1987 Tim Homan

Book design by David Russell
Illustrations by Bill Drath
Cover photo by Floyd Jillson

Revised Edition

Ninth printing (1995)

Manufactured in the United States of America

ISBN 0-931948-11-8

Library of Congress Cataloging–in–Publication
Data

Homan, Tim.
        The hiking trails of north Georgia.

        1. Hiking—Georgia—Guide-books.
2. Trails—Georgia—Guide-books. 3. Georgia—
Description and travel—1951-   —Guide-books.
I. Title.
GV199.42.G46H65   917.58   80-20946

CONTENTS

*Hemp Top: This trail leads to Big Frog Mountain and
trails in the Big Frog Wilderness.*

INTRODUCTION

Both dayhiking and backpacking have grown tremendously popular in recent years. As a result of this growing interest, more than 250 miles of trails have been added in the North Georgia region since 1975. These additional hiking opportunities have helped to ease congestion on many of the well-known, older trails. They have also increased the need for accurate, easily available information.

A simple listing of trails, especially by those who have not walked them, will not help hikers very much. They need to know exact starting and ending points, trail difficulty, distances specified one-way or round trip, hazards likely to be encountered and other facts so obviously important to the planning and enjoyment of a hike.

With these needs in mind, I have researched, walked and detailed all of the trails described in this guidebook. It is the goal of this book, then, to describe accurately the more than 438 miles of hiking trails located within its selected sphere of interest. This comprehensive guide includes 92 trails, ranging in length from the 0.1-mile Helton Creek Falls Trail to the beginning 79-mile segment of the Appalachian Trail.

Trail difficulty ranges from sidewalk-flat to long, steep stretches of physically demanding terrain, comfortably attempted only by those in good condition.

With few exceptions, the forests of North Georgia are laced with dirt roads, old logging roads and jeep trails. Footworn paths branch from them in all directions and continue for unknown distances. Countless other paths created primarily by sportsmen meander along streams and often end in a tangle of rhododendron. To avoid confusion, the word "trail" as used in this book must be defined. Trails detailed in this guide have definite starting and ending points; they are closed, where possible, to vehicular traffic; they are maintained or used often enough to be a suitable width, and their length is known. I wish I could state that all trails are clearly marked and easily followed, but unfortunately that is not the case. Unmarked turns and other problems likely to cause uncertainty, however, are noted as much as possible.

For a number of reasons — mountains, clear streams and wilderness areas among them — the scope of this book is limited to Georgia's north-ernmost 26 counties. Most of the state's longer trails are located on public land within this northern tier of counties. These trails are the most popular, the most frequently inquired about and the most scenic. They offer us beauty, knowledge and spiritual enrichment, adventure and physical challenge. And if we need it — solitude, escape.

The Rating System

Difficulty ratings are inherently subjective. The most useful rating systems are those that achieve consistency by limiting this subjectivity to a single source. To this end, I have walked and rated all of the trails described in this guide. Even if you do not agree with my ratings, I hope that you will find them consistent and, after a trip or two, useful.

This rating system does not apply to the extreme ends of the fitness scale — those in superb condition and those in poor condition. People who can run 5 or 10 miles with little trouble already know that rating systems are meaningless for them. Conversely, people who can barely make it up a flight of stairs or two would find the ratings equally inaccurate, although much harder to ignore. The system used in this guide is designed to accommodate the approximately 80 percent who are somewhere between the two extremes.

Three difficulty ratings are used throughout this guide: Easy, Moderate, and Strenuous. Many trails have been given two designations. These double designations are used to help span fitness levels when trail difficulty falls between classifications. For example, a trail may be rated Moderate to Strenuous. The person in superb shape would probably rate the trail Easy. The person in good to average condition would find the trail around Moderate, and the person in average to poor shape would judge the trail Moderate to Strenuous. People in the bottom 10 percent would probably wish they had chosen an easier trail.

There are no precise definitions for the general fitness classifications (good, average, poor) just mentioned. They are approximations, devised to bridge the gap in ability levels. The decision to hike a certain trail is a common-sense personal judgment. When planning a hike, you should be aware of the trail's difficulty, not afraid of it; you should think of it as advice, not a warning. If you walk at a leisurely pace and allow plenty of time for rest stops, you will greatly improve your chances of having a pleasurable hike. If you want to hike a trail and think you can, give it a try. Sore muscles last a few days; memories last a lifetime.

Adopt-a-Trail

The U.S. Forest Service has instituted an "Adopt-a-Trail" program, which gives individuals, families and groups the opportunity to do something worthwhile, to become forest service volunteers. The forest service provides all the paint and equipment — saws, shovels, axes, shinguards — you could possibly use or carry. Volunteers provide the time, energy and enthusiasm needed to blaze and brush out their adopted trail.

If you are interested in becoming the foster parent of a trail, or of a section of a long trail, call or write the Forest Supervisor's Office in Gainesville or the appropriate Ranger District. Addresses and phone numbers are provided in the back of this book. Don't worry, there are still plenty of trails to go around.

Blazes

The majority of trails in North Georgia are now blazed, either with metallic diamonds or, more commonly, with painted rectangles. The use of both single and double blazes is rapidly becoming standard practice. The single blaze simply marks the trail; the double blaze — one directly in line with and above the other — serves as a turn signal, giving notice that the trail is going to make a sharp or potentially confusing turn.

Forest Service Policy on Trail Corridor Protection

Wilderness and Scenic Area Trails are completely protected from management activities such as logging and road building. This policy applies, however, only within the actual boundaries of these areas. Trails do not receive protection before they enter or after they leave. The corridor of the Appalachian National Scenic Trail is also protected.

All other national forest trails, including National Recreation Trails such as the Bartram, are subject to normal management activities along or through their corridors.

Litter

I realize that most people who buy or read hiking guides are not the kind who play Hansel and Gretel with Budweiser cans. But you are the kind, I hope, who will help clean up the mess. Take a plastic bag in your daypack. Pick up the trash and carry it out. Please.

Let's add to the adages. Pack it in — pack more out. Take only pictures and litter — leave only footprints.

As always, the preservation of beauty is the responsibility of those who cherish it.

Trail Distances

During 1986 I walked all of the trails included in this guide with a measuring wheel. Using this method, I was able to record distances in feet — such as 69,078 feet for the Conasauga River Trail in the Cohutta Wilderness — then convert the large numbers to the nearest tenth of a mile. If a measurement fell exactly between tenths, such as 3.55 miles, I rounded the figure upward to 3.6.

All mileage figures given in the trail narratives that are not prefaced with "approximately" have been derived from wheeled measurements.

I would like to thank all those who brightened my days with their questions and comments:

"You be careful riding that thing around here" (Cloudland Canyon).

"Couldn't you afford a bike?"

"Are you going to ride that unicycle down this mountain?" (Brasstown Bald).

"Where's the pedals, in your pack?"

"You must work for the government."

"You're him, you're the guy my brother told me about."

"You know, you would do better if you had another wheel."

I would also like to extend special thanks to the U.S. Forest Service for loaning me their measuring wheels, and for not charging me for the one that stopped working.

1
NATIONAL FOREST SCENIC AREA TRAILS

Introduction

The U.S. Forest Service has designated seven tracts of land within the Chattahoochee National Forest as scenic areas and protects them from logging and road building to assure the preservation of their natural values. They range from 170 to 1,600 acres in size, and six have maintained hiking trails.

Clear, cold, fast-flowing water characterizes these preserved tracts. All seven areas have at least one river, creek or branch. Four of the six areas with hiking trails have at least one waterfall.

Hunting, fishing (in season) and primitive camping are allowed within their boundaries; motorized vehicles are not.

ANNA RUBY FALLS
SCENIC AREA

Chattooga Ranger District
White County
Two Trails

ANNA RUBY FALLS NATIONAL RECREATION TRAIL (0.4 mile one way to the falls). Easy to Moderate.

Combined with adjoining Unicoi State Park and situated near Helen, Anna Ruby Falls is by far the most frequently visited scenic area in the Chattahoochee National Forest. This steeply sloped scenic area lives up to its designated status throughout the year, for it is always "scenic." In addition to the uninterrupted splendor of the falls, each season brings its own beauty to the 1,600-acre tract. The spring blossoms, the shady lushness of summer, the autumn foliage and the sparkling snow and unobstructed views of winter make the Anna Ruby Falls area a great place to visit in all seasons.

The asphalt path — which has numbered posts and a corresponding pamphlet that identifies common plants — begins at the upper end of the parking lot next to the information booth and bulletin board. The trail follows Smith Creek upstream through a predominantly hardwood forest to the base of the twin waterfalls. Along the way, the turbulent brook swirls below the path, picking its way downhill through a maze of boulders. On sunny days the creek is a dazzling mixture of glinting white and green, alternately light with fast-flowing chutes and dark with short pools. Above the path, large rock outcrops

3

and their improbably rooted trees further enhance the short walk.

The trail ends at the base of two waterfalls. To the left, Curtis Creek drops 153 feet in two stages, and to the right, York Creek plunges in a 50-foot column. Both streams originate from springs high upon the slopes of Tray Mountain; below their falls they mingle to become Smith Creek, a tributary of the Chattahoochee River. Collectively known as Anna Ruby Falls, the paired cascades were named for the only daughter of Colonel John H. Nichols, who purchased the land surrounding and including the falls shortly after the Civil War.

There are two observation decks — one on either side of Smith Creek. The lower deck is nestled close to the bottom of the 153-foot falls. Standing at the forward railing, you see tree trunks, boulders, surging white water bisecting a framing forest; feel water-powered wind and mist.

Across the creek a gravel path leads to the upper deck for a closer look at the smaller falls. On clear days, especially when the sun is overhead, rainbows quiver on the edges of plummeting York Creek.

Please stay on the paved trail. "Take only pictures — leave only footprints" is a good motto for long trails that receive little use. But here, along this short, heavily used trail through a preserved "scenic area," leaving your footprints upon the wildflowers takes beauty away from photographers and everyone else, and eventually leaves only mud.

Directions: Take Georgia 75 North through Helen to the Robertstown Community. At Robertstown, turn right onto Georgia 356 toward Unicoi State Park. After traveling 1.3 miles on Georgia 356, turn left at the sign for Anna Ruby Falls just before the Unicoi

Information Office. Follow the signs to the parking lot.

SMITH CREEK TRAIL (4.5 miles one way between access points). Anna Ruby Falls to Unicoi State Park: Easy to Moderate; Unicoi State Park to Anna Ruby Falls: Moderate.

For an obvious reason, you might expect this trail to follow Smith Creek downstream to the lake in Unicoi State Park. Beyond the first 0.1 mile, however, you can no longer see the creek; beyond the first 0.5 mile, you can no longer hear it. And that's it: The trail does not come close to Smith Creek again. Hickorynut Ridge would be a more descriptive name for this trail.

Smith Creek can be walked from either end. This description starts at Anna Ruby Falls at approximately 2,180 feet and ends at Unicoi State Park at approximately 1,760 feet.

From Anna Ruby Falls the blue-blazed trail gently ascends the lower slopes of Smith Mountain through a diverse deciduous forest with many large, maturing oaks and hickories. Approximately 1.8 miles of Smith Creek Trail are within the boundaries of the Anna Ruby Falls Scenic Area. Most of what is now the scenic area was logged early in the century, from 1900 to 1915, and has not been logged since. Thus it is likely that most of the larger trees beside the beginning half mile of the trail were either too small to bother with when the tract was logged or have grown since that time.

The trail quickly swings eastward along the lower flank of Smith Mountain, continuing above an unnamed branch until it reaches an easy place to cross the branch at the head of its ravine. After crossing this small stream at 0.7 mile, the trail gradually climbs to Hickorynut Ridge at mile 1.3. Much of the mountainside from the stream to the ridgetop is a wonderful wildflower garden during late May and early June. Here the trail tunnels through dense thickets of catawba rhododendron, also known as mountain rosebay — a tall heath shrub that has many large deep pink or pink-purple blossoms.

Both trail and ridge run more or less north and south. For most of the next 0.8 mile the trail heads southward either on top of Hickorynut Ridge or along its western slopes slightly below ridgeline. At mile 2.1, after half-circling a knob, the trail crosses a gap in the ridge, then angles down its eastern side. The path approaches and then turns to the right away from a dirt road at mile 2.5 before it loops down to a seepage area where a rivulet begins. For the next 1.3 miles the trail, descending moderately at first, follows and then closely parallels this rapidly growing stream.

Two easily identified ferns — the beech and the New York — are common beside the stream. The lower frond segments are diagnostic for both: The beech fern's bottommost frond segments fold sharply forward; the New York fern's lower segments become progressively smaller.

The trail crosses the unnamed stream and Hickorynut Ridge Road, a four-wheel-drive dirt road, at mile 3.9, then remains nearly level to its southern end within Unicoi State Park.

Directions: To reach the northern (upper) end of the trail, walk the Anna Ruby Falls Trail 0.4 mile to the falls. Smith Creek Trail starts behind the sign along the path to the upper observation deck overlooking the smaller of the two falls. (See directions to Anna Ruby Falls.)

To reach the southern (lower) end of the trail, take Georgia 75 North through Helen to the Robertstown

Community. At Robertstown, turn right onto Georgia 356 toward Unicoi State Park. After traveling 1.3 miles on Georgia 356, you will see the road that leads to Anna Ruby Falls and the Unicoi Information Office. Continue on Georgia 356 past the information center, cross the dam, then turn left immediately on the first paved road beyond the dam. Continue on that road for slightly more than 0.5 mile. Just beyond the camper registration booth look for the trail's sign and initial blue blaze to the right of the road next to the sign for Little Brook Camping Area.

COLEMAN RIVER
SCENIC AREA

Tallulah Ranger District
Rabun County

COLEMAN RIVER TRAIL (0.9 mile one way to the end of the easily walked trail). Easy.

This enjoyable, highly scenic trail originates just before the bridge by the "Artificial Lures Only" sign and closely follows Coleman River upstream into the 330-acre scenic area. Shortly after entering the forest, the path comes to a commemorative plaque embedded in a huge boulder. Near the plaque, rockcap ferns grow from the moss on the rock.

By nature, mountain streams are beautiful — the Coleman, bordered by room-sized boulders and wide enough to let the sun in, is especially so. Near the end of the trail the river's fast, shimmering water rushes from cascade to cascade.

Impressive white pine and hemlock flank the Coleman. At 0.2 mile, one of the largest white pines along the trails of North Georgia stands to the left of the path. Its circumference at $4\frac{1}{2}$ feet is slightly less than 10 feet; the height of its arching tip may be as much as 150 feet, perhaps even higher.

White pines are the tallest trees in eastern North America. Judged by the original standard that no longer exists — but is slowly returning in protected areas — the Coleman River pine would hardly be worth mentioning. In America's virgin forests white pines commonly exceeded 160 feet in height; some spired to over 200 feet. On the present site of

Dartmouth College, a specimen 240 feet in height was measured.

Two-tenths of a mile farther upriver from the pine, look up and to the right of the path. Tucked away in moist pockets between and below trailside boulders are maidenhair fern, Indian cucumber-root, Vasey's trillium and showy orchis. The trillium and orchis usually begin blooming during the first two weeks of May.

Above the log steps the path narrows, then ends in a jumble of rhododendron and deadfalls.

If you continue slightly more than 7.0 miles farther northward from Coleman River on F.S. 70, you will reach an iron gate that blocks the road from further vehicular travel. The old road continues on the other side, into the 23,339-acre Southern Nantahala Wilderness.

Directions: After traveling slightly more than 8.0 miles on U.S. 76 West from Clayton, turn right onto paved Persimmon Valley Road at the volunteer fire department and sign for Tallulah River Recreation Area. Continue for approximately 4.2 miles on Persimmon Valley Road, then turn left onto F.S. 70. There is a large sign for Coleman River W.M.A. and another sign for Tallulah River Recreation Area at the entrance of F.S. 70. Travel F.S. 70 for 1.6 miles. A few hundred yards past the camping area a bridge crosses over the Coleman River. The trailhead, marked with its sign and an "Artificial Lures Only" sign, is to the right of the road immediately before the bridge.

DESOTO FALLS
SCENIC AREA

Chestatee Ranger District
Lumpkin County

DESOTO FALLS TRAIL (one way distances: Lower Falls 0.2 mile, Middle Falls 0.7 mile, Upper Falls 1.6 miles). Lower Falls: Easy to Moderate; Middle Falls: Easy; Upper Falls: Moderate to Strenuous.

The falls and the 650-acre scenic area got their name from mountain folklore. Early settlers — so the legend goes — found a piece of Spanish armor in the vicinity of the falls and believed it was left behind by Hernando DeSoto or one of his men.

Like several other scenic areas, DeSoto Falls combines with a National Forest Recreation Area bearing the same name. Access to the scenic area and trail is gained through the recreation area on U.S. 129. The trail begins across the bridge over Frogtown Creek; a sign with arrows and distances to the three falls marks the path.

If you hike to all three waterfalls — from the trailhead (elevation 2,080 ft.) to the Lower Falls, from the Lower Falls past the trailhead to the Middle and Upper Falls, then back to the trailhead — you will walk 3.7 miles.

The Lower Falls spill and splash 30 to 35 feet. Nine-tenths mile away, the Middle Falls drop in four stages — close to 90 feet altogether. Both have large observation decks. From the second or Middle Falls at approximately 2,200 feet, the trail continues another 0.9 mile to the Upper Falls, ascending steadily and becoming much more strenuous. Along the way the path rock-hops a small stream above its cascading slide. The trail continues to loop uphill to its end (2,680 ft.) at the railing overlooking the Upper Falls, which slide at a 45° angle for more than 150 feet.

The falls come from small streams, and they do not have the water volume that most of Georgia's more famous waterfalls do. If you plan to visit these waterfalls in summer or fall, you may want to wait until shortly after a substantial rain.

Directions: Take U.S. 19 North from Dahlonega or U.S. 129 North from Cleveland toward Vogel State Park. After reaching Turner's Corner, where U.S. 19 and U.S. 129 join, continue 4.2 miles on U.S. 19-129 North. A large sign marks the left turn into the DeSoto Falls Recreation Area.

Once inside the recreation area, follow the loop to the right (as the sign requests) past the signed trailhead to the DeSoto Falls Trail Parking Area, which is marked with a stickperson hiker sign.

DeSoto Falls Scenic Area is located next to DeSoto Falls Recreation Area. When the recreation area is closed during the off-season, the entrance road is gated and no further camping is allowed. If you want to hike the DeSoto Falls Trail when the recreation area is closed, you will have to park near the gate and walk the 0.2-mile access road to and from the trailhead. The U.S. Forest Service (Chestatee District) has given hikers permission to walk its trails when the recreation areas are closed. They ask you to carry all trash back out to your car and to park so that emergency access through the gate is not impaired. During a recent year the DeSoto Falls Recreation Area closed at the beginning of November and opened back up on Memorial Day weekend at the end of May. The opening and closing dates are subject to frequent change.

HIGH SHOALS
SCENIC AREA

Brasstown Ranger District
Towns County

HIGH SHOALS TRAIL (1.0 mile one way to Blue Hole Falls and 1.2 miles one way to High Shoals Falls). Moderate.

The blue-blazed trail, starting at approximately 2,880 feet, enters the forest on wooden steps just below and to the right of the jeep trail. About 25 yards from the steps the trail turns to the right and loops its way down into the 170-acre scenic area. At the bottom of the mountain at 2,560 feet, the path turns left onto an old road and follows High Shoals Creek downstream to a wooden bridge. Across the creek, the trail curls to the left, then parallels the cascading stream as it drops more than 300 feet in a series of five waterfalls. The two largest falls are viewed easily. Three prominent side trails, veering back to the left through mountain laurel and rhododendron thickets, angle down to the two observation decks. The last two side paths head to the same deck.

A few yards past a large, jeep-blocking rock at 0.9 mile, the first side path takes you down to the deck overlooking Blue Hole — a picturesque pool more than 20 feet deep, scoured over the centuries by the falling rock and water from its accompanying 25- to 30-foot waterfall.

Less than 0.1 mile farther, the next slanting side trail drops back down to the much larger High Shoals Falls — a jagged, twisting falls over 100 feet high.

The falls are more exciting, more powerful, during periods of high water. I once visited High Shoals in late February, after heavy rain and snow had increased the water volume three to four times that of late summer. The falls were in magnificent form, ricocheting off rocks and splashing into the air, sending showers of spray downstream and onto the decks. Though it was sunny and over 50 degrees, the observation decks and vegetation along the fringes of the waterfalls were still coated in ice from the mist and chill of the night before.

Directions: From the Chattahoochee River bridge in Helen, travel Georgia 75 North approximately 11.4 miles to the road leading to High Shoals. Over the years there have been various signs marking the turn. Turn right onto Indian Grave Gap Road, F.S. 283. This road is approximately 2.0 miles north of the large parking area to the right of the highway at Unicoi Gap, where the Appalachian Trail crosses Georgia 75. It is also the first road to the right after Unicoi Gap.

Once on F.S. 283, ford the usually shallow stream and keep going straight up the hill. Approximately 1.4 miles from the turn off Georgia 75, F.S. 283 reaches a level area, the road widens and a jeep trail leads off to the left. Park there. There may or may not be a sign marking the trailhead in the clearing to the left of the road. The trailhead parking area, however, does have a sunken garbage can, and the beginning of the trail usually has a "hiker trail" or "pack it in — pack it out" sign.

The dirt and gravel road is somewhat rough; during winter, frozen ruts make it all but impassable except for four-wheel-drive vehicles. During the rest of the year, regular cars may have trouble with the stream and muddied road after a heavy rain.

KEOWN FALLS
SCENIC AREA

Armuchee Ranger District
Walker County
Two Trails

JOHNS MOUNTAIN TRAIL (3.1 miles for the entire loop). Hiked counterclockwise: Moderate; hiked clockwise: Easy to Moderate.

This trail begins next to an observation deck on a high point (1,883 ft.) along the ridge of Johns Mountain. Looking straight out, you can see Dick Ridge, Taylor Ridge and several more ridges beyond those two.

Following the loop to the right, counterclockwise, the white-blazed trail heads southward along the ridgetop. The old roadbed quickly passes a communications building, then returns to the forest, which is mostly chestnut oak, hickory and Virginia pine. This section of trail remains level or gently undulating, with an overall slight elevation loss, until it turns to the left at mile 1.3.

The loop continues level or downhill until it crosses a short wooden walkway at mile 2.3. This descending section of trail parallels a line of bluffs that rim the plateau-like top of Johns Mountain. Near the end of the descent these bluffs, which are characteristic of the ridges in northwestern Georgia, become higher and more defined. A warning sign stands guard near a straight-off drop of 50 feet.

Immediately beyond the walkway a sidetrail leads 25 yards to the Keown Falls observation deck (1,420 ft.). (See Keown Falls Trail, the next trail, for further description.)

14

While you can easily switch from Johns Mountain Trail to Keown Falls Trail, the two loops do not intersect nor are they contiguous at any point. They do, however, have short sidetrails that lead to the same observation deck. The deck is the lowest point on the Johns Mountain Trail, the highest on the Keown Falls Trail. Approximately 2.0 miles of the Johns Mountain Trail are within the Keown Falls Scenic Area.

To complete the loop continue, as you might have guessed, uphill and to the left. Most of this final segment gains elevation. The last 0.4 mile climbs moderate grades on an old roadbed.

Directions: (See Keown Falls Trail, the next trail, for directions to Pocket Road.) After turning off Georgia 136, travel approximately 4.0 miles on Pocket Road before turning right onto the Johns Mountain entrance road (F.S. 208) at its large sign. Continue approximately 2.2 miles on this gravel road to the trailhead parking area. Johns Mountain Trail is a loop with two trailheads: if you start at one sign you will end at the other. If you begin at the trailhead sign to the right, through the gap in the railed fence straight ahead as you drive into the parking area, you will hike the trail in a counterclockwise direction.

The Johns Mountain entrance road and the Keown Falls entrance road are closed during the off-season, usually on the same date. (See the directions for the Keown Falls Trail for further details.)

KEOWN FALLS TRAIL (1.7 miles for the entire loop). Easy to Moderate.

Located in the Ridge and Valley physiographic province of northwestern Georgia, 218-acre Keown Falls is the only scenic area in the separate, western section (Armuchee Division) of the Chattahoochee National Forest.

The graveled, rock-lined trail enters the forest at the Keown Falls Recreation Area. From there, at an elevation of 980 feet, the treadway immediately passes under an A-frame shelter and continues into the Keown Falls Scenic Area where it forks into a loop at 0.1 mile. Along the way, you will soon notice two things: the abundance of ground-covering rocks, which get larger as the trail progresses toward the cliffs, and the trees that appear to be shedding their bark in long, curving strips. This distinctive tree, uncommon throughout much of its range in Georgia, is the shagbark hickory.

The trail, following the loop to the right, counterclockwise, quickly approaches a small stream that gives an indication of the amount of water — if any — spilling over the falls. Both of the waterfalls in Keown Falls Scenic Area come from tiny spring-fed branches; together they form this unnamed tributary of Johns Creek. During a drought the falls may be sapped to a trickle or, worse yet, be completely dry. Winter, spring and early summer after a substantial rain are good times to visit the falls. A trailhead sign states their condition, dry or not.

After the loop trail turns away from the stream, it winds up a series of switchbacks designed to keep the the grade easy or moderate. At 0.7 mile a short, steep climb up rock steps leads to an observation deck perched atop a bluff (1,420 ft.). To the right, picturesque Keown Falls, usually divided in two, sails over a large overjutting ledge, showering the rocks 50 feet below. To the left, beyond Furnace Valley, is the long ridge of Horn Mountain.

Johns Mountain Trail, a loop that shares the view at the observation deck with Keown Falls Trail, is 25 yards to the right. (See Johns Mountain Trail, the preceding trail, for further description.)

The Keown Falls Trail leads through the hollowed-out area behind the waterfall, then continues below a line of overhanging bluffs, sometimes 40 feet high, for 0.2 mile to the second waterfall. With roughly half the flow and half the height of the first, this fall is most often a mossy slide. Fern gardens grow on the ledges to the left of the dropping water. From the second fall, the path steadily descends a rock-strewn hillside to the end of the loop.

Directions: In La Fayette, turn from U.S. 27 onto Georgia 136 East toward Calhoun. After traveling approximately 13.0 miles on Highway 136, turn right onto paved Pocket Road. This turn is just up the hill from the Forest Service Work Center in Villanow and is marked with a large green "Keown and Pocket Recreation Area" sign. Continue on Pocket Road for approximately 5.0 miles, then turn right onto the Keown Falls entrance road at its sign. This gravel road ends at the Keown Falls Recreation Area parking lot after approximately 0.6 mile.

Pocket Road also can be reached by traveling Georgia 136 Conn., then Georgia 136 West from Calhoun toward La Fayette. Look for the recreation area sign and left-hand turn approximately 19.0 miles past Calhoun.

Keown Falls Scenic Area is located next to Keown Falls Recreation Area. When the recreation area is closed during the off-season, the entrance sign is removed and the entrance road is gated. If you want to hike the Keown Falls Trail when the recreation area is closed, you will have to park near the gate and walk the access road to and from the trailhead. The U.S. Forest Service (Armuchee District) has given hikers permission to walk its trails when the recreation areas are closed. They ask you to carry all your trash back out to your car and to park so that emergency access through the gate is not impaired. During a recent year the recreation area closed at the end of October and opened back up in the beginning of April. The opening and closing dates are subject to frequent change.

RAVEN CLIFFS
SCENIC AREA

Chattooga Ranger District
White County

RAVEN CLIFFS TRAIL (2.5 miles one way to the cliffs). Easy to Moderate to the cliffs.

Beginning where Dodd Creek mingles its water and loses its name to Dukes Creek, this popular 1,589-acre scenic area follows Dodd Creek and its valley back into the mountains, gradually widening as it moves up the watershed. Alternating between creek level and hillside, the gently sloping blue-blazed trail threads its way along the cascading stream, rarely leaving the sound of the rushing water.

Beside the path watch for the Fraser magnolia, a deciduous magnolia whose large leaves — 10 to 12 inches long and 6 to 7 inches wide — emanate from the stem in a whorled arrangement, and watch for the sweet birch, whose twigs have the distinctive fragrance of wintergreen. From mid-May through early June, Vasey's trillium blooms underneath its characteristic three leaves. The flower, largest of the trillium species, is a rich carmine color. In late June, the luxuriant growths of rhododendron turn the stream borders into narrow swaths of white.

Raven Cliffs lives up to its official designation almost everywhere you look. Within the first 1.3 miles the trail passes beside numerous cascades and two waterfalls. The first fall, at mile 1.1, is over 10 feet high and pours onto a conveniently placed boulder; the second is wide, 30 to 35 feet high, and drops into a shallow plunge pool. Rock outcrops, the same color as the cliffs, dot the steep slopes above the path.

Even in summer the massive rockface is visible from a distance through the veil of trees. The cliff walls, some of them amazingly smooth, tower nearly 125 feet above creek level at their highest point.

The trail forks close to the base of the cliffs. One route rock-hops across the creek; the other stays on the right side of the stream and continues uphill to the top of the cliffs. It is here, beside the right fork, that the lower stage of Raven Cliffs Falls has knifed into the rock, splitting it in two. Called Raven Cliffs Grotto, this 40-foot waterspout is completely surrounded by cave-like walls, except for the narrow opening.

The path ascends a few yards farther, then curls sharply to the left into a gap between cliff tops. A short, root-grabbing climb takes you up to the cliffs, past the gaping hole of a chimney, to the bare rock top of the precipice. To the right is the upper Raven Cliffs Falls; straight ahead and down, the Dodd Creek Valley. The ridgeline of Piney Mountain is to the left.

Across the creek the left fork climbs the hillside, meanders behind the cliffs, then descends to one of the most fascinating scenes in Georgia. Above, the upper fall slides and splashes 75 feet and, after a short rest, plunges again, pouring down into the grotto.

I have often seen copperheads sunning themselves on the rock outcrop to the right of the trail at the second waterfall. Enough said.

The area below Raven Cliffs is botanically rich. Please stay on the main trail — no matter how muddy or slick.

Directions: Take Georgia 75 North through Helen. After driving approximately 1.4 miles beyond the

Chattahoochee River bridge in Helen, turn left onto Georgia Alt. 75 South, crossing the Robertstown bridge over the Chattahoochee River. Continue on Georgia Alt. 75 South for 2.3 miles, then turn right onto Richard B. Russell Scenic Highway (Georgia 348 North).

After traveling 1.7 miles on Richard B. Russell Scenic Highway, you will come to the sign for Dukes Creek Recreation Area. Proceed 1.3 miles past this sign to where the highway crosses Dukes Creek. Immediately beyond Dukes Creek there is a parking area marked with a trail sign to the left. From the parking area, walk downstream on the gravel road along the creek. Approximately 145 yards down the road a rivulet flows into the creek; cross the tiny stream, turn right and follow the blue-blazed trail to Dodd Creek.

Note: The Georgia Wilderness Bill of 1986 incorporated Raven Cliffs Scenic Area within the 9,113-acre Raven Cliffs Wilderness Area. Raven Cliffs trail is totally within the wilderness.

SOSEBEE COVE
SCENIC AREA

Brasstown Ranger District
Union County

SOSEBEE COVE TRAIL (actually three short, inter-connected trails — all trails combined are slightly less than 0.6 mile). Easy to Moderate.

Sosebee Cove is known primarily for two unusual features: its army-strong stand of large yellow poplars and its luxuriantly abundant wildflower displays. Although the 175-acre cove hardwood forest may look like virgin timber to some, it has not gone untouched. This tract was logged early in the century and, except for the power cut, has not been touched since. Sosebee Cove's stand of second-growth yellow poplar is reported to be the best in the nation.

Near where the loop trail heads to the left, the largest yellow poplar in the area stands a few yards to the right of the path. It has a girth of 16 feet 4 inches measured 4½ feet from the ground, making it the second largest tree growing alongside the trails described in this book. While not as big around as the Sosebee Cove champion, hundreds of other maturing poplars — actually deciduous magnolias — have reached heights of more than 100 feet. Their gradually tapering gray trunks are free of limbs for much of that distance.

Halfway up the hillside another loop branches from the first and leads back to the parking lot. As the trail approaches the road it passes beside a yellow buckeye gigantic for its species. At 4½ feet from the ground the mossy-boled tree measures 15 feet 3 inches in circumference — much larger than the current state champion as listed by the Georgia Forestry Commission.

One of the trailhead signs states that Sosebee Cove is "A Botanist's Paradise." It's true. To give even a cursory account of the cove's bewildering diversity would require a small pamphlet. In addition to those listed on the sign, numerous other wildflowers grace the cove from late March through September. There is almost always a member of the lily family in sight. They include the false hellebore, yellow mandarin, Solomon's seal, false Solomon's seal, trout lily, Turk's-cap lily and three species of trillium — large-flowered, sessile and Vasey's The three members of the barberry family — blue cohosh, umbrella-leaf and mayapple — can be easily identified by their distinctive leaves. There are mints such as crimson bee-balm and wild bergamot; orchids such as rattlesnake plantain and showy orchis. Purple-flowering raspberry, leather flower and wild columbine bloom in the sunshine of the power cut. Sourgrass, wild geranium, giant chickweed; meadow rue and rue anemone; white baneberry (doll's-eyes), foamflower, spring beauty and sweet cicely also take their turn adding to the beauty of Sosebee Cove.

It seems that no matter when you visit an area during spring, your timing is off: something better than what is blooming is always either in bud or has already blossomed the week before. There is no drive-through window for wildflowers. But from April 1 through May 15 at least one new wildflower species will open every three or four days. And there really are those good days when you time the flowers just right, when you find orchids and trilliums and more along the same path.

Many people, including myself, leave Sosebee Cove somewhat frustrated, wishing they could have identi-

23

fied more of the plants they found. Knowledge of the following three wildflowers, which are large, distinctive and common in Sosebee Cove, will at least provide a start for beginners. Uncommon throughout the mountains of North Georgia, the umbrella-leaf is abundant along the rocky seepage slopes of the cove. The non-flowering stems produce a single huge leaf, 1 to 2 feet across with jagged, deeply cut edges. The flowering stems produce two somewhat smaller leaves. Throughout much of May, the plant holds a single cluster of relatively small white flowers well above its tropical-looking leaves. The umbrella-leaf is endemic to the Southern Appalachians. An almost identical species lives in the Alps of Japan.

The plant that has the broad, fern-like leaves is sweet cicely. Its tiny white flowers bloom in a sparse cluster in early May. Sweet cicely received its name from its aromatic roots, which have a licorice-like scent when bruised.

The Turk's-cap lily is a perennial herb that reaches 9 to 10 feet in height. This splendid wildflower commonly grows 6 to 8 feet tall in Sosebee Cove. Its lanceolate leaves emanate from the stem in whorls approximately 10 inches apart, giving the plant a distinctive, tiered appearance. The Turk's-cap lily's orange to orange-red flowers (with reddish-brown, freckle-like spots) most often nod toward the ground at an angle similar to that of a showerhead. Their long, exposed stamens point downward away from the plant. Their 2- to 3-inch petals, however, flare into a reflexed arc — out from, up from, then back above the point of attachment. The Turk's-cap lily usually blooms from about July 15 to August 15.

Sosebee Cove has three short interconnected trails. The first trail, the one that enters the scenic area on wooden steps to the right of the signs, leads straight down the cove beside the seepage spring that gives rise to West Fork Wolf Creek. It is slightly less than 0.4 miles long and ends at a road. The last 0.1 mile drops sharply as it descends alongside the creek. The second trail — a loop less than 0.2 mile in length — begins to the left of the main trail 80 yards down from the parking area. This loop starts and ends on either side of a slowly rotting chestnut bole. The third trail, which is less than 0.1 mile in length, connects the loop to the trailhead parking area.

Sosebee Cove is a special place, and it is protected as a National Forest Scenic Area. Its plants are not portable. It is against the law to pluck or pull up any flower or plant, even the tiny ones that you think no one will miss. If, as is often said, ignorance is no excuse for breaking the law, then certainly arrogance is no excuse either. Over the years, most of the illegal destruction that I have witnessed in the cove has come from the hands of knowledgeable people, people carrying wildflower books, who selfishly say, in effect, "I know it's wrong, but it's okay for me." It is not okay.

Directions: Heading north from Dahlonega or Cleveland toward Vogel State Park on U.S Highway 19-129, turn left onto Georgia 180 West 0.4 mile past the entrance of Vogel State Park. Continue 3.1 miles on Georgia 180 until you come to the small parking space above the three signs describing the area.

2

**NATIONAL
FOREST
RECREATION
AREA TRAILS**

Introduction

Most recreation areas have a network of short paths wandering to and from picnic tables, campsites and nearby streams. This chapter, however, confines its description to the longer trails, those specifically constructed or converted for the purpose of hiking. For the most part, these designated trails lead away from the congested areas, enabling the user to gain a degree of solitude unobtainable at the campgrounds.

Most recreation areas are closed and their approach roads gated during the off-season. The length of the off-season, however, varies from area to area and is subject to frequent change. Most recreation areas open between late March and late May and close between early September and late November. Call or write the appropriate ranger district for the exact dates.

Although you will have to walk to their trailheads, you may hike recreation area trails during the off-season. The forest service asks two favors from winter hikers: please do not park so that you block access through the gated entrance roads, and please do not leave any trash in recreation area garbage cans.

ANDREWS COVE
RECREATION AREA

Chattooga Ranger District
White County

ANDREWS COVE TRAIL (1.8 miles one way to the Appalachian Trail). Moderate to Strenuous.

Andrews Cove — short, scenic and somewhat challenging — is an ideal warm-up hike for the springtime. Now blue blazed and easily followed, the trail climbs its cove to Indian Grave Gap, where the Appalachian Trail crosses F.S. 283. Along the way it passes through a maturing second-growth forest, dominated by an open, park-like stand of hardwoods. Andrews is dryer than coves that are higher or north facing; as a result, many of its larger trees are either oak or hickory. Flowering dogwoods are abundant at all elevations.

The trail begins on a hillside above Andrews Creek, at approximately 2,080 feet. Although the trail parallels the stream, it usually remains above it, more within earshot than eyesight. Andrews Cove Trail turns 90° to the left after following an easy upgrade for the first 0.5 mile. Beyond this turn, the path often climbs steeper, moderate grades until it levels out and dips toward the creek at mile 1.1. The remainder of the trail rises steadily toward Indian Grave Gap (3,100 ft.). The last 0.3 mile is strenuous. Angling down from the left, the white-blazed Appalachian Trail crosses the road and continues northeastward to Tray

Mountain and beyond — all the way to Maine.

Andrews Cove has a good spring wildflower display during late March and April.

Directions: Travel Georgia 75 North approximately 6.5 miles past the Chattahoochee River bridge in Helen, then turn right into the recreation area. Once inside, follow the camping loop to the right (as the sign requests). Opposite campsite No. 5 and just beyond the paved walkway to the bathrooms, turn right onto the gravel drive that leads uphill until it deadends at campsites 7 and 8. Please park straight in toward the trailhead sign so that campers can occupy the space nearest their picnic tables.

BRASSTOWN BALD VISITOR INFORMATION CENTER

Brasstown Ranger District
Union County
Three Trails

ARKAQUAH NATIONAL RECREATION TRAIL (5.4 miles one way between access points). Brasstown Bald to Trackrock Road: Moderate; Trackrock Road to Brasstown Bald: Strenuous.

This challenging, scenic trail extends from the Brasstown Bald parking lot to Trackrock Road near Trackrock Gap. At the Brasstown Bald terminus, the sign-posted path enters the forest to the left of the gravel walkway leading to the restrooms. At the Trackrock Road access point, the trail, again sign-posted, begins just before the caged rocks at Trackrock Archeological Area. (See directions for shuttle car.)

The trail's length and two-sided accessibility suggest several options for dayhiking and backpacking. Arkaquah, combined with the 0.5-mile Trail to Summit, offers hikers the opportunity to climb Georgia's highest mountain along a route that averages less than 500 feet of elevation gain per mile. Starting at Trackrock Road (2,280 ft.), the elevation gain to the top of Brasstown Bald (4,784 ft.), however, is 2,504 feet — more than any other trail or combination of trails of similar length, or shorter, in North Georgia. If you are not in decent physical condition, Arkaquah will be much easier and more pleasant if you walk it from top to bottom.

If you are planning to hike to or away from Brass-town Bald during the colder months, remember that it is regularly much colder at these elevations than the forecasts predict for areas farther south, especially Atlanta and vicinity. Be prepared for strong winds on the unprotected ridges.

Starting from its sign on Trackrock Road, the blue-blazed trail ascends easily through a predominantly deciduous forest. At 0.5 mile the path climbs very sharply, then more moderately, to a moist, botanically rich slope at mile 1.0. This north-facing slope has an open hardwood forest of tall, maturing trees. Arching Solomon's-seals and other wildflowers are common along this section of the Arkaquah. The treadway continues to work its way up the mountain-side until it curls onto Buzzard Roost Ridge at mile 1.5.

The trail, a deep forest path with no intersecting roads, remains atop the ridge for the next 1.6 miles. This segment of the ridge crest is a series of waves and troughs. After the first uphill stretch, the trail is level or descending for nearly 0.2 mile. At mile 2.1 it ascends again, occasionally sharply with level sections in between. At mile 2.6 the path is again level or descending for nearly 0.2 mile before it starts climb-ing again on easy or easy-to-moderate grades. Buz-zard Roost Ridge is often open, narrow and dotted with boulders. It is especially beautiful on sunny, late-spring days when catawba rhododendron and moun-tain laurel bloom side by side.

At mile 3.1 the trail slants off the ridgetop and winds below its crest through an area of rock outcrops and moist, fern-draped slopes. Look for the splotches of yellow lichen that decorate the eaves of the tallest outcrop.

The hard hiking is over once the path regains the ridgetop at mile 3.3. For most of the next mile the trail rises to the crest of Chimney Top Mountain — actually just a named highpoint on the ridge. The remainder of the trail, following the short descent from Chimney Top, is predominantly easy uphill or level to its end at the Brasstown Bald parking area (4,440 ft.). The footpath's uppermost elevations are dominated by heath thickets and almost pure stands of short, low-branching oaks.

Arkaquah is an excellent trail for springtime botanizing. In mid-May wildflowers, including four trillium and two orchid species, are numerous. Slightly later, in early June, the catawba rhododendron blooms along the ridge at higher elevations.

This trail is dry; its nearest and most reliable water source is the drinking fountain at its upper end. This fountain is inoperable during the visitor center's off-season.

Directions for Shuttle Car: Take U.S. 19-129 North slightly more than 2.5 miles past Vogel State Park, then turn right onto Georgia 180 East toward Brasstown Bald. Continue on Georgia 180 for approximately 2.5 miles before turning left onto Town Creek School Road at the sign for Trackrock Gap Archeological Area. Proceed approximately 5.3 miles on this paved road to a church and cemetery on the left, then turn right onto Trackrock Gap Road. Travel approximately 3.9 miles to the small pulloff area and trailhead sign to the right of the road. The caged "trackrocks" are just beyond the trailhead, farther up the hill and to the left.

Note: The Georgia Wilderness Bill of 1986, as passed by the U.S. Congress, designated 11,789 acres as the Brasstown Wilderness Area. The Arkaquah National Recreation Trail, with the exception of its

33

lowermost 0.5 mile (Trackrock Gap) and its upper-most 0.2 mile (Brasstown Bald), is a wilderness path.

JACK'S KNOB NATIONAL RECREATION TRAIL (4.5 miles one way from the Brasstown Bald parking lot to Chattahoochee Gap on the Appalachian Trail). The downhill section from Brasstown Bald to Georgia 180 is Moderate. The complete trail and all other shorter sections are Strenuous.

Trail access is at the opposite end of the parking lot from the concession buildings. An opening in the fence and a small sign prohibiting motorized vehicles indicate the exact starting point.

Like the Arkaquah, the path immediately takes you through dense rhododendron arcades. But the vegetation along the two trails soon becomes quite different, especially for trails that begin only a few hundred yards apart. It is the abundance of pines surrounding the downhill section of Jack's Knob Trail that is the most noticeable difference. The reason is relatively easy to explain. Different sides of the same mountain receive different amounts of sunlight each day. South-facing slopes, for instance, receive the most sunlight, making their soils dry. Conversely, north-facing slopes receive the least sunlight, making their soils damp. Over eons the sun, in partnership with the forest communities it helped create, has significantly altered the soil. North-facing slopes, in general, have better, thicker soils with good moisture-holding qualities. South-facing slopes tend to have poorer, thinner soils with marginal moisture-holding qualities. The pines here have adapted to the poorer soils.

This easily followed, blue-blazed trail begins at an elevation of approximately 4,440 feet. After remaining nearly level for its first 0.5 mile, the path starts its switchbacking descent, becoming progressively steeper as it runs down Wolfpen Ridge. At mile 2.3 the trail reaches its second access point — the intersection of highways 180 and 180 Spur at Jack's Gap (2,960 ft.). This access point, situated in the middle of the trail, adds the option of hiking half the trail's full distance in either direction. There is no water along this first section of Jack's Knob.

At Jack's Gap, the trail bends to the left, crosses both highways, then re-enters the forest above a grassy area surrounding a concrete drainage pipe. A trailsign across Highway 180 usually marks the exact location.

The second half of Jack's Knob Trail, like the Appalachian Trail it joins, is an undulating series of ups and downs as it follows Hiwassee Ridge toward Chattahoochee Gap. And like the Appalachian Trail, Jack's Knob does not ride the ridge crest up and over every highpoint. Instead, the trail often drops off the crest and half circles around a peak well below its crown, then rejoins the ridge where it slopes down to the next gap.

Beyond the highway, the path climbs grades that are often moderate through a hardwood forest to mile 2.7. The next section of Jack's Knob, which crosses a spring head, remains level to mile 3.0, where it starts an easy upgrade to a rich cove. After it half-loops through the cove, the trail ascends sharply to the end of a ridge at mile 3.3, then drops to a gap at mile 3.6. From the gap, the path climbs a moderate to strenuous grade along the western flank of Jack's Knob for 0.3 mile.

The trail gently undulates to mile 4.2, where it passes beside a line of large gray outcrops. The final 100 yards dip to the multiple signs at Chattahoochee Gap (3,500 ft.), where Jack's Knob ends at the white-blazed Appalachian Trail. The spring-source of the Chattahoochee River is down the slope on the other side of the gap.

TRAIL TO SUMMIT (0.5 mile one way to the visitor center). Moderate.

Paved and usually sign-posted, this trail originates between the concession building and the Brasstown Bald Interpretive Association's giftshop cabin. The macadam walkway climbs the final 344 feet to the top of Georgia's highest mountain. Perched on the crown at 4,784 feet is the Brasstown Bald Visitor Information Center. The visitor center's observation deck affords an outstanding 360° view of nearby mountains such as Blood and Slaughter and Yonah.

Mountain laurel, rhododendron, hemlock, and stunted, wind-swept oaks make up the bulk of large vegetation along the trail. The Brasstown Bald Interpretive Association has placed identifying labels on several trailside trees. In late May and early June, the catawba rhododendron blooms on the upper slopes of Brasstown Bald, primarily above 4,000 feet. (See Smith Creek Trail, Chapter 1, for a description of the catawba rhododendron.)

Birdwatching is usually good in the area around and above the parking lot at Brasstown Bald. The reason is simple: the birds are easy to see. As the elevation climbs above 4,000 feet on Brasstown Bald, as well as on similar high mountaintops across North Georgia, the trees, mostly oaks, become increasingly shorter and low-branched. So even if a bird is singing from the uppermost canopy, it is still only 10 to 15 feet above your binoculars.

Directions: From either Dahlonega or Cleveland travel north toward Vogel State Park on U.S. 19-129. A little more than 2.5 miles past Vogel State Park, turn right onto Georgia 180 East. Continue on 180 East for approximately 7.5 miles, then turn left onto Georgia 180 Spur and follow it to the parking lot. From the turn onto Georgia 180, signs point out the correct route.

COOPER CREEK
RECREATION AREA

Toccoa Ranger District
Union County
Two Trails

MILL SHOALS TRAIL (2.4 miles one way).
Moderate.

Yellow blazed at first, Mill Shoals Trail quickly gains
elevation through a forest dominated by white pine
and several species of oak, including southern red
oak. The path starts out easy, then becomes progressively steeper as it skirts the northwestern edge of
Cooper Creek Scenic Area. Its most difficult sus-
tained upgrade, however, is no harder than moderate. At 0.7 mile Mill Shoals reaches the top of a spur
ridge, where a sign marks the entrance to the yellow-
blazed trail known as Cooper Creek. This 0.4-mile
connector, which follows an old logging road to the
right, rises easily to its junction with the Yellow Mountain Trail. This junction is at mile 1.0 on the Yellow
Mountain Trail.

Mill Shoals, which switches to orange blazes beyond
the connector, continues straight ahead, down onto
the upper slopes of a hardwood cove. The chestnut
stumps in the cove are still bigger around than the
trees that have supplanted them. At 0.9 mile the path,
now out of the scenic area, dips to an old roadbed.
Guided by orange directional arrows, the trail turns
right onto the road, then almost immediately slants
down and to the left, off the road and into the
rhododendron.

The treadway remains level or gently downhill until
it reaches Millshoals Creek at mile 1.4. Along the way

the trail crosses two of the creek's rivulet tributaries and winds through pockets of tall white pine and moist, lower-slope areas of hemlock and rhodo-dendron. After it crosses Millshoals Creek, the trail turns right onto another old roadbed, then quickly works its way up to Duncan Ridge Road (F.S. 39) at mile 1.5. The trail turns right and follows the dirt road for slightly more than 0.2 mile. The left turn where it re-enters the forest is marked with a sign and blaze.

The trail's remaining distance rises gradually along the lower slopes of Spencer Ridge. Soon after it crosses a rivulet near the head of its ravine, the foot-path ends at an old logging road. A tree with three blazes designates the exact ending point.

The Cooper Creek Recreation Area is located along the boundary between two ranger districts. The recreation area is managed by the Toccoa Ranger District. Mill Shoals and Yellow Mountain Trails, which begin in Cooper Creek Scenic Area, are maintained by the Chestatee Ranger District.

Directions: See directions following the next trail, Yellow Mountain Trail.

YELLOW MOUNTAIN TRAIL (1.6 miles one way to the trail fork; the right fork is 1.5 miles one way to its end at Addie Gap; the left fork is 0.5 mile one way to its end at Shope Gap). Moderate.

The Yellow Mountain Trail begins on the western edge of Cooper Creek Scenic Area. From the trail-head it rises to the northeast until it reaches the ridgetop of Yellow Mountain, which is the scenic area's northern border. Near the end of the ridge the trail forks. The left fork heads northward away from

39

the scenic area. The right fork leads southeastward, back into the scenic area, where it remains until after it crosses Bryant Creek. If you walk all of this trail — the main trail plus both forks and back again — you will have hiked 7.2 miles. This trail has blazes of several different colors. The most recent forest service blazing is yellow.

The beginning of this footpath makes an easy to moderate climb through a stand of hemlock. Above this shady grove, the trail enters an open pine-oak forest on the dry southern slopes of Yellow Mountain. Here shortleaf pines are common. Their needles, 3 to 5 inches long, occur in clusters of two or three to the sheath; their bark is broken into irregularly shaped plates and covered with thin, reddish scales.

After its initial ascent, the path rises easily to the ridgetop and its junction with Cooper Creek Trail at mile 1.0. Cooper Creek, which angles downhill and to the left behind its sign, serves as a 0.4-mile connector between Yellow Mountain and Mill Shoals Trails. Yellow Mountain Trail continues gently uphill with the ridge crest to the level top of its namesake mountain. The large green blazes along this section of trail mark the scenic area's boundary. At mile 1.6 the treadway reaches more trail signs and a tree with a blue ring around it. This is where the trail forks.

The left fork descends moderately, then more easily through a mixed hardwood-pine forest. The trail continues straight ahead through a junction at 0.2 mile. After slightly less than 0.5 mile, the path comes to a rough, single-lane road. The official end of this fork is at Shope Gap on Duncan Ridge Road (F.S. 39), slightly over 0.1 mile to the left on the single-lane road.

The right fork continues gently downhill through a forest where chestnut sprouts are common. Beyond a regenerating clearcut at mile 0.6, it switchbacks steadily down a steep slope covered with tall white pine. This slope is laced with paths of varying sizes. Where the trail curls into a switchback, another path often leads straight downhill. You have to pay attention to the blazes and the switchback turns.

At mile 1.0 the trail crosses Bryant Creek, a Cooper Creek tributary, on a log bridge. Look for the treadway and wooden steps to the left, upstream. The path continues gradually uphill, past a clearcut made in the late 1970's, to a narrow road. Eighty yards beyond this first road, the trail ends at Bryant Creek Road (F.S. 33A) in Addie Gap.

Note: The U.S. Army regularly conducts training exercises in the Cooper Creek Wildlife Management Area. Although there is little threat of physical harm, war games complete with aircraft, marching men and small arms fire can quickly shatter the solitude you may have been seeking. To avoid such noisy encounters, phone Camp Frank D. Merrill in Dahlonega and check their schedule. The number is (404) 864-3367, extension 14 or 57.

Directions: Travel northward from Dahlonega on U.S. 19-Georgia 60. At Stonepile Gap, where U.S. 19 veers right and Georgia 60 turns left, continue northward on Georgia 60. After traveling approximately 15.0 miles beyond the gap, turn right onto a paved county road at Cavender Gap. A recreation area sign should mark the turn. Continue on the paved road for approximately 0.8 mile, then turn left onto F.S. 236. Proceed approximately 2.4 miles on F.S. 236 to Cooper Creek Scenic Area's large parking lot to the right of the road before the bridge over Cooper Creek. If you are not planning to camp at the recreation area (0.2 mile farther on F.S. 236), leave your car at the scenic area parking lot.

Both trails begin across Cooper Creek, a short walk farther along F.S. 236 toward the recreation area. Yellow Mountain begins to the right of the road 300 yards beyond the Cooper Creek bridge. Its trailhead is marked with two signs. Mill Shoals begins to the right of the road 200 yards past Yellow Mountain. You will find its two trailhead signs just beyond a large recreation area sign where the road curves to the left. There are plenty of tall white pines to admire while you walk to one of the trailheads. Although the recreation area has an off-season, F.S. 236 provides year-round access to these two trails.

DOCKERY LAKE
RECREATION AREA

Chestatee Ranger District
Lumpkin County
Two Trails

DOCKERY LAKE TRAIL (3.4 miles one way to the Appalachian Trail). Moderate to Strenuous.

Dockery Lake Trail starts behind its trailhead signs at the back of the picnic area parking lot. Starting at approximately 2,420 feet, the blue-blazed trail ascends 200 feet through a predominantly oak-pine forest in the first 0.3 mile, then turns left and slants off the ridge into a cove. Silverbells, also known as snowdrop trees, are abundant in the cove. Look for small, often stooped trees that have elliptical leaves and longitudinal yellowish streaks on their small branches. Drooping, bell-shaped white flowers open in mid-April. Blooming later, through most of May and into early June, flame azaleas are common in the trailside forest. Their blossoms vary from pale yellow to fiery orange-red.

The wide, well-marked trail continues to descend, often beside small tributary streams of Waters Creek, to mile 1.1. Almost as soon as it stops going down, it starts going up. Across a small stream at mile 1.2, the climb to Miller Gap and the Appalachian Trail begins at approximately 2,040 feet. The next 0.5 mile, which follows a moderate to strenuous gradient, is the most difficult part of the ascent. At mile 2.0 the path rises above a small cascade on a feeder stream flowing toward Pigeon Roost Creek. To the right, especially in winter, there is an excellent view of the upper Waters

Creek watershed, its valley wild and completely forested.

The path steadily works its way up to a gap at mile 2.8, then curls to the left onto a former roadbed. The remainder of Dockery Lake Trail ascends gently to its upper end sign at Miller Gap (2,980 ft.) on the white-blazed Appalachian Trail. The Dockery Lake–Appalachian Trail junction is on Appalachian Trail Section 2, Woody Gap to Neels Gap. (See Chapter 4 for additional information.)

LAKESHORE TRAIL (0.5 mile for the entire loop). Easy.

Lakeshore Trail starts next to the information board in the Picnic Area Parking Lot. From the parking area, the trail quickly winds through the small picnic area down to an A-frame picnic table shelter, where it becomes a loop that can be walked in either direction around the 6-acre lake.

Along the way, numerous short sidepaths lead to small, concrete-reinforced platforms at water's edge. These platforms were built primarily as fishing sites, but also serve as lakeside vantage points for walkers. Halfway around the lake the trail crosses over the dam and its outlet steam, an unnamed tributary of Waters Creek.

Dockery Lake is an excellent and easily accessible site for the entire family to enjoy picnicking, camping, walking and fishing. Lakeshore — easy, short and graveled through the campground — is one of the best National Forest trails for taking children for a walk.

At 2,388 feet, Dockery is a mountain lake, cold and clear enough for good trout fishing.

Directions: Travel northward from Dahlonega on U.S. 19-Georgia 60. At Stonepile Gap, where U.S. 19 veers right and Georgia 60 turns left, continue northward on Georgia 60. Slightly more than 3.6 miles beyond the gap, turn right onto unpaved F.S. 654 across the highway from the large Dockery Lake sign. Proceed straight ahead on F.S. 654 for approximately 1.0 mile, then turn left where the road forks and follow the sign for picnicking, fishing and hiking to the Picnic Area parking lot.

DUKES CREEK
RECREATION AREA

Chattooga Ranger District
White County

DUKES CREEK FALLS TRAIL (0.8 mile one way to the convergence of Davis and Dukes Creeks). Easy to Moderate.

Beginning at the rock steps on the right side of the turnaround drive at 2,120 feet, this wide, blue-blazed, easy-to-walk trail snakes down the mountainside, gently descending in elongated, flattened S-loops. The path has all the amenities: it is graded and graveled, it has a rest bench for the weary, and it has stairs to smooth out the few steep spots. It is just right for a streetshoe stroll.

When the falls are going full blast, you can hear them long before you can see them. But if you're watchful, you will discover several long-range views of the high waterfall on Davis Creek through gaps in the vegetation.

In great contrast to the luxuriant growths of hemlock and rhododendron at the bottom of the gorge, the upper portion of the trail traverses a dry ridge dominated by scraggly, contorted pines of several different species. On your way down look for the table-mountain pine, a tree occurring sporadically on the dry ridges of northeastern Georgia. This small pine's best identifying characteristic is its cone, which is usually clustered in groups of three of four, very lopsided at the base and armed with large, stoutly hooked spines.

Immediately below the last set of steps, the trail appears as if it could go either way, right or left. The right fork is a jeep trail that merges with the Dukes Creek Falls Trail for a few hundred yards. To the right, the jeep trail parallels Dukes Creek above a series of falls and smaller cascades for nearly 0.5 mile before it crosses the stream. There are no side paths dropping down to the falls, and the terrain is very steep and potentially dangerous. It is much better to turn left and follow the trail to the bottom of Dukes Creek Gorge and explore the upstream falls from there. After a short distance the path and jeep trail become separate once again. Next to a long log the path curls to the right, and the jeep trail continues straight ahead.

The trail ends on a rock directly above where the two creeks converge, a great spot to view or photograph the Dukes Creek Falls. The waterfall — actually on Davis Creek — is estimated to be around 250 feet high. The water cascades down a wide, rocky course, which dilutes the power of the falls, especially at low water levels. One prominent, rectangular piece of bedrock is still perched in the middle of the falls; it even has a few hemlock and rhododendron growing from it.

At the bottom of the gorge (1,760 ft.) further exploration is on your own. Rock-hopping upstream, you will find the several small waterfalls on Dukes Creek. Those interesting swirl holes, characteristic of mountain streams where fast water flows over rock, are found below some of the falls. Downstream the creek widens and slows its pace in a series of pools.

The U.S. Forest Service has spent a considerable amount of time, effort and money minimizing both erosion and the steepness of the grade on this trail. Please stay on the graveled path. Cutting across a switchback kills vegetation, erodes the mountainside and encourages further shortcut taking.

Directions: Travel Georgia 75 North through Helen. After driving approximately 1.4 miles beyond the Chattahoochee River Bridge in Helen, turn left onto Georgia Alt. 75 South, crossing the Robertstown Bridge over the Chattahoochee River. Continue on Georgia Alt. 75 South for 2.3 miles, then turn right onto Richard B. Russell Scenic Highway (Georgia 348 North). Travel 1.7 miles on Richard B. Russell Scenic Highway; the large sign for Dukes Creek Recreation Area is on the left.

A sign on the right side of the turnaround loop marks the trailhead. If the sign is missing, look for the trail behind the cemented rock steps and sunken garbage cans. The Dukes Creek Falls approach road remains open all year.

LAKE BLUE RIDGE RECREATION AREA

Toccoa Ranger District
Fannin County

LAKE BLUE RIDGE TRAIL (0.6 mile for the entire loop). Easy.

This short, pleasant stroll begins at the back of the parking lot by the "Hiker Trail" sign and makes a complete circle or loop, taking you near the scenic lakeshore several times. The trail passes through a mixed forest of pines and hardwoods and is an easy-to-walk, level path suitable for nearly every member of the family.

Oaks of six different species make up the greatest share of the larger hardwoods. The distinctively leaved southern red oak is particularly common. Its leaves have three to seven sharply pointed lobes; the top or terminal lobe is elongated and very narrow compared to the other lobes. The base of the leaf is bell-shaped.

Pileated woodpeckers (crow-sized birds with bright crimson crests) inhabit the area and are often seen or heard drumming.

Directions: From the city of Blue Ridge, travel approximately 1.0 mile past the Valley Village Shopping Center, to the east toward Morganton, then turn right onto paved Dry Branch Road at the large recreation area sign. Proceed approximately 2.1 miles (the last 0.8 mile is dirt) to the paved entrance of the recreation area. Just inside the recreation area's entrance, turn left toward the picnic area. After less than 0.2 mile, this road ends at a parking area. Where the road ends the loop begins at the "Hiker Trail" sign at the back end of the parking lot.

The road that passes beside the shopping center and continues to Dry Branch Road is known locally as "Old 76." To reach this road, turn onto Georgia 5 Bus. South at the U.S. 76-Georgia 5 intersection (at McDonald's) just north of Blue Ridge. Continue on Georgia 5 Bus. South to a hilltop stop light, where Bus. 5 turns right at the three-way intersection. If you turn left at this intersection, you will be on Old 76; the shopping center is less than a mile away.

LAKE CONASAUGA
RECREATION AREA

Cohutta Ranger District
Murray County
Two Trails

GRASSY MOUNTAIN TOWER TRAIL (2.0 miles one way to the Lookout Tower). Moderate.

If you intend to hike the Grassy Mountain Tower Trail but are not planning to camp, park at the picnic area parking lot and walk along the lakeshore to the trail's starting point. Rangers, quite understandably, do not want people to park at a campsite unless they intend to use it.

From the picnic area parking lot, walk down to the lake and follow the shoreline path to the left toward the trailhead at the dam. The wide, easily walked trail, starting behind the sign at 3,120 feet, is predominantly level or downhill until it ties into the Songbird Trail — a grassy road — at 0.3 mile. Here, at the T-intersection, the Grassy Mountain Tower Trail turns right onto the road and quickly crosses over a beaver-plugged culvert. The Songbird Trail ends at the culvert. The Grassy Mountain Tower Trail continues as a path straight ahead, slightly to the left and uphill. Usually an arrowed sign points the way.

For the next 1.2 miles, until it runs into a gravel road at mile 1.6, the trail usually has a nearly level stretch between each easy to moderate upgrade. Although it ascends to a mountaintop, the trail's modest elevation gain (572 ft.) allows it to do so without long, strenuous climbs.

At the gravel road, turn right and follow it uphill to terrain that no longer slopes so steeply. After 100 yards the trail enters the woods to the right of the road.

Once you reach an area of large outcrops, the end of the trail and the Grassy Mountain Lookout Tower are nearby. Although the door to the inside of the tower is usually locked, you may still climb to the first landing and gain excellent views of the mountains of Georgia and Tennessee. The Cohutta Wilderness, with its vast sweep of unbroken forest, lies to the northeast.

This trail has a good spring wildflower display. From early to mid-April, trout lilies bloom in abundance. From late April through early May, look for Catesby's trillium near the beginning of the trail and sessile trillium and lousewort higher up near the tower.

In addition to the Grassy Mountain Tower Trail, a path completely encircles the lake, connecting fishing spots, campsites and picnic areas. The path, level and less than 1.0 mile in length, becomes a gravel road in the camping area. Large hemlock, jungle-like thickets of rhododendron and bridges over green coves help offset the lack of solitude.

Directions: Take Georgia 52 West 9.5 miles from the Ellijay square. At the Lake Conasauga Recreation Area sign, turn right onto F.S. 18 and continue 3.5 miles on that road before turning right onto F.S. 68. Once on F.S. 68, proceed straight ahead, uphill. After traveling approximately 6.0 miles on F.S. 68, you will reach the three-way F.S. 68-64 junction near Potatopatch Mountain. Turn left at the Lake Conasauga sign with F.S. 68 and drive straight ahead approximately 4.4 miles to the first turn (Camping Loop A) into the recreation area. If you are not going to camp, please continue 0.9 mile farther on F.S. 68, past the turn for Camping Loop B, to the turn into the picnicking and swimming area. From the picnic area parking lot, walk the wide trail around the lake to the dam. Grassy Mountain Tower Trail begins at the edge of the dam farthest from the main campground.

SONGBIRD TRAIL (0.6 mile one way to its end). Easy.

This short, easily walked trail follows a road into the Songbird Management Area, an area of small, scattered clear cuts that provides the early successional habitat many songbirds require. To the left, where the second-growth forest remains uncut, a branch of Mill Creek parallels the trail. To the right, the plots which were cut in the late 1970's have regenerated to dense young stands, thick with shrubby undergrowth.

The trail continues straight ahead where the road forks to the right at 0.1 mile. Near its midway point, there is a beaver pond to the left, the first of a 0.3 mile-long chain. Seventy yards before the Songbird Trail ends, the Grassy Mountain Tower Trail, having come from Lake Conasauga, enters from the right. Both trails share the same treadway to the culvert, where the Songbird Trail ends. The Grassy Mountain Trail continues over the stream, then leads up the hill to the left.

The beaver ponds have greatly enhanced this walk. They have added beauty and further diversity of habitat and life. The area now supports more bird species than it did before the beavers plugged the culvert. Cavity nesters, such as the flicker, live in the gray snags; the woodcock probes the mud for earthworms; the kingfisher dives for small fish. Frogs, in one form or another, snakes and salamanders are easily seen from water's edge. Colorful dragonflies helicopter to and fro, hawking insects.

The shoreline mud registers the comings and goings of the local animals. Raccoon, deer and beaver tracks are not difficult to find. If you come upon a large, wide-palmed footprint that isn't human, you have probably found a bear track.

The best time to birdwatch along this trail is during spring migration. It is then that the males are both vocal and colorful. Mid-May is usually good.

Directions: The Songbird Trail begins in the Overflow Camping Area at Lake Conasauga. To reach the Overflow Camping Area, continue straight ahead on F.S. 68 and 49 approximately 1.2 miles past Camping Loop A. The trail starts behind vehicle-blocking mounds, 100 yards down the narrow road that leads past the overflow camping area's A-frame bulletin board.

LAKE RUSSELL
RECREATION AREA

Chattooga Ranger District
Habersham County

LAKE RUSSELL TRAIL (3.3 miles one way to its end). Easy.

Lake Russell Trail was designed as a loop that begins and ends at the Nancy Town Lake parking area. The final 1.7 miles of the loop, however, follow recreation area roads that are open to vehicular traffic. A frequently used paved road covers the first 1.5 miles of that distance. In order to remain consistent with my definition of "trail," I have chosen to end this description where the loop turns onto paved road.

The beginning of this blue-blazed trail crosses the spillway immediately below the Nancy Town Dam. Concrete steps, a stride apart, make the crossing easy. After it climbs the bank, the trail turns to the right and parallels scenic Nancy Town Creek downstream.

The wide, easily walked path reaches the upper end of 100-acre Lake Russell at 0.3 mile. For the next 1.3 miles, the trail closely follows the lake's forested southern shoreline, occasionally winding around deep, inviting coves. This nearly flat section of trail remains on the level ground between the lake and its surrounding ridges. Here the shoreline forest alternates between stands of pine — shortleaf, loblolly and Virginia, their trunks sometimes fire blackened — and smaller groves of hardwood.

At mile 1.6 the trail angles away from the lakeshore and remains away until it crosses the Lake Russell dam. The walk over the grassy dam at mile 2.1 affords a good view of the long, narrow lake. Once the trail re-enters the forest, it turns left and descends to the flood plain below the dam. Here the path crosses a bridge over Nancy Town Creek, follows the outside arc of the spillway, and then makes a short climb back to lake level.

The remainder of the trail follows a gravel road now closed to vehicular traffic. After traversing a hillside above a cove, the road bends away from the lake at mile 2.9. It ends at a paved road at mile 3.3. Here you have a choice: you can either turn left and complete the loop by road, or you can turn around and backtrack the way you came.

Directions: Near the city of Cornelia there is a major intersection involving highways U.S. 23/441 and U.S. 123. To reach the Lake Russell Trail, follow U.S. 123 North, which begins at this intersection, toward the city of Cornelia. From this intersection continue on U.S. 123 North for approximately 3.2 miles, then turn right onto Lake Russell Road, F.S. 59, at the recreation area sign. Continue approximately 2.0 miles on paved F.S. 59 before turning left toward Nancy Town Lake. This turn is marked with an arrowed sign that points to the lake and the group camping area. After slightly more than 0.1 mile, turn right into the Nancy Town Lake parking area, where the trail begins behind its sign. The road to the Nancy Town Lake parking area remains open throughout the year.

LAKE WINFIELD SCOTT
RECREATION AREA

Brasstown Ranger District
Union County
Two Trails

JARRARD GAP TRAIL (1.2 miles one way to its junction with the Appalachian Trail). Easy to Moderate.

Lake Winfield Scott's trails have been greatly changed. Both trailheads have been relocated, and both trails have been rerouted and lengthened. Jarrard Gap and Slaughter Creek now share the same trailhead (elevation 2,890 ft.) beside the lake. And they also share the same treadway for slightly more than 0.2 mile.

After 0.1 mile of level walking near Slaughter Creek, the blue-blazed trail turns left immediately before a footbridge. The path continues through rhododendron beside the creek, then crosses it on a single split log. Once across, it quickly reaches a wide dirt road, where the trails split. Slaughter Creek continues straight across the road; Jarrard Gap turns right and follows the road for 0.2 mile to a three-way intersection. The trail angles across the road that enters the intersection from the right, returning to the woods on an old single-lane road blocked by boulders. The road's entrance is marked with a double blaze and a trail sign.

For the next 0.4 mile the trail follows Lance Branch up its ravine. Most often, it remains on the hardwood slopes above the Slaughter Creek tributary. This section gains elevation gradually; its steepest grade is short and only moderately difficult.

57

At 0.8 mile the path rock-steps across the branch. The remainder of the trail, still a combination of old roadbed and new path, rises to the gap. Again, the steepest grade is short and only moderately difficult. The trail turns right onto a single-lane dirt road 35 yards before its end at Jarrard Gap (3,300 ft.) on the Appalachian Trail. This road provides access to nearby private property.

If you want to take a longer dayhike from Lake Winfield Scott, Jarrard Gap can be walked as the first leg of a 6.2-mile loop that begins and ends at the lake. Once you've reached Jarrard Gap, turn left onto the white-blazed Appalachian Trail and continue 2.3 miles to Slaughter Gap, where you turn left onto Slaughter Creek Trail. (For more information, see Section 2 of the Appalachian Trail in Chapter 4.)

SLAUGHTER CREEK TRAIL (2.7 miles one way to its junction with the Appalachian Trail at Slaughter Gap). Easy to Moderate.

Slaughter Creek and Jarrard Gap share the same treadway for their first 0.2 mile. (See the first two paragraphs of Jarrard Gap Trail for a description of that segment.) Like Jarrard Gap, and all other Appalachian Trail approaches, Slaughter Creek is blue blazed. And again like Jarrard Gap, the new Slaughter Creek Trail is a series of old roadbeds connected to one another by recently constructed paths.

Slaughter Creek gains 1,000 feet in elevation, but does so gradually over its 2.7-mile length. There are no grades more strenuous than moderate. Most of the ascent is accomplished by easy or easy-to-moderate gradients, which often alternate with sections that are level or dip slightly to stream crossings.

58

After slightly more than 0.2 mile, Slaughter Creek Trail continues straight ahead across the road. Back into the evergreen thickets of rhododendron and laurel, the path quickly rises to the slopes above Slaughter Creek, where it remains until it dips to a creek-level junction at 0.7 mile. Here the trail turns right at the intersecting roadbeds and continues to follow Slaughter Creek up its watershed. Beyond this turn, in winter, you can see the prominent rock slabs that extend up Slaughter Mountain's southwestern flank.

At mile 1.7 the trail angles onto a rocky, old logging road that closely follows Slaughter Creek up a hardwood cove. After the heath thickets disappear, the stream becomes much more visible, the forest more open. Stumps from past logging days still dot the cove. Those stumps and logs bleached light gray are wrecks from the chestnut blight.

The trail crosses its namesake creek, the last of many stream crossings, at mile 2.2. Forty-five yards farther, it turns uphill toward the gap. The final 0.3 mile climbs a moderately difficult slope that supports a forest increasingly dominated by oaks.

Slaughter Gap is a major trail junction. The Appalachian Trail enters the gap, then turns 90° to the right. The gap is also the eastern terminus for the blue-blazed Duncan Ridge National Recreation Trail, which quickly leads to Vogel State Park's Coosa Backcountry Trail.

For a longer dayhike from Lake Winfield Scott Recreation Area, connect Slaughter Creek Trail with a 1.0-mile segment of the Appalachian Trail to reach the top of Blood Mountain. If you want to walk toward Blood Mountain and its superb vistas, do not turn right onto the Appalachian Trail. Instead, walk Slaughter Creek Trail almost straight across the opening and follow the white-blazed trail after it has turned to the right.

The trail from Slaughter Gap to the crest of Blood Mountain is surprisingly easy, considering that Blood Mountain (4,458 ft.) is one of Georgia's highest peaks. While the trail does wind steadily uphill, there are no long, uninterrupted steep grades. Actually, after you have reached Slaughter Gap — at 3,900 feet a very high gap in Georgia — much of your elevation gain has already been accomplished.

If you plan to continue walking from the end of Slaughter Creek Trail, you may want to remember that the last source of easily obtainable water is at mile 2.2, where the trail crosses Slaughter Creek.

Directions: Lake Winfield Scott Recreation Area is located on the section of Georgia 180 between Georgia 60 and U.S. 129. Travel Georgia 60 North from Dahlonega. Approximately 7.5 miles past Stonepile Gap, where U.S. 19 and Georgia 60 split, turn right onto Georgia 180 East. Continue on Highway 180 for approximately 4.5 miles, then turn right onto paved F.S. 37 at the recreation area sign.

Travel U.S. 129 North from Cleveland toward Vogel State Park. Proceed approximately 0.4 mile beyond Vogel State Park before turning left onto Georgia 180 West. Continue approximately 7.0 miles on Highway 180, then turn left into the recreation area. This turn is approximately 0.5 mile beyond Lake Winfield Scott.

After turning off Highway 180, follow F.S. 37 straight ahead for approximately 0.5 mile. Immediately beyond the guardrails at the lake, turn right into the trailhead pulloff area next to an A-frame bulletin board. Both trails, Jarrard Gap and Slaughter Creek, start at the sign. F.S. 37 remains open all year.

PANTHER CREEK RECREATION AREA

Chattooga Ranger District
Habersham County

PANTHER CREEK TRAIL (3.5 miles one way from U.S. 441 to the base of the large waterfall; 5.5 miles one way from U.S. 441 to the eastern terminus near Yonah Dam). Easy to Moderate to Falls; Moderate beyond.

The blue-blazed trail, which follows Panther Creek downstream toward its confluence with the Tugaloo River, begins across the highway from the recreation area on U.S. 441. A sign marks the trailhead. After slightly less than 0.1 mile, take the left fork uphill away from the creek. Until it crosses the bridge, the path usually remains on the steep slopes above the stream, within earshot of the fast-flowing shoals and low cascades. At 0.9 mile a sidetrail drops down to noisy cascade that finishes its run with a long sliding chute.

You will reach the third set of trail-crowding outcrops slightly less than 0.1 mile beyond the cascade. This time, instead of continuing straight ahead beneath the overjutting rock, the trail curls up and to the left, between the narrow gap in the outcrop. At mile 1.4 the path crosses the creek at the first of the small signs that guide hikers to the falls. The old guy-wire, rock and fallen-tree crossing has been replaced with a wooden bridge, courtesy of Boy Scout Troop 650. Beyond the bridge, the stream becomes calm and the trail becomes sidewalk flat, at least for a while.

Do not mistake the high shoals at mile 2.3 for the waterfall. Panther Creek Falls, still slightly more than a mile away, past a path-narrowing bluff, is much more impressive. Not knowing what to expect, most people are surprised by the beauty, size and power of the waterfall — really a series of falls, with a splashing slide in the middle. The trail skirts along the upper falls on the outer edge of a large outcrop, then descends to the small, swirling pool that catches the waterfall's first drop. From here the path becomes somewhat steep, sloping down to the bottom of the falls and the unusually large, enticing pool at its base.

The trail continues for 2.0 more miles. Below the falls Panther Creek becomes even more scenic: the forest becomes taller and more diverse; shoals are more frequent; boulders, occasionally table-top flat, are larger and more numerous; pools are longer, deeper and greener. Unfortunately, as it is now designed, the trail takes hikers away from the creek for half of the remaining distance.

After remaining alongside the creek for 0.6 mile, the trail comes to a low waterfall and its miniature gorge. Forty-five yards beyond this falls, the path turns to the right and climbs away from the creek beside a tributary rivulet. The path crosses the rivulet at mile 4.3, then sharply ascends a hillside for slightly more than 0.1 mile before it reaches the level top of a dry, piney ridge. (Watch for the double blue blazes which signify sudden changes in trail directions.) Descending from the ridge through a forest dominated by mature oak, yellow poplar, basswood and beech, the trail returns to Panther Creek with a 0.3-mile walk to the bridge, which marks its end.

The U.S. Forest Service has designated two parcels of land along the Panther Creek corridor as Botanical Natural Areas. These tracts, which total 598 acres, preserve and protect unique vegetative communities.

The first area, which is the much larger of the two, begins below Panther Creek Falls and continues downstream a short distance beyond where the trail ends. The second area is further downstream, across the section of privately owned land that separates the two tracts.

Spring wildflowers, including three species of trillium, are abundant on the moist, open slopes downstream from the falls. One of North Georgia's rarest wildflowers — the gay wing or bird-on-the-wing — blooms by the thousands along the first few miles of the trail. This perennial herb often grows with partridge berry, forming dense mats of dark green and orchid pink. Gay wings usually bloom in mid-April.

Directions: Panther Creek's western trailhead is on U.S. 441, north of Hollywood and south of Tallulah Falls. Look for the recreation area's sign, paved entrance road and large parking area to the left of the highway approximately 9.5 miles north of where U.S. 441 turns right in Clarkesville. The recreation area lies at the bottom of a long downhill stretch of highway that crosses Panther Creek, then starts uphill again.

The trail, which follows Panther Creek downstream, begins on the right side of U.S. 441 (facing north), beyond the recreation area entrance and across Panther Creek. The trail's entrance is behind its sign, to the right of the dirt road.

To reach the eastern trailhead at Yonah Dam, travel Georgia 106 North into the city of Toccoa. Where Highway 106 ends, just before a bridge inscribed "Southern," turn right onto Georgia 17 toward Westminster. Drive 1.0 mile to the third traffic light on Highway 17, then turn left onto Georgia 17 Conn. After traveling 0.5 mile on Highway 17 Conn., turn left at the stop sign, then turn onto the first road to the right, Prather Bridge Road.

Continue straight on Prather Bridge Road for 9.7 miles before you bear left immediately after the bridge near Yonah Park and Dam. After traveling 0.7 mile beyond the bridge, turn left onto a dirt road. Continue straight on this rutted road for 1.5 miles to near where it fords Panther Creek. Park at the pulloff area to the right of the road. (If the road is muddy, it is better to park near the power cut on the hill above the ford.)

The road forks at the ford. Follow the narrow road on the right side of the creek, cross a small stream, and continue on a path up Panther Creek to the trail sign and bridge. The trail starts on the other side of the bridge. It is 0.4 mile from the pulloff to the trailhead.

POCKET
RECREATION AREA

Armuchee Ranger District
Floyd County

POCKET TRAIL (2.6 miles for the entire loop). Easy.

"The Pocket" is a large, horseshoe-shaped piece of nearly level land flanked on three sides by the steep ridges of Horn and Mill Mountains. Most of the low-lying ground inside the loop trail has an elevation of 900 feet. The area's many spring-fed streams are headwaters to Johns Creek, which flows out of the open end of the horseshoe.

The first section of this trail passes beside an area of seeps and small streams. Here the forest's diversity becomes quickly apparent. To the left, there are mois-, ture-loving trees such as sycamore, beech, sugar maple and witch hazel; to the right on the hillside, there are trees — black gum, sassafras, shortleaf pine, several species of oak — that prefer drier sites.

At 0.4 mile the trail crosses a short wooden bridge, its second, then turns left. Twenty or 30 yards to the right of the bridge, the two largest trees along the loop, an impressive loblolly pine and an equally thick white oak, stand side by side. Although much more abundant in the Piedmont, the loblolly is also common in the southernmost districts of the Chattahoochee National Forest, particularly on south-facing slopes.

The loblolly is fairly easy to recognize. It is a large pine, often over 100 feet high with a tall, straight trunk. Spraying upward from branch ends, its nee-

dles are 6 to 9 inches long and occur in bundles of three to the sheath. The wide, light reddish-brown cones are often 4 to 6 inches in length; and, characteristic of the species, the bark changes as the tree matures. The bark of a young loblolly pine is dark and furrowed, but as the tree grows older, the bark thickens, turns bright orange-brown and becomes divided by shallow fissures into broad, flat plates.

Beyond the two big trees, the loop begins its pattern of rising slightly to drier ground, dipping to the next stream or seepage area, then rising again. Although often only 10 feet higher than the nearest stream, the upland areas are dominated by pines and scrubby hardwood species, such as blackjack oak, associated with poorer soils.

At 0.7 mile, the loop crosses a road and continues gently uphill or level along several low ridges before slanting down toward water. The trail crosses a 65-yard-long boardwalk over a seepage area at mile 1.5. Beyond this first boardwalk, the path rises through a predominantly pine forest, then dips to a second one at mile 2.0. The loop ends at the one-way road in the camping area, directly across from the picnic area parking lot where it started.

Directions: After turning off Georgia 136, travel approximately 7.0 miles on Pocket Road before turning left into the Pocket Recreation Area at its large sign. Shortly after entering the one-way camping loop, turn right into the large picnic area parking lot opposite the bathroom building on the left of the road. This parking lot is approximately 0.3 mile from the entrance gate on Pocket Road.

Cross one of the bridges leading from the back of the parking area to the springs. To the left of the concrete spring cover, you will see the trail sign and first white blaze.

See Keown Falls Trail, Chapter 1, for directions to Pocket Road. Also see Keown Falls Trail directions for information regarding the off-season closure of Pocket Recreation Area.

RABUN BEACH
RECREATION AREA

Tallulah Ranger District
Rabun County
Two Trails

RABUN BEACH TRAIL (0.9 mile one way to Angel Falls). Easy to Moderate.

This wide, rhododendron-shaded trail closely follows Joe Creek upstream. Almost immediately, the brook exhibits a small-scale preview of what's ahead. Just above the first bridge, a gentle, stairstep cascade pours over the same smooth, level ledges that characterize the much higher falls to come.

The easily followed path reaches Panther Falls after slightly less than 0.6 mile. The fall — wide and 35 to 40 feet high — is surprisingly large for such a small and usually peaceful stream. A bedrock ledge serves as a convenient seat at the base of this isolated waterfall.

After it switchbacks beside the upper portion of Panther Falls, the trail continues to a rock crossing where it becomes a loop. From here it is only a short distance to the wooden observation bridge in front of Angel Falls — higher (65 ft.) and narrower than Panther. At normal water levels Angel is a peaceful series of small falls and slides, framed by rhododendron and other moisture-loving plants. On cloudless days the late-morning sun bathes the upper falls, fusing with the white water to produce a stunning brilliance.

Joe Creek is small, and its waterfalls are usually at their best in winter and spring. During the leaf season of late summer and early fall, especially during drought, you may want to choose a waterfall trail that follows a large stream.

Directions: From the Post Office (to the right of U.S. 441 North just before the bridge over the dam on the Tallulah River) in the city of Tallulah Falls, travel northward on U.S. 441 for approximately 1.7 miles, then turn left at the Rabun Beach sign immediately before the third bridge. Continue on this paved road for approximately 2.5 miles before turning left at a three-way intersection. Proceed approximately 4.7 miles, then turn right into Rabun Beach Campground No. 2.

Once inside the campground gate, turn right and follow the paved road past the restrooms. Beyond the restrooms, proceed a short distance (past two roads to the left) to a three-way intersection. The signed trailhead is directly across the junction.

FALL BRANCH TRAIL (0.2 mile one way to Minnehaha Falls). Easy.

This trail does not begin or end at the recreation area, but because of its close proximity, many people like to walk to beautiful Minnehaha Falls while they are in the area. Tall white pines, thickets of laurel and, closer to the falls, rhododendron border the short, smooth, easily walked trail.

Like the two waterfalls at Rabun Beach, Minnehaha cascades down numerous rock ledges, but with more exuberance, force and noise. A bench-like boulder near the base of the wide 50- to 55-foot high upper falls makes a handy seat. If you have some time, spend a few minutes watching the kaleidoscopic water patterns and listening to the "laughing waters" — the Minnehaha. Below the sitting rock, the stream careens down the mountain again, this time more slide than falls.

Directions: Continue past Rabun Beach Camping Area No. 2 for approximately 1.6 miles. At the Georgia Power and Flat Creek Baptist Church signs, turn left onto the paved road that drops down to Seed Lake. Continue on the paved road across the bridge, then, where the paved road curls to the right, follow the gravel road (Bear Gap Road) straight ahead. After traveling 1.5 miles on Bear Gap Road, begin looking to the right for stairs cut into the roadbank. There is a small pulloff area on the left just before the steps. The trail sign has disappeared frequently in recent years. If you have traveled 2.0 miles on Bear Gap Road and haven't found the trailhead, turn around and try again.

WARWOMAN DELL PICNIC AREA

Tallulah Ranger District
Rabun County

WARWOMAN DELL INTERPRETIVE TRAIL (0.4 mile for the entire loop). Easy.

This interpretive trail, with its 25 numbered posts and corresponding pamphlet, identifies many of the plants common to Warwoman Dell. Although the pamphlet limits its scope to one small wooded valley, it serves as a primer for the Southern Appalachian forest. The markers identify 17 tree species (witch hazel and big bay rhododendron are included in that number), almost all of them common across the North Georgia mountains. The pamphlet also provides a short summary of the area's rich human history, including the probable origin of the word "warwoman."

The trail enters the forest over a wooden walkway beside Warwoman Creek. After the trail crosses a bridge over the creek, its loop begins and ends immediately before the picnic tables. The numbered markers continue in a counterclockwise direction to the far-right side of the picnic area. At its halfway point, at marker 15 and the small waterfall, the trail curls to the left and down, back toward the beginning of the loop.

From late March through April, the moist area between the pavilion and the waterfall has a good wildflower display. Bloodroots and violets bloom in late March. A month later, in late April, Vasey's trilliums, with their large leaves and carmine-colored flowers, bloom along the path.

The pamphlets are not available when the picnic area is closed during the off-season.

In addition to having a trail of its own, Warwoman Dell Picnic Area serves as an easily accessible starting and ending point for those walking either of Georgia's two long segments of the Bartram National Recreation Trail. The trail crosses Warwoman Road and passes through the picnic area at a point nearly midway along its 37-mile length. (See Chapter 4 for information on the Bartram Trail.)

Directions: In Clayton, where U.S. 76 turns west, turn east onto Warwoman Road. If you are traveling north on U.S. 441, the turn will be to your right near the Hardee's, which is the second building to the right on Warwoman Road. Once on Warwoman Road, turn right at the stop sign and proceed on Warwoman Road past the Georgia Power Building. After traveling approximately 3.0 miles on Warwoman Road, turn right into the sign-posted recreation area and continue 0.3 mile. The gravel road ends at the pavilion parking lot. The trail begins next to its pamphlet box in the far-right corner of the parking area.

3
COHUTTA
WILDERNESS
AREA TRAILS

Introduction

As described in the Wilderness Act of 1964, wilderness is "an area where the earth and its community of life are untrammeled by man, where man himself is a visitor who does not remain." This definition is the guiding principle behind the most foresighted land-ethic legislation since the formation of the National Forest System. Designated wilderness represents a progression of concern, an inkling that the earth has its own heritage and its own unimpeachable right to live, a willingness by the majority to let some parcels of land become what they will, unmanipulated by man. The act of preservation is a tithing of wildness for ourselves, a beginning reparation for the earth's land and its diminished existence.

Cohutta Wilderness Area Trails

Officially designated on January 4, 1975, the 34,102-acre Cohutta Wilderness — 32,307 acres within Georgia and the remainder in Tennessee — is located northeast of Chatsworth, primarily in Fannin and Murray counties.

Although much of this wilderness area was logged earlier in the century, the forest has returned, healing the scarred land and obliterating all but the smallest traces of man's past exploitation. With continued wilderness designation and the passage of time, the forest will slowly regain its former magnificence.

A network of 15 trails totalling 87 miles penetrates this rugged wilderness, where elevations range from 950 to 4,200 feet. All but two of these trails lead to or follow the scenic Jacks and Conasauga rivers, whose headwaters are protected by National Forest land in and around the wilderness. These two rivers are among the few larger streams in North Georgia that still offer quality wild-trout fishing.

Note: The Georgia Wilderness Bill of 1986 added 2,940 acres, all within the Chattahoochee National forest, to the Cohutta Wilderness. It now totals 37,042 acres. This new designation extended the Cohutta to the northeast, from Dally Gap along Forest Service 22 to the Tennessee line.

The 8,055-acre Big Frog Wilderness in Tennessee's Cherokee National Forest borders the northern tip of the Cohutta, across Big Frog and Chestnut Mountains.

CONASAUGA RIVER TRAIL (13.1 miles one way between trailheads). From Betty Gap downstream to northwestern trailhead at F.S. 17B: Easy to Moderate; from F.S. 17B upstream to southeastern trailhead at Betty Gap: Moderate.

Starting at Betty Gap (3,040 ft.), the initial 0.2 mile descends very sharply, the first of only two difficult grades on this predominantly level trail. A small spring-fed stream — the first of many — emerges beneath a stand of large white pine near the top of the descent. For the first 1.3 miles, until it reaches the river, much of the yellow-blazed trail wanders through a maze of gathering rivulets, headwaters of the Conasauga. Especially after a rain, this upper section of the trail is part water, closely following, crossing, and rock-hopping down the middle of the many shallow, intertwining streams.

Along this same 1.3-mile segment of trail stand the two largest hemlocks in Georgia. These hemlocks, huge for their species, are the two largest trees near the 15 trails in the Cohutta Wilderness.

In the spring of 1985, the Conasauga River Trail had a sign designating the hemlock I had measured years before as the official state record. In the summer of 1986 I saw the same sign, but I couldn't find the tree. I soon saw another sign, 45 yards or so straight downhill, across a small stream. This sign was posted near the base of a noticeably large tree. At first I was confused and thought the trail had been rerouted. But as soon as I walked down the hill and saw the tree, I realized that it had replaced the other giant as state record hemlock.

After measuring the new champion I continued walking; 35 yards farther along the trail, I found the old record holder, to the left of the path and easily recognized as usual. The new record-holding hemlock measured 15 feet, 1 inch in circumference, 4½ feet up from the ground; the old, 15 feet, 7 inches. First-place trees, however, are not determined solely by circumference. The overall largest tree of a given species is calculated using a point system derived from three measurements: circumference, height, and width of crown. Thus the thicker but shorter old champion lost on points, and the forest service simply moved the "state record tree" sign back up the trail 100 feet.

The Eastern hemlock is a slow-growing, long-living tree. The record age, rings actually counted, is near 1,000 years. The two Conasauga River hemlocks, skipped over by loggers as worthless wood, have lived to become venerable relics — vestiges from the days when bison, cougar, elk and wolf roamed the incredible forests of what was to become Georgia. After researching hemlock growth patterns, I believe these two trees are between 400 and 500 years old. This is a conservative estimate; they could quite possibly be older.

Should the sign somehow disappear, it would be much easier to find the old record tree first. Begin looking for it at 0.4 mile, where the land to the left of the path slopes downhill for the first time. You will walk past two or three lesser hemlocks farther away from the trail than the old giant. Keep looking to the left of the trail as you walk; you will soon notice the tree's dead top and, as you move closer, the growths that ring its lower trunk.

Once it reaches the river, the trail fords the Conasauga 38 times — 18 to Bray Field, 20 beyond. Most of the fords are shallow and present no problem other than slipping and getting wet. But in winter and early spring before the leaves bud out, when the river normally has its strongest flow, the current can reach mid-thigh depth and become surprisingly powerful. Do not plan to hike the Conasauga River Trail immediately after heavy rains or when heavy rains are predicted. Steep-sided mountain rivers, like the Conasauga and Jacks in the Cohutta Wilderness, rise rapidly following a substantial rainfall and quickly become too dangerous to ford, leaving hikers stranded between river crossings.

Usually there is a blaze marking the trail's return to dry land across the river from each ford. These guiding blazes, however, are not always easily found. You must often angle downstream while fording the river to locate the blaze and worn spot on the opposite bank. And occasionally, at an apparent ford, you have to walk 20 or 30 yards downstream along the bank before spotting the trail across the river. Just remember that the trail, even on islands, always heads downriver.

The generally level trail closely follows the scenic Conasauga River between fords. This crystalline mountain stream, dropping over 100 feet per mile to Bray Field, is a rocky succession of white shoals and green pools. By mid-morning the fast-flowing riffles beside the shaded path are sparkling silver.

As soon as the air above the Conasauga warms, tiger swallowtails begin their daily flutterings up and down the river corridor. Below these colorful yellow and black butterflys, rainbow trout face upstream to feed, holding steady in the slowed currents of the pools.

After its 18th ford at mile 4.9, the trail climbs up and over a hill, descends to and crosses Tearbritches Creek, and then enters Bray Field. Bray Field (1,920 ft.), former cabin site and now grassy camping area, is the most important trail junction in the western half of the wilderness. One trail, Tearbritches, ends here; two trails, Conasauga and Hickory Creek, pass through the small clearing, and the lower access point of a fourth trail, Panther Creek, is nearby. Possibilities for extended hikes from Bray Field are numerous.

From Bray Field at mile 5.4 the yellow-blazed trail continues downriver another 7.7 miles and another 20 crossings. In the middle of the field the trail, turning to the left away from the river on an old gravel road, becomes contiguous with the white-blazed Hickory Creek Trail. Follow the road as it winds around an abandoned beaver pond, then returns to the river. The trails split 1.3 miles from Bray Field; Hickory Creek turns left with the road, Conasauga River continues straight ahead on the path. Here the river fords begin again.

Watch carefully for the trail blazes on the second river crossing below Bray Field. As you ford the river from right side to left, look for a gap in the rocks a few feet in from the bank. The trail cuts through the gap at a right angle away from the river.

The path continues its pattern of crossing, then paralleling the river until the 38th and final ford (the 20th below Bray Field) at mile 11.9. Here, at approximately 1,260 feet, the trail leaves the Conasauga River. Twenty-five yards beyond this last ford, the trail turns 90° to the left and begins to climb. The remaining 1.2 miles are predominantly level or uphill, with several moderate grades and one short steep pitch near the end. After it levels out, the trail turns left onto an old road, then ends in the gravel parking lot (1,640 ft.) of F.S. 17B.

The Conasauga has the cleanest, clearest water of any river its size in Georgia. Its clarity — like wilderness rivers out West — gives it the illusion of being shallower than it is. This is how other mountain rivers were, should be still.

Below Bray Field the sluices, slides, shoals, boulders, bluffs and pools are continuous along the lower Conasauga. Although this trail lacks the single-feature scenery of a waterfall, its last 7.7 miles have more "everywhere-you-look" beauty, mile after mile, than any other long stretch of river trail in Georgia.

Starting from its southeastern terminus at Betty Gap, the distances to Conasauga River's trail junctions are as follows: Chestnut Lead, 1.9 miles; Panther Creek, 4.9 miles; Tearbritches, 5.4 miles; Hickory Creek, 5.4 miles; Hickory Creek, 6.7 miles. From mile 5.4 mile to mile 6.7, Conasauga River and Hickory Creek Trails share the same treadway.

Directions: To reach the Conasauga River Trail's southeastern trailhead at Betty Gap, take Georgia 52 West 9.5 miles from the Ellijay square. At the Lake Conasauga Recreation Area sign, turn right onto F.S. 18 and continue 3.5 miles on that road before turning right onto F.S. 68. Once on F.S. 68, continue straight ahead, uphill. After traveling approximately 6.0 miles on F.S. 68, you will reach the three-way F.S. 68-64 junction near Potatopatch Mountain. Turn right onto

F.S. 64 and proceed 1.4 miles to the Conasauga River Trail sign and parking area.

To reach the Conasauga River Trail's northwestern trailhead at Forest Service 17-B, take U.S. 411 North from Chatsworth, past Eton toward Tennga. From the Georgia 52-U.S. 411 intersection in Chatsworth, travel U.S. 411 North approximately 13.4 miles to the town of Cisco. In Cisco, turn right onto the paved road immediately before the Cisco Baptist Church, which is also on the right. This road was once part of Georgia 2 and is now known as Old Highway 2. This road, which is opposite the current Georgia 2-U.S. 411 junction, is also F.S. 16. Continue on F.S. 16 (the pavement ends; stay to the right at the fork) for approximately 3.2 miles, then turn right onto F.S. 17 at the Lake Conasauga sign. Proceed straight ahead (17A turns right) on F.S. 17 for approximately 3.6 miles before turning left onto F.S. 17B at the Conasauga River Trail sign. After 0.2 mile F.S. 17B ends at the Conasauga River parking area and trailhead.

CHESTNUT LEAD TRAIL (1.8 miles one way to its junction with Conasauga River Trail). From trailhead to Conasauga River Trail: Easy to Moderate; from Conasauga River Trail to trailhead: Moderate.

Chestnut Lead is the shortest trail in the Cohutta Wilderness and is the second easiest of the four Conasauga lead-in trails. It starts at 3,280 feet and, like the others, drops steadily to the river. But compared to Tearbritches and Panther Creek Trails, which lose 2,000 feet in elevation, the grades of Chestnut Lead (which loses 1,000 feet) are almost easy.

Chestnut Lead descends through a diverse forest. Upland ridge, north-facing cove and riverine communities follow each other in quick succession. Within the first mile you can find black locust, black gum, sourwood; sassafras, persimmon, white pine; two species of hickory and four species of oak. In the moist cove there is a different forest. Sugar maple, striped maple, basswood; yellow poplar, yellow buckeye and black cherry flourish there. Down at the creek and river there are, among others, hemlock, sweet birch, sweetgum and red maple.

The trail's namesake tree is still there — but only as a shrub or sapling. Once the dominant species of the Southern Appalachian forest, the American chestnut has been virtually destroyed by the chestnut blight, an introduced fungus disease affecting the bark. Some of these former giants of the eastern forest are still standing — broken, hollowed and bleached. More often, their rot-resistant trunks lie prostrate on the forest floor, slowly building new soil that may, with the help of our science, once again nourish healthy chestnuts. But for now, the blight still kills each and every sapling. You can recognize living chestnut trees by their proximity to their dead forebears, and by their long, narrow, sharply toothed leaves.

After slightly less than a mile, Chestnut Lead turns left and descends into a sheltered cove. In the wake of the blight and the saw, the hardwood forest, now dominated by yellow poplar, is coming back straight and tall. In 100 to 150 years, if they are still protected, the yellow poplars will reach a huge size — over 130 feet high and more than 20 feet in circumference. If you don't think you can wait that long, visit Joyce Kilmer-Slickrock Wilderness in North Carolina and explore a virgin grove of enormous yellow poplars.

At the bottom of the cove Chestnut Lead curves to the right and parallels a Conasauga headwater stream. After a short distance, the trail dips to the left and crosses the creek at mile 1.2. Watch for this turn; a path continues straight ahead where the trail turns left and down. Chestnut Lead reaches the river slightly more than 0.2 mile beyond where it crosses the creek for the fourth time. The trail ends at its sign in a camping area across the normally shallow Conasauga. To the left, downstream, it is 3.5 miles on the yellow-blazed Conasauga River Trail to Bray Field. To the right, upstream, it is 1.9 miles to Betty Gap, the Conasauga River Trail's southeastern terminus.

Chestnut Lead has a good spring wildflower display. Large-flowering trillium, common along much of the trail, blooms in early May.

Directions: Take Georgia 52 West 9.5 miles from the Ellijay square. At the Lake Conasauga Recreation Area sign, turn right onto F.S. 18 and continue 3.5 miles on that road before turning right onto F.S. 68. Once on F.S. 68, continue straight ahead, uphill. After traveling approximately 6.0 miles on F.S. 68, you will reach the three-way F.S. 68-64 junction near Potatopatch Mountain. Turn left toward Lake Conasauga with F.S. 68 and proceed 2.0 miles to the Chestnut Lead sign and parking area.

PANTHER CREEK TRAIL (3.4 miles one way between access points). From Conasauga River Trail to Panther Creek Falls: Moderate; from Panther Creek Falls to East Cowpen Trail: Strenuous; from East Cowpen Trail to Conasauga River Trail: Moderate.

The first 30 yards of this lightly used scenic trail ford the Conasauga River at approximately 1,940 feet. Once across, the blue-blazed trail follows Panther Creek upstream to its headwaters high in the mountains, crossing the stream frequently along the way. For the first 1.1 miles the trail gradually rises beside

Panther Creek, but after crossing the brook to the left below a long cascade, the trail suddenly changes.

Here it becomes not only steep but rocky as it ascends to the falls through a boulder field. This is the most rugged section of trail in the Cohutta Wilderness. Because the trail is often impossible to detect on the bare rock, you must search for the guiding blazes on the tree trunks.

You can easily walk down to the bottom of Panther Creek Falls. Above, the wide waterfall drops, then slides 60 to 70 feet. The sun-faceted water glistens intensely in contrast to the deep green of the surrounding forest. Below, the creek hurtles down the mountainside, twisting and tumbling, splitting and rejoining in a continuous cascade hundreds of feet in length.

From near a giant hemlock, the trail curls upward to the left beneath Panther Bluff to the top of the falls at mile 1.4. Here, where Panther Creek disappears over the brink, rock ledges provide one of only two trailside vistas within the Cohutta Wilderness. There are no roads, houses or smokestacks in sight, and miles of unbroken wilderness stretch out in front of these isolated falls. The view alone is well worth the effort.

If you intend to hike farther up the mountain, walk near the left side of Panther Creek until you find a blaze or see a muddy gap in the rhododendron, where the trail crosses the stream. For the next 0.5 mile, the path gradually ascends Panther Creek's cove-like valley. Although it doesn't open to the north, this cove supports an unusually diverse forest: sweet birch, yellow buckeye, black cherry, mountain silverbell, sugar maple and four species of deciduous magnolia — yellow poplar, cucumbertree, Fraser magnolia and umbrella magnolia — occur, among others, in this fertile area.

The trail, which reaches approximately 2,800 feet at the top of the falls, climbs to near 3,800 feet at its eastern access point. At mile 1.9 the path makes a short, very steep ascent, the first, and by far the shortest, of three sharp upgrades that gain much of the remaining elevation to East Cowpen.

Directions: Panther Creek is an interior trail that has both of its access points along other trails, Conasauga River and East Cowpen. Its Conasauga River access point is 4.9 miles from the Conasauga River Trail's southeastern trailhead at Betty Gap, and 8.2 miles from Conasauga River Trail's northwestern trailhead off F.S. 17. Its East Cowpen access point is 2.3 miles from East Cowpen's southern trailhead at Three Forks Mountain, and 4.7 miles from East Cowpen's northern trailhead at Rice Camp Trail's parking area. (See East Cowpen and Conasauga River Trails, also in this chapter, for directions to their trailheads. See Rice Camp Trail for directions to East Cowpen's northern trailhead.)

If you walk north from East Cowpen's Three Forks trailhead, Panther Creek's upper-elevation access point will be to your left along a level stretch of trail. A sign and blue blaze usually mark Panther Creek's entering gap into the woods.

If Panther Creek's lower access sign is missing, its initial blue blaze along the Conasauga River may be difficult to find. If you hike from Betty Gap toward Bray Field, you will find Panther Creek's sign (if it's there) and beginning blaze 75 yards past the end of the 18th river crossing. You will be on the left side of the river as you face downstream. Look for Panther Creek's access point to the right of the trail near the Conasauga River. Panther Creek Trail crosses the Conasauga over what is usually an island.

If you are walking upstream toward Panther Creek from Bray Field, you will climb up and over a hill. From the bottom of the hill (upstream side), it is slightly less than 0.2 mile to Panther Creek Trail. Fifteen yards before it reaches Panther Creek's sign and blaze, the Conasauga River Trail enters a wide campsite, then angles to the right. If you come to a ford on the Conasauga River, you have walked past Panther Creek Trail.

TEARBRITCHES TRAIL (3.4 miles one way to Bray Field and its junction with Conasauga River and Hickory Creek trails). From trailhead to Bray Field: Moderate; from Bray Field to trailhead: Strenuous.

Beginning at 3,606 feet, orange-blazed Tearbritches climbs 0.4 mile, sharply at first, then more moderately, to the broad top of Bald Mountain (4,005 ft.). The last time I hiked Tearbritches, early one mid-June morning, Bald Mountain was in the middle of a low-scudding cloud. When I reached the top, I breathed in a familiar fragrance — the Christmas-tree scent of the spruce-fir forest in North Carolina. To the left of the trail, in what was a clearing when the Cohuttas become wilderness, there were six small fir trees, probably Fraser firs, which are not native to Georgia. A road once led to the clearing, so my guess is that someone planted the trees there.

The short climb to Bald Mountain is the only upgrade on the way down to Bray Field and the Conasauga River. Tearbritches continues across the eastern side of the mountain's crest, then begins its descent. For the next 2.7 miles, from mile 0.5 to mile 3.2, the trail alternates short, level stretches with longer downslopes that become more abrupt toward the base of the mountain. From mile 2.0 to mile 2.9, the trail makes a particularly steep downridge plunge. Tearbritches loses approximately 2,040 feet along this 2.7-mile section of trail.

At mile 3.0 the trail splits. Follow the left fork and continue downhill to the level ground beside Tearbritches Creek at mile 3.2. From here, the trail crosses its namesake creek immediately beyond a prominent camping area, then quickly arrives at its signed junction with the Conasauga River Trail on the edge of Bray Field (1,920 ft.).

Bray Field is the most important trail junction in the western half of the wilderness. Tearbritches ends at the field; two other trails — Conasauga River and Hickory Creek — pass through it, and the lower access point of a fourth trail, Panther Creek, is nearby.

The upper slopes of Bald Mountain have an open oak forest similar to the high ridge areas on the Appalachian Trail. The broken canopy allows an abundance of sunshine to reach the forest floor. This, in turn, allows an abundance of vegetation — ferns, shrubs and, occasionally, blackberry briers — to crowd the trail. Although there are brier patches along the upper portion of the trail, they are not as bad as the trail's name might suggest.

From early to mid-June, hundreds of Indian pinks bloom along either side of the trail starting at 0.9 mile. These perennial herbs, which often grow 2 feet tall, descend with the trail for nearly 0.1 mile. The Indian pink's unusual flower resembles a trumpet-shaped tube, red on the outside and bright yellow-green on the inside. At its uppermost end, the throat of the trumpet flares into five narrow, reflexed lobes, yellow-green on top, red on the bottom.

Directions: Same as for Chestnut Lead Trail except you must travel 1.5 miles farther toward Lake Conasauga on F.S. 68. A large sign marks the trailhead. (See Chestnut Lead Trail for directions from Ellijay.)

If you are walking the Conasauga River Trail from Betty Gap, you will find Tearbritches's sign and initial blaze to the left of the trail just after it crosses Tearbritches Creek and begins to enter the upstream edge of Bray Field.

If you enter Bray Field on its downstream side, Tearbritches's sign may be difficult to find. Start where Hickory Creek Trail begins to leave Bray Field by crossing the Conasauga. Walk approximately 50 yards upstream on the path beside the river. When you reach a campsite fire ring, turn right and continue a few feet to the next path away from the Conasauga. This path is the Conasauga River Trail. You will find the Tearbritches sign before the Conasauga River Trail crosses Tearbritches Creek.

HICKORY CREEK TRAIL (8.6 miles one way between trailheads). From F.S. 630 to Conasauga River Trail at Bray Field: Easy; from Bray Field to western trailhead on F.S. 630: Moderate; from Bray Field to northern trailhead on F.S. 51: Easy to Moderate walked in either direction.

Hickory Creek is the third longest trail in the Cohutta Wilderness, and most people who hike the trail do not walk its entire length. Instead, they walk from either access point to the scenic Conasauga River, which the trail fords. Hickory Creek's western trailhead provides the shortest and easiest route to the Conasauga downstream from Bray Field.

Starting from this western access point (2,300 ft.), the wide, white-blazed trail, actually an old road, descends gradually through a predominantly hard-wood forest. After the first mile the trail swings to the left beside Rough Creek (there are two Rough Creeks in the Cohutta Wilderness). The rocky old road parallels this lively brook until crossing it at mile 1.6. The trail continues 75 yards to the Conasauga, where it turns right and follows the road upstream beside the river. From this turn and for 1.3 miles to its crossing of the Conasauga in Bray Field, Hickory Creek Trail is contiguous with the yellow-blazed Conasauga River Trail.

The two trails closely parallel the western bank of the Conasauga for 0.7 mile. This segment affords many largely unobstructed views of this beautiful mountain river. At mile 2.4 the trail slants to the right away from the river and half-circles a chain of abandoned beaver ponds. Hickory Creek fords the Conasauga (usually knee deep or lower), through the gap of the former road across Bray Field, at mile 3.0.

The remaining 5.7-mile segment is the Cohutta's easiest long stretch of trail without river crossings. From the Conasauga at an elevation of 1,920 feet, Hickory Creek loses only 120 feet to its East Cowpen access point. There are no long, strenuous grades on this section of trail. There are, however, numerous ups and downs, most of them short and easy. These undulations follow a pattern. The trail meanders through a terrain of low, flat-topped ridges frequently notched by streams and gaps. Thus Hickory Creek dips to a stream, rises to the side or top of a ridge, dips to a gap, rises to the side or top of the next ridge, then dips to a stream.

The only potentially confusing point along this section of trail occurs at mile 4.1, where the trail crosses a rocky stream, then turns right at a fire ring and follows a roadbed. This stream is Thomas Creek, the first large enough for a name beyond the Conasauga.

By mile 6.7 the trail becomes predominantly level as it follows a former road to East Cowpen. This last 2.0-mile section crosses over several branches of Hickory Creek.

The 5.7-mile segment of Hickory Creek to the east of the Conasauga winds through an unbroken, isolated forest. Here oaks, hickories, yellow poplars and white pines are slowly regaining their former size. There are more stands of tall white pine along this seldomly walked section than on any other trail in the Cohutta Wilderness.

Two deciduous magnolias — Fraser and umbrella — grow in the moist areas near streams. Their leaves, which are larger than the leaves of all other trees in North Georgia, emanate from branch ends in a circular, whorled arrangement. The leaf of the Fraser magnolia is readily identified by its auriculate (eared) base.

Directions: Hickory Creek has two trailheads; both can be reached by traveling north on U.S. 411 from Chatsworth. The western trailhead is less than 2.0 miles from the Conasauga River. The northern trailhead is 5.7 miles from the Conasauga.

To reach Hickory Creek's northern trailhead, park at the Rice Camp trailhead, then walk approximately 140 yards on the East Cowpen Trail to the Hickory Creek sign to the right. As you approach the Rice Camp trailhead on F.S. 51, East Cowpen is the trail that continues straight ahead into the wilderness. (See Rice Camp Trail, also in this chapter, for further directions.)

To reach Hickory Creek's western trailhead, take U.S. 411 North from Chatsworth past the town of Eton. From the Georgia 52-U.S. 411 intersection in Chatsworth, travel approximately 7.3 miles on U.S 411 North to the "Crandall" sign on the right side of the highway. At the sign, turn right onto the paved road and continue over the railroad tracks before turning right again. After this second right turn, proceed 0.1 mile, then turn left onto F.S. 630 (Mill Creek Road) toward Lake Conasauga Recreation Area. Stay on F.S. 630 (it turns to gravel) for approximately 9.0 miles to the F.S. 630-17 intersection. Continue straight through this intersection on F.S. 630; the Hickory Creek Trail parking area is 0.3 mile ahead.

If the "Crandall" sign is missing, ask for directions to F.S. 630 in the Dewberry Baptist Church-Gallman's Grocery area.

EAST COWPEN TRAIL (7.0 miles one way between trailheads). From Three Forks Mountain to its northern trailhead on F.S. 51: Easy to Moderate; from F.S. 51 to its southern trailhead at Three Forks Mountain: Strenuous.

East Cowpen serves as the main artery through the middle of the wilderness, leading directly to five trails and indirectly to all trails except Hemp Top. Starting at its southern trailhead at Three Forks Mountain (3,500 ft.), East Cowpen follows an easy to moderate upgrade to 4,100 feet near the top of Cowpen Mountain at mile 1.3. The remainder of the trail, except for two or three easy uphill grades, is level or downsloping all the way to its northern trailhead at the Rice Camp Trail parking area (1,740 ft.). Beyond its first 3.5 miles, East Cowpen makes numerous sharp descents.

As many of you already know, East Cowpen Trail is actually a road — old Highway 2, unmaintained (except by those who use it) but still legally open to the public. Neither iron bars nor signs prevent or prohibit motorized vehicles from entering the

Cohutta Wilderness. The reasons this road still bisects an area that was officially declared wilderness in 1975 are too numerous and convoluted to discuss in this guide. I can say that progress, such as the rerouting of Highway 2 out of the wilderness, has been made, and that the U.S. Forest Service is actively seeking a solution to the problem.

Starting at its southern end at Three Forks Mountain, the distances to East Cowpen's trail junctions are as follows: Rough Ridge, 0.5 mile; Panther Creek, 2.3 miles; Hickory Ridge, 4.4 miles; Hickory Creek, 6.9 miles; Rice Camp, 7.0 miles.

Note: On July 24, 1987 the U.S. Forest Service gated Old Georgia 2 — East Cowpen Trail — preventing vehicular access through the heart of the Cohutta Wilderness. Please join me in congratulating the Forest Service on a difficult task finally done.

Directions: To reach East Cowpen's southern trailhead at Three Forks Mountain, continue northeastward on F.S. 64 (farther away from the F.S. 68-64 intersection at Potatopatch Mountain) approximately 2.9 miles beyond the Conasauga River Trailhead at Betty Gap. East Cowpen is the road that enters the wilderness to the left in the middle of a sharp curve. (See Conasauga River Trail, also in this chapter, for directions to Betty Gap.)

At present, East Cowpen does not have a trail sign. The directions to its northern trailhead, however, are exactly the same as those to the Rice Camp Trail. The two trails share the same parking area, which is in front of Rice Camp's sign and bulletin board. East Cowpen is the trail/road that continues straight ahead where F.S. 51 ends at the Rice Camp trailhead. (See Rice Camp Trail, also in this chapter, for directions to East Cowpen's northern trailhead.)

91

JACKS RIVER TRAIL (16.7 miles one way between trailheads). From Dally Gap downstream to northwestern trailhead in Alaculsy Valley: Easy to Moderate; from Alaculsy Valley upstream to southeastern trailhead at Dally Gap: Moderate.

Jacks River is the longest and wettest (40 fords) trail in the Cohutta Wilderness. The river it follows and crosses is also the most popular destination in the wilderness. A network of seven trails leads dayhikers and backpackers directly to this trail and its river.

If you are interested in walking this trail from end to end, you may want to start at its southeastern (upstream) Dally Gap Trailhead (2,578 ft.). This route travels downriver and downhill, losing approximately 1,050 feet to Beech Bottom at mile 8.6 and slightly more than 1,600 feet to its other end in Alaculsy Valley.

The orange-blazed Jacks River Trail follows a wide, easily walked old road from Dally Gap. For the most part, this first section of trail is a gentle downhill stroll to the Jacks River and its tributary, Bear Branch. Although it parallels Bear Branch from the gap, the trail does not approach close enough for a view until mile 1.6. Three-tenths of a mile farther, the trail trades streams and turns to follow the Jacks as it winds toward the northwest. This turn is only a few hundred yards from where the river enters the wilderness.

At mile 2.3 the trail crosses the Jacks — the first of 20 fords to the falls, the first of 40 fords to complete the trail. As on the Conasauga River Trail, there is usually a blaze guiding the trail's return to dry land across the river from each ford. These blazes, however, are not always easily found. Part of the challenge of hiking this trail, besides trying to keep your balance on the slippery rocks of the riverbed, is figuring

92

out where the fords begin and end. For a helpful description of the fords, how to find them, what time of the year to cross them and their potential dangers, see the Conasauga River Trail, also in this chapter. Although the Jacks is the wider stream, trail conditions and the depths of the fords on these two rivers are nearly identical.

Much of today's trail, including some of the fords, follows the path of a former logging railroad used to transport timber out of the Cohutta Mountains until 1935. In places, parallel rows of the slowly rotting ties are still plainly visible, and observant hikers still find hand-forged railroad spikes of several different sizes. If you are walking on an aisle-like section of trail — straight, level and wide — you are probably on the former railroad bed.

Along the riverbanks near many of the fords, look for the piled-rock buttresses that mark the locations of the bridges that once spanned the Jacks River. A flood washed these bridges away nearly 55 years ago.

The high shoals below the second ford begin the Jacks's most turbulent stretch. For nearly a mile the river, especially at higher water levels, is one long, ricocheting cascade, more white than not. Here the Jacks exhibits the steep-sided, V-shaped profile of a youthful river cutting into mountain. Where the Jacks descends, so does the trail. It may climb a hillside first, but it always drops back down to the river.

Starting with the fourth crossing at mile 4.6, the trail makes you wade the river 15 times in 2.5 miles. These fords come in quick succession, most only 0.1 or 0.2 mile apart. The trail remains nearly level and parallel to the river between crossings to its 18th ford at mile 7.1. The Penitentiary Branch Trail junction is in the campsite across the 18th ford.

Beyond the next (19th) ford, the trail climbs a short distance up and away from the river, then descends to where it crosses Rough Creek at mile 8.0. Rough Ridge Trail ties into the Jacks River Trail immediately across the creek. If you turn left and follow the creek upstream, you will be walking on Rough Ridge Trail. The Jacks River Trail turns right and closely parallels the creek downstream before swinging to the left, above and then away from the river. Once it leaves the Jacks, the trail gently ascends to a spur ridge, then downslopes to its 20th and final ford before the falls. The section of trail between the 19th and 20th fords twice gives the appearance of leading up and away from the river. But it is actually the river that twice meanders away from the trail. And both times, instead of following the river, the trail takes the short-cut straight across the gap.

Beyond the 20th crossing, the Jacks River Trail reaches two trail junctions, one right after the other, at mile 8.6. The first, to the left, is yellow-blazed Hickory Ridge. The second, to the right 45 yards farther downstream, is unblazed Beech Bottom. The end of Hickory Ridge Trail has been rerouted since it was originally drawn on the Cohutta Wilderness Map. If you are walking the Jacks River Trail downstream toward the falls, you will now reach the Hickory Ridge junction 45 yards before you come to the Beech Bottom junction.

The trail continues to follow the river downstream to the cliffs above Jacks River Falls at mile 9.2. Dropping in stages at the head of a wide gorge, this waterfall is the most scenic and most visited single feature in the Cohutta Wilderness. It is also the most powerful falls beside the trails of North Georgia.

If you would like to see and hear the Jacks River Falls at its frothing, roaring best, wait until winter or early spring, after several days of heavy rains. It is then, on a sunny day, that the falls becomes one long, crashing, upwelling run of brilliant whitewater. Beech

Bottom Trail enables you to reach the falls without having to cross the river.

Beyond the falls, the trail follows an obvious railroad cut back down to river's edge. It reaches the 21st ford, the first in 1.8 miles, at mile 10.3. Here the pattern of crossing and paralleling the river begins again. Only this time the trail remains level or slightly downhill between crossings.

Downstream from the start of the 26th ford, you will see the first of several tall bluffs along the lower Jacks. The gap at the top of this bluff is Horseshoe Bend Overlook. If you want a good look at the sheer rock around the bend, keep walking down the bank after this crossing.

Beyond the 40th and final ford at mile 14.8, the last section of trail remains close to the river, occasionally close enough for long range views. Here, as it flows toward its meeting with the Conasauga just outside the wilderness boundary, the Jacks becomes wider and less turbulent, its pools longer and deeper. The Jacks River Trail ends next to a bridge in Alaculsy Valley (966 ft.).

Starting from its southeastern terminus at Dally Gap, the distances to the Jacks River's trail junctions are as follows: Sugar Cove, 3.9 miles; Penitentiary Branch, 7.2 miles; Rough Ridge, 8.0 miles; Hickory Ridge, 8.6 miles; Beech Bottom, 8.6 miles; Rice Camp, 10.4 miles; Horseshoe Bend, 13.1 miles.

If you are planning to hike the Jacks River Trail, I recommend that you leave your boots at home and wear tennis shoes you don't mind getting wet instead. A sturdy hiking stick will help you keep your balance on the slick river rocks.

Directions: To reach the Jacks River's northwestern trailhead in Alaculsy Valley, travel U.S. 411 North from Chatsworth, past Eton toward Tennga. From the Georgia 52-U.S. 411 intersection in Chatsworth, travel U.S. 411 North approximately 13.4 miles to the town of Cisco. In Cisco, turn right onto the paved road immediately before the Cisco Baptist Church, which is also on the right. This road was once Highway 2, so it is now known as Old Highway 2. This road is also F.S. 16. Continue on F.S. 16 (the pavement ends; stay to the right at the fork; pass Hopewell Church; cross the Conasauga River; continue straight ahead where F.S. 51 turns right) for approximately 8.7 miles to the suspension bridge over the Jacks River. The Jacks River Trail parking lot is to the right, across the river in Tennessee.

To reach the Jacks River's southeastern trailhead at Dally Gap, travel Georgia 5 North from Blue Ridge toward McCaysville. From the U.S. 76-Georgia 5 intersection just north of Blue Ridge, proceed approximately 3.8 miles on Georgia 5 North before turning left onto a paved road at the "Old Highway 2" sign. Continue on this road for approximately 10.5 miles (the pavement ends after 7.5 miles) to the major forest service intersection at Watson Gap. Turn hard right at the gap onto F.S. 22 (one lane) and drive approximately 3.6 miles to the trailhead at Dally Gap.

SUGAR COVE TRAIL (2.2 miles one way between access points). From Rough Ridge Trail to Jacks River Trail: Moderate; from Jacks River Trail to Rough Ridge Trail: Strenuous.

One of the three seldom-used interior trails, Sugar Cove requires a 2.6-mile walk — 0.5 mile on East Cowpen and 2.1 miles on Rough Ridge — just to reach its upper access point. But if you are interested in hiking this trail, don't let the additional distance discourage you. The 2.6 miles are easily walked and quickly completed.

Beginning at approximately 3,600 feet, Sugar Cove Trail immediately plunges into a beautiful, steep-sided cove. The upper portion of the cove has an open hardwood forest, allowing largely unobstructed views of 50 to 60 yards. Past the beginning patches of sweetshrub, the forest floor is often covered with arching fern fronds.

As you continue to descend into this isolated cove, the forest becomes more dense and the individual trees become taller and thicker. Here, beside the normally dry headwater streambed of Sugar Cove Branch, the second-growth cove hardwoods — black cherry, yellow buckeye, sweet birch, sugar maple and yellow poplar — have grown to larger dimensions than along any other trail in the Cohutta Wilderness. The yellow poplars have become perceptibly larger over the last decade. The largest are now 11 to 12 feet in circumference and 110 to 120 feet tall.

The abundance of the sugar maple — a tree at the southern limit of its range across the northernmost counties of our state — is the cove's most distinctive feature. These maples occur less and less frequently from west to east in the mountains of Georgia. Although they are fairly common from the Cohuttas westward, sugar maples are rare in the trailside forests of northcentral and northeastern Georgia.

Near the bottom of the cove the sugar maple becomes co-dominant with the yellow poplar, just as common and almost a big. The largest sugar maple along the trail is 10 feet, 7 inches in circumference and perhaps 100 to 110 feet tall. This tree has a blackened base and is located a few feet to the right of the trail at 0.8 mile. Once its height and crown are measured accurately, this tree will probably become the new state record sugar maple.

The sugar maple leaf has smooth margins (especially compared to the red maple), is dark green above and usually has five long, pointed lobes. If you have seen the Canadian flag, you have seen the shape of the sugar maple leaf.

The trail loses nearly 1,100 feet during its first 1.2 miles. The beginning 0.3 mile drops very sharply. Beyond that initial plunge, the downgrades become less severe as the trail slopes down to its first crossing of Sugar Cove Branch at mile 1.1. After crossing the branch, the path crosses a tributary, then returns to and crosses the branch for the second time. (Sugar Cove Branch usually has a steady flow below the tributary.)

Immediately after it crosses Sugar Cove Branch for the fifth time at mile 1.5, the trail veers to the left and climbs, steeply at first, a hillside high above the Jacks River. The path scarcely levels out before beginning its slow, winding, 0.5-mile descent to the river.

The trail crosses the Jacks (elevation approximately 1,900 ft.), then quickly reaches its lower-end sign where it meets the orange-blazed Jacks River Trail. To the right, upstream, it is 3.9 miles to Dally Gap, the Jacks River Trail's southeastern terminus.

Directions: Sugar Cove is the only interior trail that requires you to hike portions of two other trails to reach one of its ends. To reach Sugar Cove's upper access point, you must first walk 0.5 mile on East Cowpen Trail starting at Three Forks Mountain, then walk 2.1 miles on Rough Ridge Trail.

The right turn onto Sugar Cove is marked with a sign and a white blaze, which may be faint. The sign is in an 8-by-8-foot worn spot and has a flat rock just right to sit on behind it. (See East Cowpen and Rough Ridge Trails, also in this chapter, for further directions. The directions to East Cowpen's southern trailhead at Three Forks Mountain begin at Betty Gap. See Conasauga River Trail for directions to Betty Gap.)

PENITENTIARY BRANCH TRAIL (3.5 miles one way to its junction with Jacks River Trail). From trailhead to Jacks River Trail: Easy; from Jacks River Trail to trailhead: Moderate.

One of seven trails guiding hikers to the Jacks River, Penitentiary Branch, like the others, loses elevation along the way. But even though it loses 1,380 feet, compared to most of the other Jacks River lead-in trails, especially Rough Ridge and Hickory Ridge, the descent is mild.

This trail doesn't roller-coaster to the river; it is level or downhill the entire way. So if you're searching for an easy, enjoyable and uncongested route to Jacks River and its trail, try Penitentiary Branch.

The trail, beginning at 3,060 feet, is wide, yellow blazed and easily walked. As long as you stay on the former jeep road and ignore the side paths, you should have no difficulty following the trail down to the river.

For most of the first 3.0 miles a canopy of oak, hickory, maple and Virginia pine shade the trail. Underneath these taller trees, a great variety of herbaceous plants, ferns, shrubs and smaller trees form a dense understory. Against this solid, hedge-like background of green, the remaining clusters of bright orange flame azaleas are especially showy in mid-June.

Scattered alongside the trail, Virginia pine thrive in pockets of dry, rocky soil as they do throughout much of North Georgia. Often they grow on granite ledges where no other tree can. Usually 30 to 50 feet high and somewhat scraggly in appearance, Virginia pines are readily identified. Their yellow-green needles — two to the sheath, 1 to 3 inches long and twisted — are shorter than those of any other native pine in the mountains. Also characteristic of the Virginia pine is the reddish-brown bark which is broken into small scales.

After 3.1 miles, the trail rock-steps across the normally inches-deep Penitentiary Branch and follows it toward the river. In the moist coves near Jacks River, the composition of the forest abruptly changes. Here tall hemlock, beech, sweet birch and yellow poplar shade the trail. Penitentiary Branch ties into the orange-blazed Jacks River Trail at a large campsite clearing. To the right (downstream) it is two river crossings and 2.0 miles to Jacks River Falls; to the left (upstream) it is 7.2 miles to the southeastern terminus of the Jacks River Trail at Dally Gap.

Directions: From Dally Gap, continue straight ahead (northward) on F.S. 73. F.S. 73 curves to the left from Dally Gap. After traveling approximately 2.4 miles on F.S. 73, you will come to the trailhead parking area on the right side of the road. Penitentiary Branch Trail begins across the road from the parking area. (See Jacks River Trail, also in this chapter, for directions to Dally Gap.)

ROUGH RIDGE TRAIL (7.0 miles one way between access points). From East Cowpen Trail to Jacks River Trail: Moderate to Strenuous; from Jacks River Trail to East Cowpen Trail: Strenuous.

Along Rough Ridge Trail, as well as throughout the wilderness, you may occasionally notice small, pulverized patches of bare dirt. These patches are made by the rooting of an exotic species, the fabled European wild boar (*Sus scrofa*). Introduced at Hooper's Bald, North Carolina, in 1912, the original stock of 14 animals escaped from their fenced game refuge. They have since multiplied, interbred with the half-wild mountaineer swine and spread throughout much of the Southern Appalachians.

Although they now have a mixed genotype, European wild boar in the Cohutta Wilderness retain much of their original phenotype. The European wild boar, unlike domestic swine, has a heavy, bristly coat which varies in color from reddish-brown to black. And whereas domestic swine are usually heavy through the hindquarters, the wild boar has massive shoulders and a mane of bristles running along the back of the neck, giving the animal a humped appearance. The mane stands up when the boar is excited or angry. The young, looking much like giant chipmunks, have horizontal stripes and blotches of brown and yellow on their sides. Both sexes have tusks.

Where living close to man, boar are usually nocturnal, but in remote areas like the Cohutta Wilderness, they often become active during the day. I saw five wild boar — a female and her four young — the last time I hiked Rough Ridge. Keep in mind that the European wild boar is a large and formidable animal. The larger, solitary males range from 300 to over 400 pounds. Do not molest or antagonize them or their young, in any way. And if you plan to walk with a hound that has more bravado than brains, remember that these wild boar are renowned for their ability to defend themselves against entire packs of hunting dogs.

Blue-blazed Rough Ridge is the longest of the seven Jacks River lead-in trails. Starting along East

Cowpen Trail at 3,760 feet and ending at 1,620 feet, it also loses more elevation than the other Jacks River approaches. Most people who have carried a heavy pack up or down this trail agree that the ridge it follows is aptly named.

The trail stays on or near the top of Rough Ridge for much of its length. For the first 4 miles it often follows wide, grassy roadbeds. But soon after beginning its series of steep descents, the trail narrows to forest path, often winding and occasionally rocky.

For the first 2.1 miles, to the Sugar Cove access point, Rough Ridge gently undulates through a hardwood forest with witch-hazel, sassafras and a deciduous holly common in the understory. Beyond the Sugar Cove sign the trail begins to descend, alternating nearly level stretches with moderate downgrades for 1.6 miles. At mile 3.7 it climbs moderately for less than 0.2 mile, levels off, then drops below the ridge.

The trail crosses two shallow streams at mile 4.4, then starts its second and last climb — a sharp 0.1-mile ascent back to ridgetop. From here, Rough Ridge becomes a downhill roller coaster, alternating level stretches or easy downgrades with steep pitches to mile 6.3, where it enters a cove dominated by hemlock. Along this last section of trail you may catch glimpses of Big Frog, a 4,200-foot mountain 3 or 4 miles to the northeast in Tennessee.

After reaching the cove, the path turns left and dips to an unnamed tributary of Rough Creek. It parallels both the feeder stream and creek before crossing Rough Creek at mile 6.7. The remainder of the trail closely follows the creek downstream to a sign, which marks its lower access point on the Jacks River Trail.

Rough Ridge Trail does not cross Rough Creek a second time; it ends where the Jacks River Trail crosses Rough Creek. If you continue from the Rough Ridge sign downstream along the creek, you will tie into the Jacks River Trail on its way to Jacks River Falls, 1.2 miles downriver. If you cross Rough Creek at the trail junction, you will be on the orange-blazed Jacks River Trail as it heads upstream, back toward Dally Gap.

A section of Rough Ridge Trail approximately 2.0 miles in length has been rerouted. The last part of the trail — before it reaches the Rough Creek tributary — was moved to the west, down from the sharply descending ridgetop to the mountainside closer to Rough Creek.

Rough Ridge Trail's only water source, two small, spring-fed streams at mile 4.4 from East Cowpen, may be dry during the summer and fall.

Directions: Rough Ridge is an interior trail that has both of its access points along other trails, Jacks River and East Cowpen. Its Jacks River access point is 8.0 miles from the Jacks River Trail's southeastern trailhead at Dally Gap, and 8.7 miles from the Jacks River Trail's northwestern trailhead at Alaculsy Valley. Its East Cowpen access point is 0.5 mile from East Cowpen's southern trailhead at Three Forks Mountain, and 6.5 miles from East Cowpen's northern trailhead at Rice Camp Trail's parking area.

(See East Cowpen and Jacks River Trails, also in this chapter, for directions to their trailheads. See Rice Camp Trail for directions to East Cowpen's northern trailhead. East Cowpen's directions to its southern trailhead at Three Forks Mountain start at Betty Gap. See Conasauga River Trail for directions to Betty Gap.)

HICKORY RIDGE TRAIL (3.5 miles one way between access points). From East Cowpen Trail to Jacks River Trail: Easy to Moderate; from Jacks River Trail to East Cowpen Trail: Strenuous.

Hickory Ridge starts at 3,200 feet on the shoulder of Buckeye Mountain, deep within the Cohutta Wilderness. To reach its closest access point, you must walk 2.6 miles on East Cowpen Trail.

Yellow-blazed Hickory Ridge Trail is easy to describe. The lightly used path starts out level, then descends to another level stretch, then descends again. The rest of the trail, alternating between nearly level sections and downridge pitches of varying length and steepness, repeats this pattern down to the Jacks River. Hickory Ridge leads uphill half a dozen times, but these upgrades are so short and easy, that by Cohutta Wilderness standards, they are hardly noticeable or worth mentioning.

On your way down the trail, the higher ridge to the right, a mile to the east, is Rough Ridge.

Although hickories, mockernut and pignut, are more common than usual on North Georgia ridges, the oaks — northern red, scarlet, black, white and chestnut — still dominate the trailside forest for most of its length. Chestnut oaks, preferring the dry, rocky soils of ridges and mountainsides, are especially common along the upper portion of the trail. These slow-growing oaks are the thickest trees on Hickory Ridge. They have dark brown, deeply furrowed bark; large, often twisted limbs; and leaves with numerous wavy, rounded teeth or lobes. Many of them are starting to hollow.

At mile 3.2 the trail descends through a belt of rhododendron and hemlock, turns parallel to a small stream, then drops quickly down to the Jacks River (1,560 ft.) by way of the streambed. If it has not been blazed recently, the last 0.2 mile of Hickory Ridge, from where it first reaches the river to its end, can be confusing. Once you come to the river, turn right and follow the Jacks upstream. After you duck under rhododendron, walk over a rocky, washed-out section of shoreline, pass a path that angles to the left into deep water, you will again find the trail's treadway. Make the ford where you see the worn bank and yellow blaze.

Hickory Ridge ends at its junction sign on the Jacks River Trail. Jacks River Falls is 0.6 mile to the left, downstream.

Directions: Hickory Ridge is an interior trail that has both of its access points along other trails, Jacks River and East Cowpen. Its Jacks River access point is 8.6 miles from the Jacks River Trail's southeastern trailhead at Dally Gap, and 8.1 miles from the Jacks River Trail's northwestern trailhead at Alaculsy Valley. Its East Cowpen access point is 4.4 miles from East Cowpen's southern trailhead at Three Forks Mountain, and 2.6 miles from East Cowpen's northern trailhead at Rice Camp Trail's parking area. (See East Cowpen and Jacks River Trails, also in this chapter, for directions to their trailheads. See Rice Camp Trail for directions to East Cowpen's northern trailhead.)

If its initial blaze has become faint and if its sign has been vandalized, Hickory Ridge's East Cowpen access point is difficult to find. You will find Hickory Ridge Trail in the middle of a horseshoe curve that almost doubles back on itself. On the outside of the curve the road widens and leads to a rotting log. The trail starts next to the log.

BEECH BOTTOM TRAIL (4.0 miles one way to its junction with Jacks River Trail). Easy to Moderate walked in either direction.

Beech Bottom Trail, really an old road blocked to vehicular traffic, is now 0.5 mile longer than it was originally. The forest service has moved its trailhead out to Forest Route 62, where there is now a sign, bulletin board and large graveled parking area.

Even though it has been lengthened, Beech Bottom is still the most easily walked trail in the Cohutta Wilderness. It is also the only trail that leads to the most scenic single feature in the wilderness — the wildly churning Jacks River Falls — without forcing hikers to ford the Jacks at least once. These two facts predictably account for another: Beech Bottom is the most heavily used trail in the Cohuttas.

The unblazed yet easily followed old road gradually loses elevation as it winds around steep ravines to mile 1.0, where it crosses an unnamed branch. Across the first branch, the trail follows another upstream. Along this section of trail, there are two large, slow-growing trees — a beech and a hemlock — that escaped the logging earlier in the century. Beech Bottom continues level or gently uphill to mile 2.4, where it begins its gradual descent to the Jacks River. The middle of the trail often winds along dry ridges where the forest changes to oak and Virginia pine.

At mile 3.3 the trail turns sharply to the right, then quickly crosses Beech Creek. To the right before Beech Creek, the clearing quickly returning to forest is the former site of a large hunting cabin. The intertwining rocky paths across the creek all head in the same direction. After they come together, continue through Beech Bottom — a flat flood-plain area just east of where Beech Creek joins the Jacks River — on the dirt path to the left. The site of an old homestead,

Beech Bottom was once cleared, fenced and farmed. Now the buildings have been removed and the forest is rapidly reclaiming the bottom.

Continue straight ahead on the path until it meets the orange-blazed Jacks River Trail. To the right, downstream, it is 0.6 mile to the cliffside overlook above Jacks River Falls.

Directions: From the Jacks River Trailhead in Alaculsy Valley, continue farther into Tennessee on Forest Route 221. Slightly more than 1.0 mile past the suspension bridge over the Jacks River, where F.S. 16 enters Tennessee and becomes F.R. 221, make a sharp right turn onto F.R. 62. Continue approximately 4.5 miles on F.R. 62, then turn into the large graveled parking area above and to the left of the road. (See Jacks River Trail, also in this chapter, for directions to its northwestern trailhead in Alaculsy Valley.)

RICE CAMP TRAIL (3.9 miles one way to its junction with Jacks River Trail). Easy to Moderate walked in either direction.

Yellow-blazed Rice Camp Trail follows the clear, cold, often sliding water of small streams for the first half of its length. Almost from its beginning at 1,740 feet, the wide and always wet trail parallels a tributary of Rice Camp Branch. After crossing this headwater rivulet for the third time at mile 1.1, the trail trades streams and follows Rice Camp Branch.

The path, after nine Rice Camp Branch crossings and 1.9 miles of nearly level terrain, turns to the left away from the stream. It then ascends moderate and more gradual upgrades until it makes a short, sharp drop to a muddy rivulet at mile 2.7. Look for the smooth, light gray bark of the last few large beech trees still standing beside the small stream.

The remainder of Rice Camp follows a succession of low, dry ridges through a predominantly oak-pine forest. The resulting series of ups and downs are easy to moderate. The land beside the trail often slopes away gradually on small spur ridges or falls away suddenly into moist ravines to either side of the ridgetop.

Rice Camp descends through a belt of rhododendron and hemlock to 1,350 feet, where it ends at the orange-blazed Jacks River Trail above a normally shallow tributary. Jacks River Falls is one ford and 1.2 miles to the right, east and upstream, on the Jacks River Trail.

Directions: Travel U.S. 411 North from Chatsworth, past Eton toward Tennga. From the Georgia 52-U.S. 411 intersection in Chatsworth, travel U.S. 411 North approximately 13.4 miles to the town of Cisco. In Cisco, turn right onto the paved road immediately before the Cisco Baptist Church, which is also on the right. This road was once part of Georgia 2, and is now known as Old Highway 2. This road, which is opposite the current Georgia 2-U.S. 411 junction, is also F.S. 16. Continue on F.S. 16 (the pavement ends; stay to the right at the fork; pass Hopewell Church; cross the Conasauga River) for approximately 7.9 miles, then turn right onto F.S. 51. Proceed approximately 4.8 miles (make two shallow fords) to Rice Camp's trailhead sign, bulletin board and parking area on the left. As you approach the Rice Camp trailhead on F.S. 51, Rice Camp trail is to the left and East Cowpen is the trail that continues straight ahead into the wilderness.

HORSESHOE BEND TRAIL (3.0 miles one way to its junction with Jacks River Trail). From trailhead

to Jacks River Trail: Easy to Moderate; from Jacks River Trail to trailhead: Moderate to Strenuous.

Horseshoe Bend Trail, named for its scenic overlook, originates in the Chattahoochee National Forest, slightly less than 2.0 miles outside the Cohutta Wilderness. That the beginning portion of this trail does not enjoy protected status is only too obvious. Horseshoe Bend has been rerouted and shortened by approximately 0.5 mile. The first 0.9 mile of the trail now follows a logging road through an area where the forest has recently been thinned or cut over.

The white-blazed trail, which starts at 1,560 feet, turns left at 0.1 mile. After a short, steep uphill climb that ends at mile 1.1, it turns right onto an old road, continues 70 yards, then turns left into the woods. Beyond these two turns, Horseshoe Bend gradually rises to approximately 1,840 feet on one of the low ridges collectively known as Ken Mountain. For the next few tenths of a mile the trail is level or gently undulating as it heads northward along the wilderness boundary.

The trail begins a gradual descent at mile 1.9. After turning east into the wilderness, it loops steadily downhill to a small open area on the sloping edge of a precipitous bluff. This is Horseshoe Bend Overlook. The canopied landscape, the ridges overlapping into the haze, the shining river below — the solitude — all are characteristic of the rugged Cohuttas. The view is pictured on the back of the wilderness map.

The trail is easily walked to the overlook, but after it bends away from the view, the remaining 0.4 mile makes a short, steep climb to 1,600 feet, then drops very sharply to 1,120 feet at the river. Here Horseshoe Bend ends at the sign marking its junction with the orange-blazed Jacks River Trail. To the right, upstream, it is 3.9 miles to Jacks River Falls; to the left, downstream, it is 3.6 miles to the Tennessee line and the northwestern terminus of the Jacks River Trail.

Directions: The directions to Horseshoe Bend Trail are almost the same as those to Rice Camp Trail. Rice Camp's trailhead is farther down the same road. After you turn onto F.S. 51 from the F.S. 51-F.S. 16 junction, continue approximately 2.7 miles on F.S. 51 to the Horseshoe Bend Trailhead. Look for Horseshoe Bend's sign, trailhead bulletin board and primitive campground to the left of F.S. 51. (See Rice Camp Trail, also in this chapter.)

HEMP TOP TRAIL (2.1 miles one way to near the top of Big Frog Mountain). Strenuous.

Hemp Top serves as the wilderness boundary line for most of its length and is the only trail originating in Georgia's share of the Cohutta Wilderness that does not directly or indirectly lead to the popular Jacks and Conasauga Rivers. This fact, combined with its difficulty and long dirt-road drive to its trailhead, has kept Hemp Top lightly used.

Hemp Top, starting at 3,580 feet at the site of an old lookout tower, begins in Georgia on the northeastern edge of the Cohutta Wilderness and heads almost due north to its end in Tennessee. Easy to follow despite its faded white blazes, the trail quickly descends to a former jeep road. If you have any doubts or can't find a blaze, continue straight ahead at the infrequent junctions.

Except for three uphill grades along the way — two short and easy, the other longer and moderate — the trail steadily descends to Double Spring Gap (3,180 ft.) at mile 1.2. Double Spring Gap is bisected by the Tennessee Valley Divide. Downhill to either side of the gap is a spring. The newborn branches flow in opposite directions, into different watersheds, different river systems and, finally, into different parts of the Gulf of Mexico. The spring to the right (east) of the trail adds to the Tennessee River.

Less than 100 yards above Double Spring Gap, a sign welcomes you to Tennessee and the Cherokee National Forest. Beyond that sign, Hemp Top serves as the boundary between Tennessee's 5,055-acre Big Frog Wilderness on the right and the Cohutta Wilderness on the left. It is also beyond that sign that Hemp Top begins its strenuous, uninterrupted climb up Big Frog Mountain. There are no switchbacks to decrease exertion, the old road, blazed with rusty wildlife management area signs, ascends straight up — and up.

Near the top of Big Frog Mountain, the terrain levels and the trail winds to its northern terminus in a small clearing. But where Hemp Top ends at 4,100 feet, two other trails begin at another sign. To the right (with your back to the end of Hemp Top), Lick-log Trail descends to the northeast, into the Big Frog Wilderness. To the left, Wolf Ridge Trail reaches the top of Big Frog Mountain within 0.5 mile. Like Hemp Top, Wolf Ridge follows the Tennessee Valley Divide, which is the boundary between the two wilderness areas across the crest of Big Frog Mountain and for several miles beyond. Both wilderness areas claim Big Frog, at 4,200 feet, as their highest point.

If you walk ridgetop trails such as Hemp Top from late April through June, you will no doubt hear the ovenbird — a sparrow-sized (6 inch) ground-nesting warbler that breeds no farther south than the mountains of North Georgia. You will hear the ovenbird because it is abundant and loud. Most bird guides

111

describe its song as *teacher, teacher, teacher . . .*, repeated up to 10 times louder and louder, in crescendo. Georgia birds, however, sing with a regional variation. They leave off the *"er"* and chant *teach, teach, teach . . .*, most often an emphatic, ringing staccato.

The normally secretive ovenbird lacks the tropical coloring and flashy flight patterns characteristic of most wood warblers. From the neck down it resembles a small, olive-brown thrush. For a positive identification you must see the diagnostic band-stripe-ring color pattern on its head. The band is a mohawk brushstroke of bright orange-brown from the base of its bill back across the top of its crown. The stripe is a thin black eyebrow, bordering the band and accentuating the white of the eye ring below.

The ovenbird weaves its nest — a flattened dome with a walk-in, ground-level entrance — in the undergrowth of dry, predominantly deciduous forests.

Directions: From Dally Gap, continue straight ahead (northward) on F.S. 73, which curves to the left from Dally Gap. After 4.1 miles F.S. 73 ends at the turnaround loop on Hemp Top. The trail begins behind its sign on the left side of the loop less than halfway around the circle. (See Jacks River Trail, also in this chapter, for directions to Dally Gap.)

4

LONG TRAILS
AND THEIR
APPROACHES

Introduction

Four long footpaths — the Appalachian, Bartram, Benton Mackaye and Duncan Ridge — offer hikers over 160 miles of isolated trail in the mountains of North Georgia. These trails traverse land that is almost all within the Chattahoochee National Forest.

Whenever possible, I have divided the long trails into sections between paved access roads. These sections, ranging from 6.8 to 20.8 miles, make excellent dayhikes or two- or three-day backpacking trips.

Also included in this section are long trail approaches or sidetrails that have not been described in Chapter 2. The trails that have been detailed in Chapter 2 are noted for reference in the long trail sections.

Appalachian National Scenic Trail

The Appalachian Trail — with its southern terminus at Springer Mountain, Georgia, and its northern terminus at Mount Katahdin, Maine — winds its way along the Appalachian Mountains for more than 2,000 miles through 14 states. Georgia's segment of the trail, from Springer Mountain to Bly Gap on the North Carolina border, is 79 miles in length.

Wide and easily followed, the trail is marked with white blazes; double white blazes, one above the other, warn hikers of potentially confusing turns or sudden changes in direction. Water sources and shelters off the main trail and major sidetrails are marked with blue blazes. Blue W's with arrows indicate water.

Because of its national reputation, the Appalachian Trail is the most heavily used long footpath in Georgia. Those who want a large degree of solitude may want to consider other trails in this guide.

The Georgia Appalachian Trail Club (G.A.T.C.), a volunteer organization, maintains Georgia's portion of the trail.

Bartram National Recreation Trail

The 36.8-mile segment of the Bartram Trail in Rabun County is but a small link of an envisioned 2,550-mile trail that may someday wind through eight southeastern states. The goal of this trail is to trace, wherever possible, the exact route of 18th-century naturalist William Bartram. From 1773 to 1776, Bartram traveled an estimated 920 miles in Georgia. He explored portions of what is now Rabun County in 1776, when "bears, tygers, wolves and wildcats were numerous."

I have described the Bartram Trail from north to south — from Hale Ridge Road to Georgia 28 — because it is considerably less difficult hiked in this direction. Of the four long trails described in this chapter, the Bartram is by far the least strenuous.

Benton MacKaye Trail

Benton MacKaye, a forester, was the first to envision a continuous trail along the crest of the entire Appalachian Mountain chain. His completed dream, the Appalachian Trail, is now 50 years old. MacKaye also foresaw the need to create major loop trails that would join the Appalachian. In 1980, a trail association was established to make the idea of a major Southern loop — the Benton MacKaye Trail — a reality.

If it is completed as proposed, the 250-mile footpath will have its southern terminus at Springer Mountain and its northern terminus at Davenport Gap, on the northeastern edge of Great Smoky

Mountains National Park. Scheduled to be completed by the summer of 1988, Georgia's portion of the trail will wind approximately 75 miles to the northwest, from Springer Mountain to Big Frog Mountain on the northern boundary of the Cohutta Wilderness.

The Benton MacKaye Trail Association, a volunteer organization, is building and maintaining the trail.

APPALACHIAN
APPROACH TRAILS

Three Trails

Brasstown Ranger District
Union County

BLOOD MOUNTAIN SPUR TRAIL (0.7 mile one way to its junction with the Appalachian Trail at Flatrock Gap). Easy to Moderate.

The blue-blazed Blood Mountain Spur Trail quickly tunnels through a thicket of mountain laurel and rhododendron, crosses one of the headwater forks of Shanty Branch, then gently rises beside the other fork. Shanty Branch is a tributary of Helton Creek, which is a tributary of Nottely River, which flows into the Hiwassee, which unites with the Tennessee, which joins the Ohio, which merges with the Mississippi — 350 miles northwest of Blood Mountain as a crow flies, hundreds of miles more as the rivers flow.

At 0.2 mile the path (at a double blaze) curls away from the stream and begins the first of two switchbacks that climb to an old roadbed at 0.4 mile. After 0.1 mile of easy walking, the spur trail angles away from the road and ascends moderately through a forest with a predominantly oak canopy and white pine understory. The Blood Mountain Spur soon deadends at the Appalachian Trail, forming a three-way T-intersection on the mountain side of Flatrock Gap (3,460 ft.). To the left, it is 1.0 mile to Neels Gap; to the right, it is 1.5 miles and 1,000 feet up to the top of Blood (4,458 ft.).

The Georgia Appalachian Trail Club (G.A.T.C.) built the Blood Mountain Spur Trail, and they did an excellent job; the trail is wide, well marked and easily followed. The G.A.T.C. constructed this spur trail to alleviate car and hiker congestion at Neels Gap. They urge Blood Mountain dayhikers to begin their walk at the Byron Reece Picnic Area (3,040 ft.) rather than at Neels Gap, the usual starting point. The spur trail is shorter and only slightly steeper than the Appalachian Trail from Neels Gap (3,109 ft.). The spur is 0.7 mile long and gains 420 feet in elevation to Flatrock Gap; the section of the Appalachian Trail from Neels Gap is 1.0 mile long and rises 350 feet to meet the spur.

Directions: Starting from the Walasi-Yi Center at Neels Gap (see directions for Section 3 of the Appalachian Trail), travel north on U.S. 19-129 for approximately 0.4 mile before turning left onto the paved road that enters the Byron Herbert Reece Memorial Picnic Area. After traveling approximately 0.1 mile on the paved road, which makes a loop through the picnic area, you will see the trailhead sign to the left before you reach the gravel parking area.

———

Chestatee Ranger District
White County

LOGAN TURNPIKE TRAIL (1.9 miles one way to its junction with the Appalachian Trail at Tesnatee Gap). Moderate to Strenuous.

The Logan Turnpike Trail follows a short but historic section of the first road to lead southward out of Union County. I have read four accounts of the

Logan Turnpike, and each one differs, not in the main points but in specific details such as dates, from the others. Therefore, I must begin this description with a disclaimer as to its strict historical accuracy.

In 1821, the Union Turnpike Company received a state charter to construct a toll road that would join existing roads north and south of Tesnatee Gap. Completed by 1840, the Union Turnpike was the final link of a continuous road — the forerunner of U.S. 129 — that stretched from Gainesville to Cleveland and over the mountains to Blairsville. Shortly after it was finished, Major Francis Logan bought the rights to operate the turnpike. He built his home, his lodge and a tollgate 0.8 mile south of the Kellum Valley trailhead, near the house with the "Tollgate" sign. In 1871 Major Logan bought 220 acres, which included a segment of the turnpike north of his tollgate, in western White County. It was probably then that the road took his name. The toll road remained under Logan family management until it was abandoned in 1922, the year the state completed the highway over Neels Gap.

The section of road that became known as Logan Turnpike was roughly 10 miles long, from near Loudsville through Tesnatee Gap to Ponder. "Tesnatee" was the Cherokee word for turkey. Ponder was located in a valley the Cherokees had named "Choestoe," their way of saying "Land of the Dancing Rabbits." The story of rabbits dancing, told by Indians, heard by pioneers, was no doubt thought to be mythological — a wonderful folklore image handed down from an old tribal legend or mountaintop vision. To the Cherokee, however, the story represented special knowledge gained from actual observation of natural phenomena. In its text describing the eastern cottontail, *The Audubon Society Field Guide to North American Mammals* states: "On midwin-

121

ter nights, groups of cottontails have been seen frolicking on crusted snow; as they are not mating aggregations, they may be purely playful gatherings to provide release after periods of forced inactivity."

In its day, Logan Turnpike was one of the major north-south roads through the mountains of North Georgia. Wagon trains loaded with produce rumbled south to Gainesville, then returned to the mountains full of merchandise. The turnpike served as a mail route; the stagecoach that traveled from Athens, Tennessee, to Augusta, Georgia, crossed over Tesnatee Gap. Over the years a colorful parade of travelers — Confederate soldiers; gold prospectors; famous politicians; drivers of turkey, cattle and hogs; chestnut hunters; early photographers, and organ grinders with tame bears or monkeys — passed by Major Logan's tollgate.

I believe that John Muir, who walked alone, quickly and quietly, was among the turnpike travelers in the early fall of 1867. He kept a journal of his adventures, which later became the source for his book *A Thousand Mile Walk to the Gulf*. In this book Muir tells us that he passed through Blairsville during the morning of September 21. The next day, I would guess in the early afternoon, he reached "the last mountain summit" on his way to Florida. That last climb was probably to Tesnatee Gap. After crossing this last summit, Muir states that he walked downhill "in the wake of three poor, but merry mountaineers — an old woman, a young woman, and a young man — who sat, leaned, and lay in the box of a shackly wagon that seemed to be held together by spiritualism, and was kept in agitation by a very large and a very small mule." He spent the night of September 22 at Mount Yonah, which is about 8 miles due east of Loudsville. By nightfall of the next day John Muir, who would

122

later gain fame as an explorer, naturalist, conservationist and writer, had reached Gainesville.

The Logan Turnpike Trail has either-end access. The lower, southern access point is in Kellum Valley; the upper, northern access point is Tesnatee Gap. This description starts at the Kellum Valley trailhead (approximately 1,960 ft.) and ends at Tesnatee Gap (3,138 ft.).

Immediately beyond the yellow "Wildlife Management Area" signs, the trail follows the blue blaze to the left of the old tollroad past the first set of dirt mounds, then crosses over to the right side of the road before the next set. After the second set of mounds, the trail drops down to the middle of the roadbed, where it remains for another 1.1 miles. The turnpike trail soon parallels Town Creek, here near its undisturbed headwaters a clear, cold mountain stream rushing noisily around rocks luxuriant with moss. This thick moss is a sign of health. During times of high water, silt from upstream erosion can scour the moss from the rocks. In general, the bigger, faster and muddier the stream, the less moss on its rocks.

The mountains to either side of the trail have long funneled travelers, including the Cherokee whose path the road followed, up the cove to the gap in the ridge. To the left or west is Cowrock Mountain, its highest point 3,841 feet. Cowrock's cliffs are visible from the trail in winter. To the right is Wildcat Mountain.

At 0.6 mile the trail starts to gain elevation, alternating between easy and moderate grades. The old roadbed, which is often rocky and wet, continues beside Town Creek and its linear forest of hemlock. Where the road cut turns to the right at 1.2 miles, the trail stays straight ahead, uphill. Here it really begins to climb, becoming increasingly steep as it rises toward the gap. The last 0.3 mile, which seems twice as long, gains elevation as quickly as the most rugged sections of trail in Georgia. Below the cove hardwoods, flowering dogwoods are abundant along this ascending section of trail.

The Logan Turnpike ties back into the trail near the gap. Although the former road was not quite as steep as the last 0.8 mile of the trail, it sloped enough to present special problems to those going either up to or down from Tesnatee Gap. Wagoners, and later auto drivers, often had to tie logs to the backs of their vehicles to help brake them down the mountain. This braking was crucial to the wagoner, for if there weren't enough dragging weight behind the wagon on a downhill pitch, it could run over the animals in front of it. Before cars had fuel pumps, drivers who started up to the gap with less than half a tank of gas often had to drive their Model T's in reverse to gravity-feed the fuel. On their return trip, they frequently backed down the steep section to avoid damaging their brakes.

Directions: To reach the trail's lower, Kellum Valley access point, take U.S. 129 North from the Cleveland Square for approximately 7.7 miles, then turn right onto Kellum Valley Road. Watch for the road sign after you crest the hill past the Town Creek Bridge. After the Kellum Valley Road becomes dirt at approximately 1.2 miles, proceed straight ahead another 0.9 mile to where the road splits just before the "Toll Gate" house on the right. Continue on the narrow dirt lane past the house for approximately 0.8 mile. The trail begins at the yellow "Wildlife Management Area" signs and the blue trail blaze. You don't have to worry about missing the trailhead or driving too far: less than 50 yards beyond the trailhead, the road, which becomes the trail, is blocked by dirt mounds and felled logs. Sections of the last 0.8 mile are rough, rocky and often wet, but the road is still passable for all but the lowest-to-the-ground passenger vehicles.

Note: Logan Turnpike is totally within the 9,113-acre Raven Cliffs Wilderness Area.

Toccoa Ranger District
Primarily Dawson and Gilmer Counties

SOUTHERN TERMINUS APPROACH FROM AMICALOLA FALLS STATE PARK (8.1 miles one way to the southern terminus of the Appalachian Trail atop Springer Mountain). Strenuous.

Because of the Appalachian Trail's popularity and allure, people with little or no backpacking experience often pick it for their first long hiking trip. Many of these people — with boots that are too new and packs that are too heavy — start on the Appalachian Approach Trail at Amicalola Falls State Park, eager to reach Springer Mountain and the Appalachian Trail. Slowed by blisters and aching muscles, some of these inexperienced hikers fail to make the 8.1 miles to the top of Springer Mountain the first day.

The visitor center in Amicalola Falls State Park has a scale to weigh your pack. If you are uncertain about how much weight you can comfortably carry, ask the park ranger for advice. You may want to lighten your load before starting out.

The Appalachian is a well-marked, highly scenic trail, but if you plan to walk long distances of it carrying a pack, you need to be in good physical condition and have suitable gear to enjoy it. The Approach Trail will give you a good idea of what lies ahead. If the alternating ascents and descents to

125

Springer Mountain prove to be too strenuous, you will not enjoy the Appalachian Trail.

This trail traverses a ridgeline string of knobs and named peaks collectively known as Amicalola Mountain. Beyond the state park, the trailside forest is predominantly hardwood. Oaks, hickories, American holly, flowering dogwood, black locust, yellow poplar, sourwood and sweet birch are common. On many of the low, flat-topped knobs, the forest is undergoing quick and obvious successional change. The Virginia pine, a pioneer species that formed dense stands 15 years ago, is being rapidly replaced by taller hardwoods. Their fallen trunks keep trail crews busy. By the year 2000, most will have fallen and rotted.

The blue-blazed Appalachian Approach has a trailhead you can't miss. Its beginning is the log-lined walkway that leads away from the back of Amicalola's visitor information center (1,820 ft.). The initiation starts immediately: the trail's first 0.5 mile makes an easy to moderate climb to East Ridge Spring, then switchbacks up sharper grades to a left turn onto an old road at 0.8 mile. The road's open left side affords good views of valleys and ridges.

The approach continues straight ahead (past the bathrooms) and becomes path again where it skirts what used to be the shoreline of Amicalola Lake. At mile 1.4 the footpath crosses Little Amicalola Creek and the dirt road that turns into F.S. 46. Across the road the trail ascends moderately for 0.3 mile to the ridge. On the way up, at the painted trees, it leaves the park and enters the Chattahoochee National Forest. Once the treadway reaches the ridge, it does what the ridgetop does: it runs level, then easy up, to a low crest (2,940 ft.) at mile 1.9; it runs level along the crest and then gently down to a gap at mile 2.4; then it travels up, over and down the next knob on the ridge.

After leaving the ridge at mile 2.8, the approach makes a moderate to strenuous climb to mile 3.0, where it crosses Cemetery Road. Once across, the path continues upward, quickly gaining the next ridge and rising to the top of a flat-headed knob at mile 3.2. The trail slides off the ridge again at the next gap. Instead of proceeding straight ahead, the approach gains elevation gradually along the western flank of Frosty Mountain to mile 3.9, where it curls onto an eastward-running ridge that leads to the mountaintop. Here the treadway ascends moderately to the mountain's western peak at mile 4.3. Two-tenths of a mile farther, across a saddle, it enters the clearing at Frosty Mountain's high point (3,382 ft.). The wide walkway to the right of the clearing, a former fire-tower site, heads to water.

Continuing toward Springer Mountain, the footpath descends steadily until it crosses F.S. 46 at mile 4.9. After a short level stretch, the trail starts an easy to moderate upgrade over the double humps of Woody Knob (3,390 ft.). There is a campsite (mile 5.5) immediately before the steep, rocky, down-ridge run to Nimblewill Gap (3,049 ft.) at mile 5.8. The approach crosses the gap at a Forest Service junction — F.S. 46 ends at the gap, F.S. 28 passes through it.

From Nimblewill the path rises on grades alternately strenuous then easy to the ridgecrest of Black Mountain (3,610 ft.) at mile 6.6. Following a very steep descent to a gap (camping, water; 3,190 ft.) at mile 7.1, the approach trail starts its final climb to the beginning of many more on the Appalachian Trail. A steady, occasionally steep, 0.9-mile ascent leads to the short, wind-crooked oaks on the broad summit of Springer Mountain (3,782 ft.). Once on top, turn left at the double blue blaze and follow the final 50 yards of the approach to Springer's rock-slab overlook. Here, where the wind always seems to be blowing, a plaque commemorates the southern terminus of the Appalachian Trail. This lookoff is one of those special places where toasts are made and adventures begin.

Directions: Amicalola Falls State Park can be reached from many different directions; the three easiest routes, however, are from Dahlonega, Dawsonville and Ellijay. Travel Georgia 52 East from Ellijay, Georgia 52 West from Dahlonega or Georgia 53 West from Dawsonville and follow signs to the park.

See the Appalachian Trail, Section One, for directions to the end of the Approach Trail at Springer Mountain.

*Remote for detachment, narrow for chosen company,
lonely for contemplation, it beckons not merely north and
south, but upward to the body, mind and soul of man.*

— Harold Allen

APPALACHIAN TRAIL
SECTION 1

*Toccoa and Chestatee Ranger Districts
Primarily Fannin, Lumpkin and Union Counties*

**SPRINGER MOUNTAIN TO WOODY GAP
(HIGHWAY 60) (20.8 miles one way to Woody Gap).
Moderate to Strenuous.**

Section 1 of the Appalachian Trail is an excellent two-
or three-day backpacking trip. The beginning 8.4-
mile portion of Section 1, from Springer Mountain to
Hightower Gap, is the least strenuous (easy to moderate) long segment of the Appalachian Trail in Georgia. It is after Hightower Gap that Section 1 earns its
overall rating of moderate to strenuous. By setting up
a shuttle, dayhikers can walk to or away from Hightower Gap.

From its beginning at Springer Mountain, the trail
heads generally north to Three Forks, generally east
from Three Forks to Gooch Gap, then generally
northeast to Woody Gap. The first 12.0 miles of Section 1, from Springer to Cooper Gap, wind through
the Blue Ridge Wildlife Management Area. Overall,
the trailside forest is varied. Tall hemlock and white

129

pine are common from the first crossing of F.S. 42 through the Three Forks area. Beyond Hawk Mountain the hardwoods predominate.

The white-blazed Appalachian Trail begins amid the gnarled oaks atop Springer Mountain's overlook (3,782 ft.). The exact spot is commemorated with a plaque: "Georgia to Maine — a footpath for those who seek fellowship with the wilderness." After passing the large sign and registration mailbox, the trail heads north. At 0.2 mile a sidepath leads 80 yards to the deluxe Springer Mountain Shelter (picnic table in front, spring nearby). Sixty yards beyond the path to the shelter, Section 1 reaches its first trail junction. The A.T. follows the directions of the sign and takes the left fork. The diamond-blazed Benton MacKaye Trail, the right fork, is also described in this chapter.

Prior to the early 1980's, the Appalachian Trail was routed to the right at this junction, where the Benton MacKaye is today. Since that time, however, much of the Appalachian Trail from Springer to Three Forks has been relocated. As a result, Section 1 is approximately 1.5 miles shorter.

The treadway descends steadily from the fork to mile 1.0, where it angles to the left across F.S. 42 (3,309 ft.) and continues through a clearing. At mile 1.2 the Benton MacKaye turns onto the Appalachian Trail. For the next 0.7 mile, both trails share the same treadway along the broad ridge of Rich Mountain, through a forest dominated by tall white pine and yellow poplar. After the trails split apart, the A.T. heads downslope, turns left onto an old road at mile 2.4, continues downhill through a rhododendron thicket, then turns left onto another old road.

At mile 2.6 a sign points to the Stover Creek Shelter, approximately 60 yards to the left. Here the walkway turns right at the sign, quickly crosses a split-log bridge over Stover Creek and turns right again.

For the next 1.1 miles, the trail follows the slightly descending grade of an old road that parallels Stover Creek downstream. Even though the cascading creek is nearby, it is usually blocked from view by the dense evergreen of rhododendron. Groves of virgin hemlock — many of the individual trees at least 200 to 300 years old — line the stream's opposite corridor.

At mile 3.7 Section 1 crosses a bridge over Stover Creek and continues to lose elevation on the wide walkway of the old road. The Benton MacKaye joins in again at mile 4.1. Together they dip 0.1 mile to Three Forks (2,540 ft.), where Stover, Chester and Long creeks flow together at right angles to create Noontootla Creek. At Three Forks the trails cross a footbridge over Chester Creek, cross F.S. 58 and proceed on the gravel road as it parallels Long Creek upstream. A sign at mile 5.2 marks the blue-blazed sidepath that leads 100 yards to Long Creek Falls — a ledge-sliding drop of 20 to 25 feet.

The trails split apart (Benton MacKaye left, Appalachian straight) at another sign 0.1 mile past the waterfall. Section 1 of the blue-blazed Duncan Ridge Trail, also described in this chapter, begins at this junction. It shares the same treadway as the Benton MacKaye to Georgia 60.

On its own again, the A.T. continues on the road, crossing rivulets at mile 5.3 and mile 5.7. Immediately after this second crossing, Section 1 leaves the road and turns right onto path. It then rises through heath thickets to a ridge, ascends easily across F.S. 251 at mile 6.0 and climbs 0.5 mile to the top of a knob (3,360 ft.).

After losing elevation gradually to a slight gap (3,180 ft.) at mile 7.1, the footpath skirts the northern slopes of Hawk Mountain far below its peak. The headwater stream in the cove to the left is Long Creek. Section 1 passes beside the Hawk Mountain

131

Shelter at mile 7.9 before working its way down 0.5 mile to Hightower Gap (2,854 ft.).

The A.T. crosses Hightower Gap at the F.S. 42-69 junction. The trail continues straight across this junction, re-entering the tall hardwood forest to the right of F.S. 42. Here the footpath climbs, hard at first, then more moderately, 0.3 mile to the top of an unnamed knob (3,160 ft.). It then dips 0.4 mile to Mauldin Gap (3,020 ft.) beside F.S. 42. From Mauldin Gap the treadway roller-coasters with the ridge on easy to moderate grades to mile 10.0, where it drops sharply 0.3 mile to Horse Gap (2,673 ft.) next to F.S. 42.

Continuing to the east, Section 1 makes a steady, switchbacking, moderate ascent along the southern side of the ridge. On the way up, it passes beside a rim-like line of outcrop rock. At mile 10.9 there is an overlook open to the south. According to the Suches Quadrangle, the view should be of Conner Mountain, the headwater valley of the Etowah River and low ridges beyond. (I didn't see a thing because of fog.) The white-blazed walkway reaches the crest of Sassafras Mountain (3,336 ft.) at mile 11.3.

The A.T. crosses F.S. 42 through a stand of tall yellow poplar in Cooper Gap (2,820 ft.) at mile 12.0. Traversing rugged terrain similar to that on Sassafras Mountain, the path rises moderately by switchback for 0.6 mile to the crown of Justus Mountain (3,222 ft.). It then loses elevation for 0.3 mile to the saddle of Brookshire Gap (2,920 ft.), follows the ridge over a low peak (3,081 ft.) and descends. At mile 13.9 the trail crosses an old road, turns right onto another and quickly crosses a bridge over Justus Creek. Still on old road, Section 1 gradually rises over a low ridge before crossing another stream, Blackwell Creek, by bridge at mile 14.7.

Beyond Blackwell Creek, the wide walkway continues level or slightly uphill through rhododendron thickets to mile 15.2, where it curls to the right and climbs sharply for 0.3 mile to a highpoint (3,004 ft.) on Horseshoe Ridge. After an easy downgrade to a gap at mile 15.9, the treadway skirts the northern slopes of Gooch Mountain, rising gently for 0.5 mile before heading down. At mile 16.7, where the A.T. crosses a bridge over a rivulet, there is a blue-blazed sidepath to the Gooch Gap Shelter. At mile 17.0, just before the trail crosses F.S. 42 in Gooch Gap, another blue-blazed sidepath leads to the same shelter.

From Gooch Gap (2,784 ft.), the A.T. proceeds on easy grades around two low knobs to the stand of tall, straight-boled yellow poplars in Liss Gap (3,020 ft.) at mile 18.5. It then rises, moderately at first, 0.4 mile to Page Knob (3,233 ft.), runs down-ridge to Jacks Gap (3,020 ft.) at mile 19.1, ascends 0.2 mile to Ramrock Mountain (3,200 ft.) and drops to Tritt Gap (3,020 ft.) at mile 19.6. There is a view to the right (south) atop Ramrock Mountain. The predominantly level remainder of Section 1 swings around the southern flank of Black Mountain to Woody Gap.

Directions: To reach the Appalachian Trail's southern terminus atop Springer Mountain, travel approximately 7.6 miles on Georgia 52 East from the Ellijay square, then turn left onto paved "16 Roy Road" immediately past Stanley's Grocery and Service Station. There is a large power apparatus to the right of Georgia 52 just past the turn onto Roy Road. If you wish to approach Roy Road from the east, or set up a shuttle between Amicalola State Park and Springer Mountain, continue driving on Georgia 52 West approximately 12.0 miles beyond the Georgia 52-183 junction, then turn right onto Roy Road.

After proceeding approximately 9.5 miles on Roy Road, turn right onto another paved road at the stop sign. Travel approximately 2.1 miles on this road before turning right onto gravel F.S. 42 opposite Mount Pleasant Baptist Church. Continue approximately 6.7 miles on F.S. 42 (usually a good road) to the "Hiker Trail" sign that marks the spot where the Appalachian Trail crosses the road. Park in the clearing to the left.

The Appalachian Trail crosses F.S. 42 and enters the parking-camping area clearing 1.0 mile from its southern terminus atop Springer Mountain. If you are in the right spot, you should find the wide, stair-step gap, the double white blaze and the sign for Springer to the right of the road 15 or 20 yards beyond the left turn into the clearing.

Shorter segments of Section 1 can be dayhiked by setting up a shuttle at the intersection of Forest Service Roads 69 and 42 in Hightower Gap. Depending on which segment you want to walk, and where you are driving from, there are numerous combinations of routes that will lead you to Hightower Gap. The Forest Service Administration Map, available from the Forest Supervisor's Office for a small fee, features the system roads of the Chattahoochee National Forest.

APPALACHIAN TRAIL
SECTION 2

Chestatee Ranger District
Lumpkin and Union Counties

WOODY GAP (HIGHWAY 60) TO NEELS GAP (U.S. 19-129) (11.5 miles one way to Neels Gap). Moderate.

This section, with only one long, steady uphill grade, makes an excellent dayhike or a leisurely weekend backpacking trip. Starting at the picnic area and large gravel parking lot at Woody Gap (3,160 ft.), the white-blazed trail gradually gains elevation along the western, hardwood slopes of Steel Trap and Jacobs Knobs for the first 0.5 mile. Following a short, 100-yard dip to the stand of yellow poplars at Lunsford Gap (3,330 ft.), the footpath makes a moderate to strenuous, switchbacking climb to an outcrop overlook at mile 1.0. The trail continues to rise on the eastern side of the ridge to near the crest of Big Cedar Mountain (3,737 ft.) at mile 1.3. It then descends, alternating between moderate and easy downgrades for most of the distance, to Dan Gap at mile 2.5.

Beyond Dan Gap, the path slants down off the ridge onto the western flank of Granny Top, where it remains slightly downhill or level to Miller Gap (2,980 ft.) at mile 2.9. Dockery Lake Trail (see Chapter 2 for description) ends at its sign in Miller Gap. The A.T. continues northward from the gap, gently undulating through a predominantly deciduous forest on the eastern slopes of Baker Mountain to mile 4.1. Here it ascends moderately to ridgetop, then drops to Henry Gap (3,100 ft.) at mile 4.5. For the next 1.2 miles the treadway follows the ridge up, over and down the two low knobs of Burnett Field Mountain. Both of the switchbacking upgrades are moderate.

The trail enters Jarrard Gap (3,300 ft.) at mile 5.7. Jarrard Gap Trail (see Chapter 2 for description) ends at its sign to the left of the gap. Across the new road that bisects the gap, the A.T. rises moderately by switchback to near the crest of Gaddis Mountain (approx. 3,520 ft.) before descending 0.2 mile to the next gap — Horsebone (3,460 ft.). The gap-mountain-gap pattern continues as the footpath ascends moderately, then easily, to the level top of Turkey Stamp (approx. 3,780 ft.) at mile 7.0. Beyond the short, downridge grade off the mountaintop, the treadway remains predominantly level or easy up to the next gap. At mile 7.6 the path crosses Slaughter Creek (often dry in late summer and early fall) near its source. The mountain that fills your view to the left — the one you're hoping you don't have to climb — is Slaughter.

The trail enters the small clearing of Slaughter Gap (3,900 ft.) at mile 8.0. Slaughter Gap (marked with a sign) is a major trail junction. The old road to the left is the end of the Slaughter Creek Trail (see Chapter 2 for description). The gap is also the eastern terminus for the blue-blazed Duncan Ridge National Recreation Trail (see this chapter for description), which quickly leads to Vogel's Coosa Backcountry Trail (see Chapter 6 for description). The Duncan Ridge Trail is to the left of the large campsite that is straight through the gap. A blue-blazed path on the far side of the camping area leads to the last water source before Neels Gap.

After the A.T. turns 90° to the right in Slaughter Gap, it begins the 1.0-mile-long upgrade to the short, twisted oaks and rhododendron thickets atop Blood Mountain. The remaining 558-foot elevation gain to the top of Blood (4,458 ft.), the highest point along the A.T. in Georgia, is surprisingly easy. The gradient starts out mild, then becomes moderate as the treadway switchbacks steadily up the slope. At mile 9.0 the footpath reaches "Picnic Rock" and the cabin-sized, two-room stone shelter on Blood's crest. A few yards past the shelter the trail enters Blood's sunny crown, stripped down to its backbone. The bare rock affords dramatic views of ridges and peaks and valleys to the south.

The final 2.5 miles of Section 2 loses 1,350 feet to Neels Gap. The first 1.0 mile of the descent works its way quickly down the mountain on short, steep switchbacks through rocky terrain. At mile 10.5, on the mountain side of Flatrock Gap (3,460 ft.), the A.T. reaches its intersection with the Blood Mountain Spur Trail (see this chapter for description). The last 1.0 mile is easily walked.

Section 2 of the Appalachian Trail has a good spring wildflower display. Approximately 2.0 miles before Jarrard Gap, I saw the most spectacular wildflower colony I have ever seen along the trails of North Georgia. Hundreds of large-flowered trillium carpeted a steep slope to the left of the trail, their three-petaled blooms held high by 10- to 15-inch stems. Though it was only May 2, many of the creamy white blossoms had already turned pink with age.

Marked water sources occur at regular intervals along Section 2.

Directions: Travel northward from Dahlonega on U.S. 19-Georgia 60. At Stonepile Gap, where U.S. 19 veers right and Georgia 60 turns left, continue northward on Georgia 60 approximately 5.5 miles to the gravel parking area and picnic tables at Woody Gap.

APPALACHIAN TRAIL
SECTION 3

Chestatee Ranger District
Primarily Lumpkin and Union Counties

**NEELS GAP (U.S. 19-129) TO HOGPEN GAP
(RICHARD B. RUSSELL SCENIC HIGHWAY) (6.8
miles one way to Hogpen Gap). Moderate to
Strenuous.**

This section is the shortest segment of the
Appalachian Trail between paved road crossings in
Georgia. Section 3, with only one long, strenuous
climb, makes an ideal introductory trip for beginning
dayhikers and backpackers.

Starting at Neels Gap (3,109 ft.), the trail tunnels
through the Walasi-Yi Center's white-blazed breeze-
way before ascending the lower slopes of Levelland
Mountain. Here heath thickets are common below
the open, predominantly oak forest. Mountain laurel
and pinxter-flower (*Rhododendron nudiflorum*) bloom
during late April and much of May. Also blossoming
at this time, the lousewort — an unusual wildflower
with fern-like leaves and whorled, yellow-reddish-
brown blooms — is common beside this initial segment of trail below 3,500 feet.

The trail makes a steady, easy to moderate climb
from Neels Gap to Levelland Mountain's western
highpoint at mile 1.5. Across the saddle between the
mountain's twin crests (3,900 ft.), the trail reaches the
rockslab overlook atop Levelland's eastern knob at
mile 1.7. The prominent mountain to the south is
Hogpen.

The treadway switchbacks downridge from Section 3's first vista to Swaim Gap (3,480 ft.) at mile 2.2. Here it rises up and over a low, unnamed knob (3,560 ft.), then gently undulates with the ridgecrest to the second marked campsite at mile 2.9. Less than 100 yards past this camping area, there is a climbing vine called Dutchman's pipe to the right of the trail. Look for its strongly curved, pipe-like blooms in late April and early May.

Continuing eastward, the path passes over a top and stamp — Rock Spring Top (3,570 ft.), Corbin Horse Stamp (3,680 ft.) — before it dips to a gap at mile 3.5. From this gap the trail makes a short, moderate upridge run to Wolf Laurel Top (3,766 ft.), where a sidetrail leads to an open picnic spot with a view. The trail descends a short distance to a second look-off from Wolf Laurel, then continues to lose elevation to another unnamed gap (3,540 ft.) at mile 4.0. For the next 1.0 mile the treadway heads up — easily at first, then moderately, then easily again — to the crown of Cowrock Mountain (3,841 ft.). Outcrop overlooks are at mile 4.7 and 4.9 along the way.

The sharp, switchbacking downgrade through rocky terrain to Tesnatee Gap at mile 5.8 is Section 3's steepest and longest descent. At Tesnatee Gap (3,138 ft.) the A.T. angles to the right toward Richard B. Russell Scenic Highway, parallels the pavement for a few yards, then bears off to the right, up and away from the road. Before it enters the forest again, the trail passes the always trashy entrance to an old road. That old road is the end of the historical Logan Turnpike Trail, also included in this chapter.

From Tesnatee Gap, the footpath climbs 0.6 mile to the northern crest of Wildcat Mountain (3,730 ft.). Here Section 3 gets on the elevator, earning the "strenuous" part of its difficulty rating. The first 0.4 mile of this ascent rises sharply through a scenic area of large, lichen-splotched outcrops. To the right at mile 6.3, there is a view of Town Creek Cove and the rock face of Cowrock Mountain. Two-tenths of a mile farther, on top of Wildcat, the trail comes to the sign for Whitley Gap Shelter, which is approximately 1.2 miles to the south.

Immediately beyond the sidepath to the shelter, the A.T. turns left and heads down toward Hogpen Gap on long, easy switchbacks. Near the highway, where the trail turns left again, a blue-blazed sidepath drops a short distance to the Dodd Creek headwaters. The end of Section 3 angles to the left across the highway and follows the white-blazed posts to the Hogpen Gap parking area (3,480 ft.).

Marked water sources occur at regular intervals along this section of the Appalachian Trail. The sidepath that leads to water before Hogpen Gap is much shorter and easier than the sidepath that leads to water from Tesnatee Gap.

During September and early October much of Section 3's ridgetop is an aster garden.

Directions: Take U.S. 19 North from Dahlonega or U.S. 129 North from Cleveland toward Vogel State Park. After reaching Turner's Corner, where U.S. 19 and U.S. 129 join, continue 7.6 miles on U.S. 19-129 North to the Walasi-Yi Center at Neels Gap.

Note: With the exception of its first 0.1 mile at Neels Gap, Section 3 of the Appalachian Trail is totally within the 9,113-acre Raven Cliffs Wilderness Area.

APPALACHIAN TRAIL
SECTION 4

Chattooga Ranger District
Primarily Towns and Union Counties

HOGPEN GAP (RICHARD B. RUSSELL SCENIC HIGHWAY) TO UNICOI GAP (GEORGIA 75) (14.0 miles one way to Unicoi Gap). Moderate.

Of the three long sections of the Appalachian Trail in Georgia — Sections 1, 4 and 5 — Section 4 is the shortest and least strenuous. This section, with miles of gentle grades mixed with the usual alternating ascents and descents, makes an excellent long dayhike or two-day backpacking trip.

The first 4.3 miles of Section 4 follow the typical pattern of the Appalachian Trail: the gap-mountain-gap-mountain sine wave of the ridge crest. Starting at Hogpen Gap (3,480 ft.), the trail gradually gains elevation around the eastern side of Strawberry Top before it dips slightly with the ridge to Sapling Gap (3,480 ft.) at mile 1.6. The treadway rises easily to moderately from Sapling Gap to the top of Poor Mountain (3,640 ft.) at mile 1.9, descends steadily to Wide Gap (3,180 ft.) at mile 2.6, ascends moderately to the crown of Sheep Rock Top (3,550 ft.) at mile 3.7, then drops to Low Gap (3,020 ft.) at mile 4.3. The Low Gap Shelter is 0.1 mile to the right of the trail.

Continuing northeastward, the trail follows the unexpectedly mild grades of an old road until mile 8.2, where it returns to its usual up-and-down pattern. This 3.9-mile segment — the easiest long stretch on the Appalachian Trail in Georgia — winds through a mature hardwood forest on the eastern

141

flank of Horsetrough Mountain for most of its length.

Near Cold Springs Gap (3,460 ft.) at mile 8.2, the path leaves the roadbed and makes a moderate 0.2-mile ascent to the top of an unnamed knob. Following the sharp downgrade from the first knob, the tread-way climbs 0.6 mile (the first 0.4 mile is moderate to strenuous, the rest is easy to moderate) to near the highpoint of another unnamed knob before dipping slightly to Chattahoochee Gap (3,500 ft.) at mile 9.4. Chattahoochee Spring, the official source of the Chattahoochee River, is approximately 150 yards to the right of the gap. To the left of the gap, blue-blazed Jack's Knob National Recreation Trail leads 4.5 miles to the parking lot near the summit of Brasstown Bald. (See Brasstown Bald Visitor Information Center, Chapter 2, for more information concerning Jack's Knob Trail.)

In Chattahoochee Gap the A.T. angles to the right, slants down off the ridge, then skirts the southern slopes of Jack's Knob to Red Clay Gap (3,440 ft.) at mile 10.0. Here the trail switches to the other side of the ridge and enters a moist, northslope forest on the flank of Spaniards Knob. To either side of the rock-jumbled footpath, scores of dead chestnuts have fallen into tangled windrows. Striped maples, common in cool, moist locations throughout the Blue Ridge Mountains of North Georgia, are abundant beside this richly vegetated portion of trail. A small tree, the striped maple is easily identified by the whitish, vertical stripes that line the smooth green bark of its thinner branches and by its three-lobed leaves, which have rounded or heart-shaped bases, notched margins, and long slender tips on the end of each lobe.

The treadway gradually gains elevation from Red Clay Gap to the Rocky Knob Shelter at mile 11.1. It then rises up and over a Spaniards Knob ridge and descends to Henson Gap (3,580 ft.) at mile 11.3. With the exception of two, short downhill grades, the next 1.3 miles ascend to the crest of Blue Mountain (4,020 ft.). This long grade, which angles steadily upward on mountainside before climbing hard along the ridge, is moderate in overall difficulty. The remainder of Section 4 drops steadily, occasionally sharply, down the rocky northeastern slopes of Blue Mountain to Unicoi Gap (2,949 ft.).

Water is plentiful along Section 4.

Directions: Travel Georgia 75 North through Helen. After driving approximately 1.4 miles beyond the Chattahoochee River Bridge in Helen, turn left onto Georgia Alt. 75 South, crossing the Robertstown Bridge over the Chattahoochee River. Continue on Georgia Alt. 75 South for 2.3 miles; then turn right onto Richard B. Russell Scenic Highway (Georgia 348 North). Proceed slightly more than 7.0 miles on Richard B. Russell Scenic Highway to the large parking area to the right. Hogpen Gap, marked with a sign to the left of the road, is the highest point on the highway.

APPALACHIAN TRAIL
SECTION 5

Brasstown and Tallulah Ranger Districts
Primarily Towns County

UNICOI GAP (GEORGIA 75) TO DICKS CREEK GAP (U.S. 76) (16.6 miles one way to Dicks Creek Gap). Moderate to Strenuous.

Section 5, offering scenic views and isolated forest, makes an ideal two- or three-day backpacking trip. The second half of this segment, from Young Lick to Dicks Creek Gap, follows the ridge that serves as the boundary between two wildlife management areas. Lake Burton W.M.A., 12,600 acres, is to the east; Swallow Creek W.M.A., 19,000 acres, is to the west.

Starting to the right of the commemorative plaque at the parking area in Unicoi Gap (2,949 ft.), Section 5 climbs moderately, through rocky terrain and a predominantly oak forest, to the crown of Rocky Mountain (4,020 ft.) at mile 1.3. The rivulet it crosses on the way up is the Hiwassee River. Atop the mountain, a splendid view to the right extends beyond the unmistakable profile of Mount Yonah all the way to the Piedmont.

The trail descends, with occasional short, steep pitches, to F.S. 283 in Indian Grave Gap (3,100 ft.) at mile 2.6. Andrews Cove Trail meets the Appalachian Trail in Indian Grave Gap. (See Andrews Cove Recreation Area, Chapter 2, for a description of the Andrews Cove Trail.) Across the road, the A.T. enters the evergreen tunnel of a heath thicket. Here the path slants gently upward to its crossing of F.S. 79 (Tray Mountain Road) at mile 3.3, continues 0.2 mile to ridgetop, then quickly crosses a jeep road in an unnamed gap. Through the gap, the treadway rises moderately as it winds to the northeast onto York Ridge. After the initial upgrade, the trail remains nearly level through an open forest of old, gnarled oaks to Tray Gap (3,841 ft.), where it crosses F.S. 79 again at mile 4.3. Two-tenths mile before the gap there is a good view, especially when the leaves have fallen, of Hickorynut Ridge.

Proceeding eastward from Tray Gap, Section 5 ascends moderately on wide switchbacking loops through rocky terrain. At mile 5.0, where the tread-way turns sharply to the right, there is an excellent outcrop overlook to the left. One tenth of a mile farther, the twisting footpath reaches the protruding topknot at Tray's Summit (4,430 ft.). Here, atop the second highest point on the Appalachian Trail in Georgia, the bare rock affords one of the most scenic 360° vistas in the Chattahoochee National Forest. Yonah's half-dome is to the south; Brasstown Bald's tower is to the northwest; the Nantahala's sharp peaks are almost due north.

The A.T. traverses the saddle between Tray's high-points, then descends steadily to an unnamed gap (3,780 ft.) at mile 5.9. On the way down, at mile 5.5, a blue-blazed sidepath to the left leads to the Tray Mountain Shelter and water. Beyond this first gap, the trail gently undulates on or just below the ridgeline, losing elevation through two more gaps — Wolfpen (3,580 ft.) at mile 6.7 and Steeltrap (3,500 ft.) at mile 7.3.

The downgrade from Tray Mountain is through an open, predominantly oak forest. Two of North Georgia's most brightly colored birds — the rose-breasted grosbeak and scarlet tanager — are common along this descending segment of Section 5, as well as other portions of the Appalachian Trail with similar habitat and elevations.

Continuing from Steeltrap Gap, the treadway makes a moderate, then easy, upridge grade to the crest of Young Lick (approximately 3,800 ft.) at mile 8.2. It then heads down the ridge for 0.2 mile, skirts the upper slopes of a knob and dips to a low gap — the Blue Ridge Swag (3,460 ft.) — at mile 9.1. From the swag the footpath gains elevation moderately along the eastern side of Round Top for 0.8 mile before dropping to Sassafras Gap (3,540 ft.) at mile 10.3. Here the A.T. follows a north-running ridge over a low knob and down to Addis Gap (3,340 ft.) at mile 11.1. The Addis Gap Shelter (spring nearby) is approximately 0.3 mile down the road to the right.

Section 5 climbs moderately along Kelly Knob's southern ridge to approximately 4,140 feet at mile 12.2. At that point, instead of completing the climb to its crest (4,276 ft.), the trail slants down onto the knob's eastern slopes, swings around its highpoint and descends to the stand of yellow poplar in Deep Gap (3,560 ft.) at mile 13.0. The treadway rises easily from Deep Gap for 0.6 mile to Whiteoak Stomp, where it continues on a nearly level ridge across Wolf Stake Knob (3,900 ft.). Following a 0.2-mile downgrade to McClure Gap (3,700 ft.) at mile 14.2, the path gains approximately 100 feet of elevation toward the crown of Powell Mountain before it veers off the ridge. Here the A.T. drops steadily along Powell's southeastern flank to a gap at mile 15.4.

In this gap the trail turns 90° to the right onto an old road. The remainder of Section 5 is predominantly downhill or level to Dicks Creek Gap (2,675 ft.). The last mile, most of it on the wide walkway of an old road, passes through a scenic area of steep-sided coves and small streams.

Water occurs at regular intervals along Section 5.

Directions: To reach Unicoi Gap, travel approximately 9.5 miles on Georgia 75 North from the Chattahoochee River Bridge in Helen. The gap's large gravel parking area to the right of the highway has a boulder-embedded plaque commemorating the Appalachian Trail. One sign usually marks the gap and another sign, the stickperson hiker, usually marks the trail's crossing at Georgia 75.

Note: A 6.8-mile segment of Section 5 of the Appalachian Trail, from Tray Gap to Addis Gap, passes through the 10,414-acre Tray Mountain Wilderness Area.

APPALACHIAN TRAIL
SECTION 6

Tallulah Ranger District
Primarily Rabun and Towns Counties

DICKS CREEK GAP (U.S. 76) TO BLY GAP AT THE GEORGIA-NORTH CAROLINA BORDER (9.0 miles one way to Bly Gap). Moderate to Strenuous.

The Georgia Appalachian Trail Club has rerouted the beginning of Section 6. As a result, it is slightly longer and somewhat less strenuous. There are no long, steep upgrades along this section. There are, however, a few short, strenuous grades and numerous moderate grades, both up and down, that take their toll on those carrying heavy packs. Notice the constant change and wide range of the elevations for the gaps.

Starting straight back from the picnic tables at Dicks Creek Gap (2,675 ft.), the white-blazed footpath rises moderately through a mixed deciduous-evergreen forest to the top of a sharp ridge at 0.4 mile. Here it crosses over the ridge, dips to a saddle on a spur ridge, then continues gradually upward along the southern slopes of Little Bald Mountain. At mile 1.1 the treadway angles up to the ridge and follows it easily uphill for 0.3 mile before slanting down to its western side. After crossing the ridge, the path makes a steady, predominantly moderate descent to Tom Cowart Gap (2,900 ft.) at mile 1.8. On the way down, it passes through a rich forest of basswood, buckeye and ash along the headwaters of Little Hightower Creek.

Once across the road that bisects the gap, the trail climbs moderately for 0.4 mile back to the ridgetop, where it drops to the slopes again and skirts below the highpoint of an unnamed knob. The trail then leads through a gap at mile 2.4, and rises on the easy to moderate grades of a north-running ridge for 0.5 mile. After this elevation gain, it slips off the ridge onto the upper flank of Buzzard Knob, remaining nearly level until it dips to Bull Gap (3,540 ft.) at mile 3.4.

Beyond Bull Gap, the footpath ascends for 0.1 mile before crossing over the ridge and dropping to its eastern side. The next 1.0 mile, a gradual downgrade through a cove forest to Plumorchard Gap (3,100 ft.), is the easiest walking on Section 6. The Plumorchard Gap Shelter (mile 4.5) is located less than 200 yards to the right of the trail. There is a spring a short distance down the jeep road to the left of the gap as well as at the shelter.

Continuing northward to Bly Gap, the trail climbs easy to moderate grades for 0.5 mile, then gently undulates with the ridge to the southern highpoint of As Knob (approx. 3,440 ft.). Here, instead of following the knob's crest, the treadway slides onto the mountain's western slopes and descends easily to F.S. 72 in Blue Ridge Gap (3,020 ft.). The trail enters the 23,339-acre Southern Nantahala Wilderness across Blue Ridge Gap at mile 5.8. The rest of Section 6 remains in the wilderness.

The path holds its course on moderate, then easy, upgrades to mile 6.4, where it bears to the left onto the western pitch of Wheeler Knob. Once off the ridge, the treadway is predominantly level or slightly downhill to Rich Cove Gap (3,420 ft.). From this gap at mile 7.0, the trail heads upridge for less than 0.2 mile before half-circling below the crest of Rocky Knob. After it regains the ridge at mile 7.3, the A.T.

alternates level, then ascending, grades (easy or moderate) as it climbs toward Rich Knob. At mile 8.4 the footpath leaves the ridge and undulates easily on the eastern side of Rich Knob to Bly Gap (3,840 ft.), just over the state line in North Carolina. One-tenth mile before entering the gap, the trail turns 90° to the left, travels 60 yards uphill, then turns 90° to the right. One hundred yards beyond the second sharp turn, the A.T. reaches the old road in the small clearing of Bly Gap.

Along the higher elevations of the last half of Section 6, from Plumorchard Gap to Bly Gap, you may notice small clusters of squaw-root — a common parasitic wildflower. Usually 3 to 8 inches tall, squaw-root closely resembles a slender, elongated pine cone. These unusual plants range from yellow to brown and become darker as they grow older.

The pitch pine, which ranges only as far south as the mountains in northeastern Georgia, is fairly common along this section of the trail. The pitch — usually 50 to 60 feet tall, rarely 100 — is a medium-sized pine. It is shorter than the white and shortleaf, generally taller and thicker than the Virginia or table-mountain. Its stiff, often twisted, dark yellow-green needles — 3 to 5 inches long and three to the sheath — stand at right angles to the branch. The tree's numerous horizontal branches give it a short-trunked appearance, especially when compared to the shortleaf pine.

Marked water sources occur at regular intervals along this section of the Appalachian Trail.

Directions: To reach Dicks Creek Gap, travel Georgia 75 North to its junction with U.S. 76 near Hiawassee. Turn right at this junction onto U.S. 76 East and continue approximately 7.6 miles to the picnic area and parking lot to the left of the highway at Dicks Creek Gap. Dicks Creek Gap can also be reached by traveling approximately 16.5 miles on U.S. 76 West from Clayton. A prominent stickperson hiker sign marks the Appalachian Trail crossing at U.S. 76, where the trail enters the picnic area at Dicks Creek Gap.

BARTRAM APPROACH TRAILS

Tallulah Ranger District
Rabun County
Two Trails

CHATTOOGA RIVER TRAIL (10.7 miles one way to its junction with the Bartram Trail). Moderate.

The Chattooga River Trail may not be what you would expect or want from a trail bearing such a famous name. The trail does not lead you to the wild, colorfully named rapids — Painted Rock, Roller Coaster, Eye of the Needle, The Narrows — along Floating Section III. In fact, it closely parallels the river for only 1.6 miles, from mile 6.3 to mile 7.9.

Starting from U.S. 76, the trail heads northeastward along the Georgia side of the Chattooga River. The first half of the trail frequently loops outside of the blue-blazed river corridor, where motorized vehicles are allowed on the jeep roads. The last half of the trail stays totally within the protected corridor, where motorized vehicles are prohibited except at designated access points. Alternating from constructed path to old road, the trail winds along the sloping strip of land from the river up to its enclosing ridge. Although this terrain is steep and frequently cut by streams, the trail's numerous grades are all easy or moderate. Most of the moderate grades are short.

The white-blazed Chattooga River Trail begins behind two sets of vehicle-blocking boulders, at an elevation of approximately 1,200 feet. One of the outside boulders, engraved and safe from all but the most determined of vandals, now serves as the trailhead sign. The footpath follows a former jeep road through a mixed deciduous-evergreen forest to 0.7 mile, where it curls down and to the left from the road to cross Pole Creek. Beyond this first of many streams, the treadway winds along the lower slopes of Lion Mountain for several miles, often crossing rivulets above their steep-sided coves. Occasionally you can hear the roar of powerful rapids below; the loudest comes from Bull Sluice, a Class 5 rapid.

The trail crosses Chattooga tributaries, big enough for bridges but unnamed, at mile 4.1 and mile 4.4. Beyond the second, a slow-moving stream with a flood plain, the treadway curves to the right, then passes within 40 yards of the river before veering away. From this quick glimpse the trail climbs to the ridge on an old road. Once on top, it rises and dips with the road along the Chattooga's protective boundary to mile 5.9, where it bears to the right onto path and descends to the river.

At mile 6.3 the footpath swings parallel to the Chattooga, usually green and always beautiful. For the next 1.6 miles, occasionally through dense stands of hemlock, the trail heads upstream above the river's low shoals and long, calm pools. At mile 6.8 it crosses a bridge over Licklog Creek, then continues beside the deep green of good swimming holes before crossing Buckeye Branch at mile 7.4. Sandy beaches and boulders make great spots to enjoy lunch or watch the rafts float by.

At mile 7.9 the trail bends backward to the left away from the river on an old road, climbs a hill, then turns 90° to the right onto path. Here the treadway ascends moderately to the ridge above the river, where it gently undulates on or near the ridgeline to mile 9.8. Following a 0.2-mile downgrade, the Chattooga River Trail crosses Rock Creek and Dicks Creek Road in quick succession. Another inscribed boulder marks the trail's crossing of Dicks Creek Road. The remainder of the footpath is easily walked to its Y-shaped junction with the Bartram Trail. This junction (approx. 1,640 ft.) is designated with a small rock sign inside the Y.

Directions: To reach the trail's southern access point, take U.S. 76 East from Clayton toward Westminster, South Carolina. If you are traveling north on U.S. 441, the turn will be to your right. After driving slightly more than 8.0 miles on U.S. 76 East, turn into a small gravel parking area to the left of the highway immediately before the bridge over the Chattooga River. The trail begins behind two sets of vehicle-blocking boulders at the end of the parking lot farthest from the river.

The trail's northern access point can also be reached from Clayton. In Clayton, where U.S. 76 turns west, turn east onto Warwoman Road. If you are traveling north on U.S. 441, the turn will be to your right near the Hardee's, which is the second building to the right on Warwoman Road. Once on Warwoman Road, turn right at the stop sign and proceed on Warwoman Road past the Georgia Power building.

After driving approximately 5.9 miles on Warwoman Road, turn right onto unpaved Dicks Creek Road immediately past the house with the A-shaped, gable-like roof over its door. Inside the entrance to Dicks Creek Road, bear right with the main dirt road, continue approximately 0.7 mile from the pavement, and then turn left across a road-level bridge. After this left turn, proceed approximately 3.7 miles to the Bartram Trail sign — an engraved rock to the right of the road.

The northern end of the Chattooga River Trail ties into the Bartram Trail near Dicks Creek Road. If you end your hike at this junction, turn sharp left onto the

Bartram and walk the 100 yards to Dicks Creek Road at the Bartram sign. If you wish to walk the Chattooga River Trail north to south, park at the Bartram Trail sign, walk the Bartram to the left (from the way you came) 100 yards, then turn right onto the Chattooga River Trail.

In addition to being fairly rough and rutted, Dicks Creek Road fords the creek twice before reaching the Bartram Trail sign. The second ford may be too deep for low-to-the-ground conventional cars.

RABUN BALD TRAIL (2.9 miles one way to its junction with the Bartram Trail). Strenuous.

Starting at the sign (Rabun Bald 3.0, Three Forks Trail), this infrequently blazed but easily followed trail works its way up to the summit of Rabun Bald (4,696 ft.), Georgia's second highest peak. See Three Forks Trail, Chapter 5, for an explanation of the trail sign.

This remote, challenging footpath rises steadily almost from the beginning, ascending nearly 2,200 feet along its 2.9-mile length. The level stretches and short dips between climbs are just long enough to let you catch your breath. The final grade to Rabun Bald is very steep. I am not sure if it is the steepest pitch along North Georgia's trails, but I am sure there are none steeper.

Beginning at approximately 2,500 feet, the trail rises steadily through a dense forest where mountain laurel thickets and galax patches are common. Galax, an abundant wildflower in the mountains, is easily identified by its shiny green (copper-red in winter), leathery, heart-shaped leaf. Their colonies can often be detected by their scent — a peculiar, sweet skunky fragrance — even before you see them.

At mile 1.5 there is a rivulet to the left of the path. This is the only water source on the way to the top, and it probably goes dry during drought. Beyond the streamlet, the treadway leads through an open oak forest before it enters an area of boulders and laurel thickets. At mile 2.1 the footpath crosses a grassy glade where louseworts are common. This fern-leaved wildflower received the first part of its name from the old belief that livestock became infested with lice upon contact with the plant.

The trail climbs steeply from the glade for slightly less than 0.2 mile before leveling out on a spur ridge. Often tunneling through rhododendron, the final 0.3 mile ascends very sharply. The path enters the small clearing atop Rabun Bald on the side opposite the observation tower's stairs. Here atop Rabun Bald's crest, a few mountain ash grow among the short, twisted oaks that surround the manmade clearing. This is the only place where I have seen this tree along the trails in this guide.

The Rabun Bald Trail ends at its junction with the Bartram Trail (see the following trail for description).

On clear, hazeless days the high-perched observation tower offers a superb 360° panorama. The long sloping ridges and unbroken forests of the 14,000-acre Warwoman Wildlife Management Area spread away to the south. To the east, South Carolina's Lake Keowee shimmers in the distance. To the northeast, near Cashiers, North Carolina, you can see the sheer rock face of Whiteside Mountain. At most other points on the compass, except where the view reaches the rolling landscape of the Piedmont, overlapping rows of ridges and peaks become indistinct in the blue distance.

If streams are full, and if you have binoculars, see if you can spot the waterfall over toward the cliff faces in North Carolina. One more thing: the large crows that call "crunk" rather than "caw" are ravens.

Directions: In Clayton, where U.S. 76 turns west, turn east onto Warwoman Road. If you are traveling north on U.S. 441, the turn will be to your right near the Hardee's, which is the second building to the right on Warwoman Road. Once on Warwoman Road, turn right at the stop sign and proceed on Warwoman Road past the Georgia Power building.

After traveling approximately 10.0 miles on Warwoman Road, turn left onto F.S. 7 (Hale Ridge Road). F.S. 7 is the first public road to the left past Allen's Grocery. Continue 5.5 miles on F.S. 7; you will see the back of the trail sign on the left side of the road. There is a small pulloff area just beyond the sign to the right.

BARTRAM NATIONAL RECREATION TRAIL SECTION 1

Tallulah Ranger District
Rabun County

HALE RIDGE ROAD (F.S. 7) TO WARWOMAN ROAD AT WARWOMAN DELL RECREATION AREA (17.6 miles one way to Warwoman Road). Moderate to Strenuous.

Beginning 0.1 or 0.2 mile from the North Carolina line, Section 1 of the Bartram Trail maintains a meandering, southwestward course for most of its length. This isolated footpath winds through a predominantly hardwood forest, much of it dominated by stands of mature oak. There are no signs of recent logging. From Rabun Bald to Courthouse Gap, the Bartram follows the northwestern boundary of the 14,000-acre Warwoman Wildlife Management Area.

Starting at an elevation of approximately 3,280 feet, this wide, well-constructed trail gently undulates — dipping slightly to a stream, rising, then dipping to the next stream — through a diverse, mature forest to Beegum Gap. At 0.4 mile a rivulet slides over rock to the right of the path. This small waterfall comes from one of Holcomb Creek's many headwater streams that cross this initial segment of Section 1. Slightly more than 0.1 mile beyond the waterslide, a look over your left shoulder will give you a good view (when the leaves are gone) of rock-faced mountains in North Carolina.

A short distance after crossing a narrow dirt road, the Bartram reaches Beegum Gap (3,640 ft.), where it turns left onto an old firetower road at mile 2.7. Here the trail climbs steadily for the next 1.5 miles to the summit of Rabun Bald (4,696 ft.), the second highest mountain in Georgia. This is the longest, most difficult upgrade on the Bartram Trail; however, because the rocky road loops up the steeper slopes, the ascent is not as difficult as you might expect.

Following his discovery of "a new and beautiful species of that celebrated family of flowering trees," William Bartram named a nearby "exalted peak" Mount Magnolia. Authorities believe that Bartram's Mount Magnolia is our Rabun Bald. That beautiful species — the Fraser magnolia — is common along the lower elevations of the Bartram Trail.

The observation tower atop Rabun Bald provides views of the Blue Ridge Mountains to all points of the compass. To the northeast, east and south, you can see many square miles of heavily forested, mountainous landscape that remain largely wild. The narrow path that enters the clearing opposite the tower's steps is Rabun Bald Trail. (For more information concerning this trail and the view from the observation tower, see Rabun Bald Trail, also in this chapter.)

If you spend some time on Rabun Bald's crown, you will probably see or hear the "crunk" of one of north Georgia's rarest birds: the raven. Noticeably larger than the common crow, the raven's thick bill and wedge-shaped tail make it easy to identify. The raven, which is increasing its range in the Southern Appalachians, flies alternately flapping and gliding like a hawk.

Guided by the first of its nearly vandal-proof trail signs — an engraved rock — the Bartram loses elevation easily through rhododendron, then drops off the ridge and switchbacks steadily down hardwood slopes to Saltrock Gap (3,740 ft.) at mile 5.9. Continuing to the southwest, the trail ascends the eastern side of Flat Top to near its crest (4,100 ft.) at mile 6.5 before

descending again. At mile 7.1, on the western flank of
Wilson Knob, a 20-foot sidepath leads to a sunny
outcrop open to the west. Here is another view well
worth the walk. The rock faces a high valley, wild and
completely forested, hemmed in by higher ridges all
around. This valley, which is named Ramey Field, was
once cleared and farmed.

Following a sharp 0.3-mile downgrade, the treadway turns to the west, gradually rises along the northwestern slopes of Double Knob, then dips to
Tuckaluge Road in Wilson Gap (3,220 ft.) at mile 8.5.
The Bartram follows this road (F.S. 153) to the right
and downhill to mile 9.1, where it angles to the right
away from the road. Look for this turn where the
main road curves sharply to the left at a jeep-road
junction.

Back in the forest again, the path climbs moderately on the eastern side of Rattlesnake and Blacks
Creek knobs before descending easily to Windy Gap
(3,180 ft.) at mile 10.5. The trail continues gently up
and down to Rock Mountain Gap (3,260 ft.) at mile
10.9, then makes an easy to moderate 0.5-mile ascent
to the crest of Rock Mountain (3,680 ft.). After a
sharp descent to an unnamed gap (2,900 ft.) at mile
12.3, the treadway loses elevation on easy grades
along the southern flank of Raven Knob to mile 13.9,
where it drops 0.1 mile to Courthouse Gap (2,540 ft.).

Beyond Courthouse Gap to the end of Section 1 at
Warwoman Road, the Bartram forms a 3.6-mile semi-
circle, open to the west. The trail rises sharply from
the gap (a wide bare spot) for a short distance on an
old road. After the road levels out, the treadway
angles to the left through a gap in the vegetation as
the road turns to the right. Here the footpath works
its way down through rhododendron thickets to Mar-
tin Creek Falls at mile 15.6. A short sidetrail curls back
to the left to an open view. The 45-foot waterfall,

narrow and framed by hemlock, freefalls twice over ledges.

Section 1 continues downhill beside the clear, cascading creek for 0.3 mile before turning away from the stream. After the path swings parallel to Warwoman Road, it passes through an area recovering from fire, then dips to a junction above Becky Branch. The Bartram Trail turns right and heads upstream to the bridge in front of a 20- to 25-foot sliding falls. The last 0.1 mile of Section 1 descends above the branch to Warwoman Road (approximately 1,920 ft.).

Directions: To reach the Bartram Trail's northernmost point in Georgia at Hale Ridge Road, travel U.S. 441 North from Clayton past Mountain City and Dillard. Slightly more than 1.0 mile north of Dillard, turn right onto Georgia 246 toward Highlands, North Carolina. Continue on highways 246 and 106 (it changes to Highway 106 at the North Carolina line) for approximately 7.0 miles, then turn right onto a paved road just before the green "Scaly Mountain" city sign. This turn is after the ski lifts (uphill and to the right) and before the Scaly Mountain Post Office, which is the second building on the right beyond the turn. This unmarked road is locally known as Bald Mountain Road.

After traveling 2.1 miles on Bald Mountain Road, you will come to a Y-shaped fork — gravel to the left, paved to the right. Take the left fork — F.S. 7, Hale Ridge Road — and proceed 1.1 miles to the large Bartram Trail sign on the right side of the road.

To reach Warwoman Dell Recreation Area, travel U.S. 76 or U.S. 441 to Clayton. In Clayton, where U.S. 76 turns west, turn east onto Warwoman Road. If you are traveling north on U.S. 441, the turn will be to your right near the Hardee's, which is the second building to the right on Warwoman Road. Once on

161

Warwoman Road, turn right at the stop sign and proceed on Warwoman Road past the Georgia Power building. The Warwoman Dell sign and entrance will be on the right after you have traveled nearly 3.0 miles on Warwoman Road. The Bartram Trail crosses Warwoman Road just before a pulloff parking area to the left a few hundred yards before the entrance of Warwoman Dell Recreation Area.

BARTRAM NATIONAL RECREATION TRAIL SECTION 2

Tallulah Ranger District
Rabun County

WARWOMAN ROAD TO GEORGIA 28 (19.2 miles one way to Georgia 28). Moderate.

Section 2 of the Bartram Trail is a good two- or three-day backpacking trip. Dicks Creek Road, which divides this section into segments of nearly equal length, provides opportunities for dayhikers.

From Warwoman Dell to Dicks Creek Road, the Bartram travels west to east. From Dicks Creek Road to its end at Highway 28, the trail generally follows the Chattooga River corridor to the northeast. The trailside forest is most often a mixture of deciduous and evergreen species.

From Warwoman Road to Dicks Creek Road, Section 2 winds its way up, along and over a series of low, unnamed ridges as it heads toward the Chattooga. This 9.4-mile segment is constantly undulating. All the long upgrades are easy or moderate. The downgrades are occasionally steep.

This portion of the Bartram Trail is the least strenuous long section of trail (over 15.0 miles) in North Georgia. It is especially mild in comparison to sections of the Duncan Ridge and Appalachian Trails of similar length. Because the highest point on Section 2 is less than 2,800 feet, I have not included elevations as in the descriptions of other trails where there are substantial and frequent changes.

Section 2 begins beside the "Bartram" historical marker to the right of Warwoman Road a few hundred yards before the entrance to Warwoman Dell Picnic Area. There is a small pulloff parking area on the left side of the road opposite the sign (see directions for Bartram Trail, Section 1). The trail descends from Warwoman Road into the picnic area, turns right onto the road and follows it to the pavilion parking lot. The treadway continues up and to the left of the parking lot, behind the Bartram and Blue Ridge Railroad signs.

Beyond the dell, the footpath makes an easy to moderate climb, winding through coves to the top of a ridge at mile 1.1, then descending 0.4 mile to a dirt road. Here Section 2 turns right onto the road and follows it for 65 yards before re-entering the forest to the right. At mile 1.9 the Bartram crosses the road and continues to ascend to the next ridge at mile 2.7. It then roller-coasters on easy to moderate grades to where it crosses over another ridge at mile 4.0.

After dropping sharply for 0.2 mile, the trail rises back onto the ridge, undulates with its crest to mile 5.4, then steadily loses elevation to Pool Creek Road at mile 5.9. Across the road, the treadway gains elevation moderately for 0.4 mile through a forest dominated by Virginia pine and blackjack oak. In winter, gaps through these trees afford views of Rabun Bald to the north.

At mile 7.2 the path angles to the left across an old road. Beyond this road the Bartram is predominantly level or downhill until it crosses Dicks Creek Road at mile 9.4. Section 2's remaining 9.8 miles stay mostly within the blue-blazed corridor of the Chattooga National Wild and Scenic River.

Approximately 100 yards past the road, the Chattooga River Trail ties into the Bartram at a Y-shaped junction marked with a sign of stone. (For more information see Chattooga River Trail, also in this chapter.)

164

Section 2 descends easily through a stand of tall white pine, crosses a bridge over Dicks Creek at mile 9.8, then quickly enters a small clearing. To the right of this clearing, across a small bridge, an old road leads 200 yards to one of North Georgia's most beautiful scenes — Dicks Creek Falls. Here the creek's final run splashes 60 feet down a solid slide of rock to the Chattooga. In front of the waterfall, the wide river booms over a bank-to-bank ledge, a Class 4 rapid known as Dicks Creek Ledge. A steep path drops to the boulders at the base of the falls.

Continuing straight ahead from the clearing, the treadway gradually rises over a low ridge before winding down through coves to the river at mile 10.5. For the next 0.6 mile, the Bartram closely parallels the Chattooga, an enticing dark green where it deepens, on an old road through hemlock. The trail continues to follow the easy grades of the old road as it swings away from the river and heads to Warwoman Ford. After paralleling Warwoman Creek, the wide walkway reaches Earls Ford Road and a trail-sign rock at mile 12.2. Here Section 2 turns right onto the road, fords the wide, knee-deep creek and continues on the road.

Slightly less than 0.1 mile beyond the ford, the Bartram turns left onto a blocked jeep road, immediately slants back to the right onto path, then ascends moderately for 0.3 mile to a ridge. The trail's next 2.1 miles wind along the Chattooga's protective boundary, well away from the river. Easily walked, this segment alternates between old road and constructed footpath on the lower ridges and slopes of Willis Knob.

At mile 14.7 the treadway crosses a bridge over Laurel Branch. It then heads up to another ridge-running road, quickly turns to the right onto path and drops to the bridge over Bynum Branch at mile

15.6. The Bartram crosses a bridge over Adline Branch at mile 16.2, then turns right onto an old road. Section 2's remaining 3.0 miles mostly follow old roads through a flood plain, close to but usually out of sight of the river. This flood plain area, Long Bottom, was fenced and farmed until perhaps the 1960's. The pine plantation will give you an idea of when the open land returned to forest.

At mile 16.5 the trail approaches close enough for a view before bending away from the river. Four-tenths mile beyond that point, the walkway turns to the left onto another old road. The entrance to this road may look like a path. If you continue straight ahead and miss this turn, you will have overshot it by 130 yards when you reach the Chattooga River.

The treadway crosses a bridge over Holden Branch at mile 17.8, then closely parallels the Chattooga one more time before curling beside the west fork. At mile 18.8 the Bartram fords the West Fork Chattooga River below a Class 2 rapid called Big Slide. This ford is nearly twice as wide as the one on Warwoman Creek, and can be mid-thigh depth or deeper. It is potentially dangerous after heavy rains.

Once across the ford, Section 2 follows the West Fork downstream, turns to parallel the main river, and soon ends at Russell Bridge on Georgia 28.

Directions: To reach the end of Section 2 from Warwoman Dell Recreation Area, travel 11.2 miles northeastward (away from Clayton) on Warwoman Road, then turn right onto Georgia 28 toward Walhalla, South Carolina. Continue 2.2 miles on Georgia 28 to where it crosses the Chattooga River. You will see a Bartram Trail emblem and sign to the right of the highway on the Georgia side of the river just before Russell Bridge. There is a parking area on the opposite side of the highway.

Dicks Creek Road divides Section 2 into segments of nearly equal length. For directions to the Bartram Trail crossing at Dicks Creek Road, see the Chattooga River Trail, also in this chapter.

BENTON MACKAYE TRAIL
SECTION 1

Toccoa Ranger District
Fannin County

SPRINGER MOUNTAIN TO GEORGIA 60 (17.5 miles one way to Georgia 60). Moderate.

Section 1 of the Benton MacKaye makes a good two- or three-day backpacking trip. The footpath's first 7.8 miles, often paralleling streams through hemlock and rhododendron, is easily walked. After winding away from Long Creek, however, it becomes a ridge and slope trail of moderate difficulty. From Springer Mountain to the Toccoa River, Benton MacKaye travels northward through the 39,000-acre Blue Ridge Wildlife Management Area.

The summit of Springer Mountain serves as the southern terminus for the two longest trails in Georgia — the Appalachian and the Benton MacKaye. Slightly more than 0.2 mile from its start, the Appalachian Trail arrives at a sign-posted, Y-shaped junction. The Appalachian Trail, blazed with white-paint rectangles, follows the left fork. The Benton MacKaye, blazed with white-plastic diamonds, begins at the right fork at an elevation of approximately 3,760 feet.

Curling to the east with the ridge, Section 1 of the Benton MacKaye starts with an easy to moderate descent to a shallow gap at 0.4 mile. Beyond this unnamed gap, the trail rises through a heath thicket, skirts the southeastern side of Ball Mountain, then continues the steady downgrade from Springer. At mile 1.2 "View" is painted on a tree to the right. A

168

short sidepath leads to an outcrop overlook, open to the southeast, that most definitely affords a view — the completely forested Jones Creek Cove and its surrounding ridges.

After crossing F.S. 42 in Big Stamp Gap (3,146 ft.) at mile 1.6, the treadway undulates on easy grades until it swings beside a rhododendron-lined tributary of Chester Creek. Section 1 parallels this stream on the wide walkway of an old road before crossing it at mile 2.1. Continuing to the northwest, the trail crosses the two forks of Davis Creek (another Chester Creek tributary) — the first at mile 2.5, the second at mile 2.6 — heads uphill for 0.3 mile, then turns left. At mile 3.2 it turns right at the sign and joins the Appalachian Trail. For 0.7 mile, both trails share the same treadway along a Rich Mountain ridge dominated by tall white pine and yellow poplar.

After the trails split, the Benton MacKaye ascends easily with the ridge, through an understory of silverbell, for 0.3 mile before dropping to an old road at mile 5.0. It follows this road gently downhill through hemlock and rhododendron on the lower slopes of Rich Mountain. Chester Creek is deeply entrenched to the right. At mile 5.9 Section 1 turns right and shares the gravel road walkway with the Appalachian Trail. Together they dip 0.1 mile to Three Forks (2,540 ft.), where Stover, Chester and Long creeks flow together at right angles to create Noontootla Creek.

At Three Forks the trails cross a footbridge over Chester Creek, cross F.S. 58, and continue on the old gravel road as it parallels Long Creek upstream. A sign at mile 6.9 marks the blue-blazed sidepath that leads 100 yards to Long Creek Falls — a ledge-sliding drop of 20 to 25 feet. One-tenth of a mile farther the trails split apart at another sign. Here Section 1 of the blue-blazed Duncan Ridge Trail begins. It shares the treadway with the Benton MacKaye for the remaining 10.5 miles to Georgia 60.

The Benton MacKaye turns left onto path at the split and quickly crosses Long Creek. It then winds through heath thickets beside a small tributary stream for 0.8 mile, swings to the west and makes a moderate, diagonal climb to a ridgetop clearing (3,260 ft.). This area is used as a helicopter pad by the U.S. Army. The view to the left is slowly being blocked by pine trees. There is still a good view to the right.

For the next 2.3 miles Section 1 roller-coasters, rising to knobs and dipping to the gaps between them, on or near the crest of an unnamed ridge. The downgrades are often steep and slope off the ridge. Most of the upgrades are easy or moderate and stay on the ridge.The clearing, at mile 8.1, is the highest elevation along this segment; the first gap north of the clearing (2,900 ft.) is the lowest. The forest is open and predominantly oak.

After an easy, 0.4-mile descent from Wildcat Ridge, the treadway enters a shallow gap at mile 10.8. Beyond this gap, the Benton MacKaye makes a 1.7-mile "S," walked south to north, around the two peaks collectively known as John Dick Mountain. Here the footpath climbs for 0.2 mile toward the southern peak, slants down off the ridge onto its eastern side, then swings to the west on its northern slopes. At mile 11.4, it turns to the right (north) and drops sharply for 0.2 mile to the middle of the S — Bryson Gap (2,900 ft.). The trail continues to the northwest, rising over a low spur before completing the half loop around John Dick's northern peak on the easy grades of an old road.

The Benton MacKaye turns left onto another old road at mile 12.5, and heads downhill through a heath thicket on a north-running spur. With the exception of a few short, up-ridge grades, the treadway steadily works its way down, losing approximately 1,000 feet in elevation to the Toccoa River (1,900 ft.) at mile 14.5. Here the path crosses the shoaling, usually green river on a deluxe, 265-foot-long suspension bridge.

The remainder of Section 1 is a long upgrade followed by a long downgrade of nearly equal length. Across the river, the trail makes a moderate, occasionally strenuous, ascent to the twin highpoints (both 2,720 ft.) of Toonowee Mountain. It then descends for 1.3 miles, winding steadily and sometimes steeply down the slopes of Toonowee to Georgia 60.

Obvious or marked water sources occur at regular intervals along Section 1 of the Benton MacKaye.

Directions: The directions to Benton MacKaye's southern terminus atop Springer Mountain are exactly the same as those for Section 1 of the Appalachian Trail, also in this chapter. After reaching the place where the Appalachian Trail crosses F.S. 42, you have two options. You can walk 0.7 mile on the Appalachian Trail to the beginning of the Benton MacKaye, or you can drive approximately 1.8 miles farther on F.S. 42 and walk 1.6 miles on the Benton MacKaye to its beginning. Springer Mountain is to the south (to the right and uphill) of F.S. 42. A trail sign marks where the Benton MacKaye crosses F.S. 42.

The directions to the end of Section 1 of the Benton MacKaye Trail are exactly the same as those to the beginning of Section 2 of the Duncan Ridge Trail, also in this chapter.

DUNCAN RIDGE
NATIONAL RECREATION TRAIL
SECTION 1

Toccoa Ranger District
Fannin County

NEAR THREE FORKS TO GEORGIA 60 (10.5 miles one way to Georgia 60). Moderate.

The Duncan Ridge National Recreation Trail was once known as the Loop Trail. But while its name grew longer, the trail became shorter. Section 1 of the Duncan Ridge Trail has been shortened by approximately 5.0 miles. In 1980, this section began atop Springer Mountain, near the southern terminus of the Appalachian Trail. Now it begins along the Appalachian Trail to the northeast of Springer Mountain, near Three Forks. Section 2 of the Duncan Ridge Trail remains unchanged.

The Duncan Ridge Trail was constructed so that it would form a loop with the Appalachian Trail. With some help, it still serves that purpose. You can walk either the Appalachian Trail or the Benton MacKaye Trail from Springer Mountain to the beginning of Section 1 of the Duncan Ridge Trail.

All of Section 1 of the Duncan Ridge Trail now shares the same treadway with the Benton MacKaye Trail. (See the Benton MacKaye Trail, also in this chapter, for a description of Section 1 of the Duncan Ridge Trail.)

Directions: There are three ways to reach the southern trailhead (near Three Forks) of Section 1 of the Duncan Ridge Trail. The first is to walk the Appalachian Trail 4.3 miles to the north (away from

Springer Mountain) from its crossing at F.S. 42. Another way is to walk the Benton MacKaye Trail 5.4 miles to the north (away from Springer Mountain) from its crossing at F.S. 42. If you want to walk the Appalachian, see the directions for Section 1 of that trail, also in this chapter. If you want to walk the Benton MacKaye, see the directions for that trail, also in this chapter.

The third way to gain access to Section 1 of the Duncan Ridge Trail is from F.S. 58. The Benton MacKaye and Appalachian Trails share the same treadway (an old road) across F.S. 58 to the beginning of the Duncan Ridge Trail. When the old road reaches the beginning of the blue-blazed Duncan Ridge Trail, Benton MacKaye turns left and shares the same treadway with Duncan Ridge. The Appalachian Trail continues straight ahead — by itself. It is slightly over 1.0 mile from F.S. 58 to the beginning of the Duncan Ridge Trail. Look for the Benton MacKaye sign and the first blue blaze of Duncan Ridge 0.1 mile beyond the sidepath to Long Creek Falls.

If you want to walk to the Duncan Ridge Trail by way of F.S. 58, follow the directions for Section 1 of the Appalachian Trail to the point where you turn right onto F.S. 42 opposite the church. Instead of turning onto F.S. 42, however, continue straight ahead on the paved road. After traveling approximately 2.8 miles beyond the entrance to F.S. 42 (after 2.0 miles the pavement turns to dirt before a bridge), turn right onto F.S. 58. A short distance beyond a church (cemetery across the road), the main dirt road forks. F.S. 58 is the right fork.

After driving approximately 5.5 miles on F.S. 58, you should come to a trail post on the right side of the road immediately after crossing Long Creek. This post has an Appalachian Trail sign, a Benton

MacKaye sign and a stickperson hiker sign. If you are in the right place, there should be an intersecting gravel road next to the sign. A triangle of large logs blocks this road to the right. To reach the Duncan Ridge Trail, walk the intersecting road to the left.

DUNCAN RIDGE NATIONAL RECREATION TRAIL SECTION 2

Toccoa and Brasstown Ranger Districts
Fannin and Union Counties

GEORGIA 60 TO SLAUGHTER GAP (20.4 miles one way to Slaughter Gap). Strenuous.

Beyond its first climb, Section 2 follows a well-defined line of named mountains, knobs and gaps — Duncan Ridge — all the way to trail's end at Slaughter Gap. From Georgia 60 this section arcs northeast to southeast to its terminus, which is almost due east from its beginning. The trail follows the northern boundary of Coopers Creek Wildlife Management Area from Rhodes Mountain to Wolfpen Gap.

Section 2 of Duncan Ridge is the most strenuous long segment of trail in Georgia. This section roller-coasters along the crest of the ridge up, over and down nearly every peak. Many of the gap-to-mountain ascents are moderate or strenuous, and many of the mountain-to-gap descents are steep. Do not plan to backpack this entire section unless you have mountain experience, are in good shape, and are seeking rugged terrain.

At Mulky Gap, F.S. 4 divides Section 2 of the Duncan Ridge Trail into segments of nearly equal lengths. If you want to dayhike or backpack one of these two segments, you can set up a shuttle and use Mulky Gap as a beginning or ending point. The trail is less strenuous hiked as it is described, from west to east.

The blue-blazed Duncan Ridge Trail shares its treadway with the Benton MacKaye Trail, blazed with white diamonds, to the top of Rhodes Mountain.

Starting near a bench mark with a recorded elevation of 2,028 feet, Section 2 immediately crosses Little Skeenah Creek, then climbs moderately toward the ridge. At mile 1.0 the trail turns right onto an old road atop Duncan Ridge and ascends sharply by switchback. Before reaching the rocky crown of Wallalah Mountain (3,100 ft.) at mile 1.6, the treadway passes beside an outcrop open to the south. The nearest mountain is Toonowee.

After descending 0.6 mile to an unnamed gap (2,730 ft.), Section 2 heads steadily upridge to the crest of Licklog Mountain (3,472 ft.) at mile 3.2. It then loses elevation to another unnamed gap (3,140 ft.) and rises to the next highpoint on the ridge — Rhodes Mountain (3,380 ft.) — at mile 4.2. Here the footpath drops sharply, climbs over a low knob, and drops sharply again to Rhodes Mountain Gap (2,980 ft.) at mile 4.7. From Rhodes Mountain Gap the trail undulates 0.8 mile on easy to moderate grades to Gregory Gap (3,060 ft.).

Continuing eastward on Duncan Ridge, Section 2 roller-coasters up, over and down two knobs — Gregory (3,360 ft.) at mile 5.8, Payne (3,420 ft.) at mile 6.3 — in quick succession. From Gregory Gap to Sarvis Gap (3,020 ft.) at mile 6.8, the treadway gains and loses 1,200 feet of elevation in 1.3 miles. The ascents are strenuous, the descents, steep.

The path angles up the northern flank of Parke Knob to approximately 3,320 feet before it dips to the clearing in Fish Gap (3,100 ft.) at mile 7.9. F.S. 88 ends at the clearing. Beyond Akin Gap (3,020 ft.) at mile 8.6, Section 2 climbs over Clements Mountain (3,500 ft.), then Akin Mountain (3,531 ft. at the bench mark) in similar fashion. Both times the trail steadily gains elevation along the southern slope of the mountain. It appears that the trail would continue below the crest, but instead it turns sharply to the left and ascends straight up to the summit.

The trail passes beside the bench mark atop Akin Mountain at mile 10.0. The long, occasionally steep downgrade to Mulky Gap has several sharp turns. The first and easiest to miss is at mile 10.4, where the footpath turns to the right off the ridge at a double blaze.

Section 2 crosses F.S. 4 in Mulky Gap (2,780 ft.) at mile 10.9. Beyond this intersecting dirt road, the treadway climbs a strenuous, switchbacking grade to Wildcat Knob (3,500 ft.) at mile 11.8, descends 0.3 mile to Wildcat Gap (3,380 ft.), rises over Buck Knob (3,540 ft.), then loses elevation easily to Bryant Gap (3,200 ft.) at mile 12.9. The trail approaches Duncan Ridge Road, F.S. 39, for the first of several times in Bryant Gap. Section 2 does not cross Duncan Ridge Road; blazed sidepaths that cross the road lead to water.

After swinging beside the road again in Buckeye Gap (3,280 ft.) at mile 13.5, the trail works its way up, gradually at first, to the highpoint of Buckeye Knob (3,820 ft.) at mile 14.5. It then heads steadily down-ridge for 1.0 mile to a slight gap, proceeds over a low knob, then dips to Whiteoak Stomp (3,460 ft.) at mile 16.2. Here, beside the road again, the long upgrade to Coosa Bald begins. The middle part of this climb is a straight-up-the-ridge grunt. Near the top, above the steep portion of the ascent, the treadway passes through a grove of yellow birch. At the southern limit of its range in northernmost Georgia, this tree is easily identified by its yellowish bark, which curls into papery strips. To the right of the path at mile 17.1, a bench mark embedded in a low knot of protruding rock designates Coosa Bald's official highpoint — 4,271 feet.

At mile 17.3 the yellow-blazed Coosa Backcountry Trail joins the Duncan Ridge Trail. These two trails share the same treadway for the next 3.0 miles. (See Vogel State Park, Chapter 6, for a description of the Coosa Backcountry Trail.)

Section 2 follows an old road down a steep grade to Wildcat Gap (3,780 ft.), where it turns left onto Duncan Ridge Road, skirts its edge for 30 yards, then returns to the forest on the left side of the road. Beyond its second Wildcat Gap, the trail ascends its second Wildcat Knob before switchbacking sharply down to Wolfpen Gap (3,260 ft.) at mile 18.7. At Wolfpen Gap it crosses Georgia 180 onto a dirt road, and immediately turns left onto blazed path. The next 0.9 mile rises to the upper slopes (approximately 4,140 ft.) of Slaughter Mountain. The first 0.5 mile of this climb is strenuous. Beyond mile 19.7, the remainder of Section 2 is nearly level until it drops to its end at Slaughter Gap (3,900 ft.). A short distance beyond the sign in Slaughter Gap, Duncan Ridge Trail rejoins the white-blazed Appalachian Trail.

After crossing Little Skeenah Creek (possibly contaminated from homes upstream) next to Georgia 60, Section 2 does not cross or closely parallel a stream for the remainder of its 20.4-mile length. Marked water sources, however, do occur at regular intervals, usually in the gaps. Designated by blue W's, sidepaths lead downhill to the nearest spring.

Directions: Travel northward from Dahlonega on U.S. 19-Georgia 60. At Stonepile Gap, where U.S. 19 veers right and Georgia 60 turns left, continue northward on Georgia 60. The Duncan Ridge Trail crosses Georgia 60 approximately 22.0 miles beyond Stonepile Gap and approximately 3.0 miles beyond Deep Hole Recreation Area. When you pass the trout farm ponds to the right of the highway, continue approximately 0.2 mile to the trailhead.

The Benton MacKaye Trail shares the same treadway with the Duncan Ridge Trail across Georgia 60. Look for blue blazes, white diamond blazes and a small trail sign. Both trails cross Georgia 60 at the entrance to F.S. 816 to the left of the highway. Section 1 of the Benton MacKaye Trail ends at Georgia 60. Section 2 of the Duncan Ridge Trail begins to the right of Georgia 60.

To reach Wolfpen Gap, where the Duncan Ridge Trail crosses Georgia 180 near its ending point, travel Georgia 60 North approximately 16.0 miles from Dahlonega, then turn right onto Georgia 180 East. (This turn is 2.0 miles beyond Woody Gap Recreation Area.) Continue 7.8 miles on Georgia 180 to a pulloff parking area on the left side of the highway. The parking area is marked with a large Cooper Creek Wildlife Management Area sign and a small sign for F.S. 39 (Duncan Ridge Road).

F.S. 4, which runs through Mulky Gap, divides Section 2 of the Duncan Ridge Trail into two segments of nearly equal length. Depending on which segment you want to hike, and where you are driving from, there are numerous combinations of routes that will lead you to Mulky Gap. The Forest Service Administration map, available from the Forest Supervisor's Office for a small fee, features the system roads of the Chattahoochee National Forest.

5
MORE NATIONAL FOREST TRAILS

Introduction

The trails in this chapter are those remaining trails that did not belong to any other National Forest category. Ranging from 0.1 to 8.8 miles in length, most of the trails included in this chapter feature mountain water, falling or flowing.

One trail, Bear Creek, leads walkers to the largest tree yet discovered in the Chattahoochee National Forest — the impressive Gennett Poplar.

Cohutta Ranger District
Gilmer County

BEAR CREEK TRAIL (0.8 mile one way to the Gennett Poplar). Easy.

Bear Creek Trail makes an interesting side trip for those who are visiting the Lake Conasauga-Cohutta Wilderness area of the Chattahoochee National Forest. The trail, an unblazed yet easily followed old road now closed to motorized traffic, follows Bear Creek upstream to the Gennett Poplar. After 0.5 mile the trail crosses Little Bear Creek, turns to the right and continues upstream along Bear Creek. The trail crosses Bear Creek 0.2 mile farther. At normal water levels both streams can be crossed dry-shod. The big poplar is located a few yards to the left of the trail 0.1 mile beyond the second stream crossing.

This stately yellow poplar, its straight trunk looking much like a massive gray column, seems out of place, dwarfing all other trees along the path. Measured 4½ feet up from the ground, this North Georgia forest giant is 17 feet, 9 inches in circumference and 5 feet, 8 inches in diameter. Even with the last 10 or 20 feet of its top gone, the surrounding branches reach nearly 100 feet high. The Gennett Poplar, a survivor of forests of the past, is the largest tree yet discovered in the Chattahoochee National Forest.

Those curious parallel rows of small holes encircling the trunk were bored by small woodpeckers — yellow-bellied sapsuckers. After tapping the holes, they return to feed on sap and small insects.

Directions: Take Georgia 52 West 9.5 miles from the Ellijay square. At the Lake Conasauga Recreation Area sign, turn right onto F.S. 18 and continue 3.5 miles on that road before turning to the right onto F.S. 68. After traveling 2.5 miles on F.S. 68, bear right on F.S. 90 at the Holly Creek Gap-Mountain Town Creek sign.

Continue for 2.0 miles on F.S. 90 before turning left onto F.S. 241, a one-lane gravel road. Follow F.S. 241 straight ahead for 2.0 miles until the road ends at a small turnaround area. The trail begins behind the post and "Closed-to-Vehicles" sign.

———

Chattooga Ranger District
Stephens County

BROAD RIVER TRAIL (4.1 miles one way between access points on Guard Camp Road). Easy to Moderate.

The Broad River Trail was originally built in the late 1930's by the Resettlement Administration, a Depression-era program that moved people off eroded, unproductive land, resettled them nearby, then hired them to restore the land they had left behind. More recently, the Youth Conservation Corps (YCC) rebuilt the trail along its old route and reopened it in 1980. They did a good job; the blue-blazed trail is wide, well cut and easily followed.

The Broad River Trail has either-end access on Guard Camp Road. Once the trail begins to follow the Broad River downstream, its general direction of travel is north to south. Although it is not difficult to walk in either direction, the trail is noticeably easier from north to south, downstream and downhill.

The trail quickly follows Dicks Creek downstream through a mixed deciduous-evergreen forest. Despite its location in the southernmost section of the Chattahoochee National Forest, where upper piedmont meets lower mountains, and despite its low elevation, Dicks Creek — with its quick, clear water, rocky cascades and hemlock-lined banks — is a mountain stream, closely resembling creeks 30 miles farther north and 1,000 feet higher in elevation. The trail and creek remain parallel until they reach a level field known as Brown Bottoms. Here, across the creek from the bottoms, after 1.0 mile, the trail turns left and follows the Middle Fork of the Broad River downstream.

The trail continues beside the Middle Fork — a shallow, relatively clear, creek-sized stream, occasionally enlivened with low shoals — for 0.4 mile before it climbs away from the river. For most of the next mile, the trail winds up, around, then back down ravines eroded by small sidestreams. Most often, it travels away from the river up one side of a ravine, crosses it up high where it narrows, then follows the other side back down toward the river. The slopes and level areas near the streams have open, cove-like stands of maturing hardwoods.

Leaving the moist ravines behind, the trail continues through a dry, open woods on or near ridgetop before dropping to the river at mile 3.7. Fifty yards after it comes parallel to the Middle Fork, the trail skirts the shoreline between the river and its rock bank. The gray-barked, low-branching trees on the other side of the river are beeches. From here, the trail slants toward its southern end across Kimbell Creek. A wide footbridge with railings has replaced the narrow, potentially dangerous single-log bridge that once added a few tense moments to the hike.

The Broad River traverses an area of rich botanical diversity. This diversity is the result not only of the trail's habitat variety but also of its location in a transition zone between physiographic provinces. During late May and early June, the pink blossoms of the catawba rhododendron transform much of the trail into a beautiful wildflower garden.

The Broad River Trail is located in the Lake Russell Wildlife Management Area, which has a high population of deer and is heavily hunted. The management area has hunts for deer or small game throughout the fall and winter. The dates of these hunts often change from year to year. For more information, call the Forest Service Ranger District or read the Wildlife Management Area section in the "Georgia Hunting Season and Regulations" pamphlet.

Directions: Near the city of Cornelia there is a major intersection involving highways U.S. 23/441 and U.S. 123. To reach the Broad River Trail, follow U.S. 123 North, which begins or ends at this intersection, toward the city of Cornelia. From the intersection continue on U.S. 123 North for approximately 13 miles, then turn right onto Ayersville Road at the

185

Milliken Plant. After driving approximately 0.9 mile on the paved Ayersville Road, turn left onto unpaved F.S. 87, Guard Camp Road, and proceed approximately 2.2 miles to the northern (upstream) trailhead. The trailhead is on the right side of the road just uphill from Dicks Creek, and is marked with a "Trail" sign that points to a larger sign in the woods below. The southern (downstream) access point is to the right of the road approximately 3.0 miles farther on F.S. 87, slightly more than 0.1 mile past a single-lane bridge and before an intersection.

All access gates to Lake Russell Wildlife Management Area are open during summer; only one, Guard Camp Road, is open all year.

Cohutta Ranger District
Murray County

EMERY CREEK TRAIL (3.2 miles one way to its end). Easy to Moderate.

Although Emery Creek is primitive — unblazed, infrequently maintained and usually without signs — it is scenic and now, for the most part, easily followed. The trail is easily followed because its sharply ascending, often confusing upper end has been eliminated. Emery Creek, which no longer has a trailhead on F.S. 68, has been shortened from approximately 4.5 miles to 3.2 miles.

The first 0.2 mile of Emery Creek Trail follows an old road, now blocked to traffic, that starts on a hillside high above Holly Creek. This section of Holly Creek, with its deep pools, cascades and huge boulders, is scenic; the disgusting amount of litter usually strewn beside it, however, is not. Soon after it descends to stream level, the trail narrows to rocky path and reaches the convergence of Holly and Emery Creeks. As you face upstream, Holly Creek is to the right, Emery to the left. The trail continues along the left bank of Emery Creek. You can either cross Holly Creek alone below the fork, or you can cross both creeks just above their confluence.

Beyond this initial crossing (which counts as one), this little-used path often parallels Emery Creek through a forest dotted with tall white and shortleaf pines and thick, uninitialed beech trees. It becomes more interesting, more isolated as it moves farther away from Holly Creek and its popular swimming holes. Shortly after its fifth crossing at mile 1.3, the trail turns right onto a gravel road, crosses a bridge, then turns left onto an old road just before a second bridge. This narrow road has a yellow "Closed to Vehicles" sign at its entrance.

Forty yards beyond the eighth crossing (most can be made dry-shod) at mile 2.2, a wide sidetrail to the left leads 125 yards to the first waterfall. Forty-five to 50 feet high and surprisingly loud and powerful for the stream's size, the fall drops from wide ledge to wide ledge to the small green pool at its base. Emery Creek Falls is both higher and longer than you might first guess. Below most of the ledges, the fall slides into a narrow pool which pours over the lip of the next ledge.

To reach the second falls, continue on the main trail as it bends to the left and ascends very sharply for 0.1 mile. At mile 2.7 the trail comes to a point where you can scramble down the hillside to explore a series of four cascades. The highest of the cascades is a waterfall of 20 to 25 feet. The trail crosses Emery Creek three more times and remains level or slightly uphill to its end at a forest service road, which remains closed during most of the year.

Directions: From the Georgia 52-U.S. 411 intersection in Chatsworth, travel U.S. 411 North approximately 4.2 miles to the town of Eton. In Eton, at the stoplight next to the Eton Branch First National Bank of Chatsworth, turn right onto Holly Creek Road, following the sign for Lake Conasauga. Continue straight on Holly Creek Road for approximately 7.4 miles (after 6.2 miles the pavement ends). Before it reaches the trailhead, Holly Creek Road parallels Holly Creek. As you start a sharp curve to the right and uphill away from the creek, look for the entrance of a narrow road on the left. Emery Creek Trail begins behind the dirt mounds that block vehicles from entering the old road. There may be a yellow "Closed to Vehicles" sign.

––––––––

Brasstown Ranger District
Union County

HELTON CREEK FALLS TRAIL (0.1 mile one way to the upper falls). Easy.

Flanked by towering hemlocks, this short but scenic trail gently descends to a pair of waterfalls on Helton Creek. The first waterfall — really a waterslide — is approximately 30 feet high. The second, a short distance upstream, is wide and approximately 50 to 55 feet high. Its twin cascades spill into a dark green wading pool.

Directions: From the Walasi-Yi Center at Neels Gap (see Appalachian Trail, Section 3 for directions to

Neels Gap), continue 1.6 miles farther on U.S. 19-129 North before turning on the first road to the right — Helton Creek Road, F.S. 118. Stay straight on Helton Creek Road for 2.3 miles. There will be a pulloff area on the right. There may not be a sign or post at the trailhead. Look for the trail entrance where the road first widens into the pulloff.

There are several pulloff areas before the trail. Make sure you have traveled the full 2.3 miles.

———

Tallulah Ranger District
Rabun County

HOLCOMB CREEK TRAIL (0.3 mile one way to Holcomb Creek Falls; 0.5 mile one way to Ammons Creek Falls; 0.6 mile one way for alternate trail to F.S. 7, Hale Ridge Road). Moderate.

From the road, this short trail quickly zigzags past several large yellow poplars, then tunnels through rhododendron thickets as it descends toward Holcomb Creek Falls. Even though you hear this isolated waterfall well before you see it, its much-greater-than-anticipated size and beauty take you by surprise. As you walk out over the bridge across Holcomb Creek, the fall comes suddenly into view. Almost as long as it is high, this 120-foot waterfall is a picturesque combination of wide freefalls, splashing cascades and quick slides that careen around raised slabs of bedrock.

The trail continues past several giant hemlocks a short distance to yet another waterfall — Ammons Creek Falls. Like many other North Georgia waterfalls, Ammons Creek is more churning cascade than

189

sheer plunge. The water drops above and below the stilted observation deck. Above, a foaming, pure white 40-foot falls begins the stream's rush down the mountainside directly in front of you; below, the longer, less vertical portion of the falls S-curves into a narrow, squirming raceway between boulders.

Forty yards before its end at the observation deck, the trail passes a sign that points to another way back to Hale Ridge Road. This alternate route coupled with a segment of Hale Ridge Road completes a loop that returns to the trailhead. The sidetrail is 0.6 mile in length; the Hale Ridge Road segment, to the left and downhill, is slightly less than 0.6 mile.

The alternate route parallels cascading Holcomb Creek all the way to the road. The trail first comes close to the creek on a hillside above the waterfall's uppermost ledge. It is a tempting and potentially very dangerous 35 yards down for a look. Before you try it, think "what if" and then be very careful or don't go.

The trail continues within earshot or eyesight of the creek. One-tenth mile from the road, a long cascade slides into its shallow, surprisingly large catch pool.

Directions: In Clayton, where U.S. 76 turns west, turn east onto Warwoman Road. If you are traveling north on U.S. 441, the turn will be to your right near the Hardee's, which is the second building to the right on Warwoman Road. Once on Warwoman Road, turn right at the stop sign and proceed on Warwoman Road past the Georgia Power building.

After traveling 14.0 miles on Warwoman Road, turn left onto F.S. 86 (Overflow Road) immediately after crossing West Fork Chattooga River. Continue approximately 7.3 miles on F.S. 86 until it ends at its Y-shaped junction with F.S. 7, Hale Ridge Road. Turn right onto F.S. 7 and park a few feet farther on the right side of the road. The trailhead, usually marked with a sign, is to the right of F.S. 7, 30 feet beyond the turn.

———

Chattooga Ranger District
White and Union Counties

HORSE TROUGH FALLS TRAIL (0.3 mile one way to the falls). Easy.

The trail begins where logs with yellow "Closed to Vehicles" signs block the road. Beyond the logs, where the road once continued, look for several large trees with blue blazes. There are no more blazes after these; none are needed. Follow the footpath upstream alongside Georgia's longest river — the Cherokee's Chattahoochee, "River of the Painted Rocks" — here only a short distance from its source-spring high in the mountains of Union County. All of the Chattahoochee's headwater branches arise south of the Appalachian Trail, only a few miles north of the falls.

From the trailhead the path quickly leads the hiker beside the uppermost Chattahoochee, 15 to 35 feet wide and usually less than a foot deep. The vegetation is typical of streamside habitats above 2,000 feet: sweet birch, basswood, hemlock and rhododendron near the river; oaks on the hillsides; white pine and yellow poplar scattered throughout. At 0.2 mile the trail passes above a small shoal and its pool. Beyond, soon after you hear the falls, the path angles down-ward through rhododendron to the river and, on the other side of the gap along the rockface, the falls.

Rather than freefall or wide cascade, Horse Trough is a narrow, frothing sluiceway, small but surprisingly noisy and powerful. The upper part of the sluiceway, foaming through a 3-foot-wide rock trough, drops 15 to 20 feet at a 45° angle. After the first drop the river races through a nearly level gutter 2 to 3 feet deep and, where the rocks squeeze the Chattahoochee to its narrowest, only a foot wide. Before slowing at the wading pool, the water drops again, but only a few feet.

Litter left by inconsiderate campers often mars the beauty of this trail. Please pack out yours and as much of theirs as possible.

Directions: From the Chattahoochee River bridge in Helen travel Georgia 75 North approximately 9.5 miles to the large parking area to the right of the highway at Unicoi Gap, where the Appalachian Trail crosses Georgia 75. At Unicoi Gap turn around back toward Helen, then turn onto the first dirt road to the right — Wilkes Creek Road, F.S. 44 — after less than 0.1 mile. After traveling slightly less than 5.0 miles (start looking after 4.5 miles) on F.S. 44, watch for a road leading to the right as F.S. 44 curves sharply to the left. Immediately before the turn you will see a stream to the right of the road around the curve and a level camping area to the left, opposite the turn.

Take the road to the right, travel straight through the grassy wildlife opening, then turn left where the road forks. After turning left, continue on the rough road (marked with blue blazes) until it is blocked with logs that have the yellow "Closed to Vehicles" signs on them. Park there. It is 0.4 mile from Wilkes Creek Road to the trailhead.

MILLS CREEK FALLS TRAIL (0.5 mile one way to the falls). Easy to Moderate.

Mills Creek Falls Trail is one of several interesting trails in the Lake Conasauga area outside of the Cohutta Wilderness. It is actually an unblazed, unconstructed but easily followed footpath created by people walking to the falls from the primitive campground on Mills Creek.

From the camping area, walk downstream between the big rocks and the creek. Continue following this sliding, cascading stream to the falls. At one point, after a large boulder to the right of the path, the trail seems to disappear into the creek. Skirt the moist slabs of rock close to the water's edge; the stream will be on your left and a rock wall will be on your right. The path, recognizable once again, returns to the forest 20 or 30 yards downstream.

Near the end of the trail Mills Creek, quickening its pace over a series of low falls and short slides, takes a running start toward its final long cascade to the falls below. It is much safer to stay away from the slide and the slippery rocks near its edge. To reach the bottom of the falls, follow the path upward to the right, then sharply downhill. Approximately 30 to 35 feet of the wide, sliding waterfall are visible from its base. The roughly circular plunge pool — deep, green and goose-pimple cold — is 35 to 40 feet across.

During early May, the fringetree, also known as old-man's-beard, blooms on the rock outcrops near Mills Creek Falls. This member of the olive family has fragrant white blossoms that hang in loose, three-flowered clusters, 4 to 8 inches long. The petals are long (1 inch) and thin, like scissor-cut fringe.

Directions: Take U.S. 411 North from Chatsworth past the town of Eton. From the Georgia 52–U.S. 411 intersection in Chatsworth, travel 7.3 miles on U.S. 411 North to the "Crandall" sign on the right side of the highway. At the sign, turn right and continue past the railroad tracks before turning right again. After this second right turn, travel 0.1 mile, then turn left onto F.S. 630 (Mill Creek Road) toward Lake Conasauga Recreation Area. Continue straight ahead on F.S. 630 for approximately 6.7 miles to F.S. 630E, which drops down and to the right (at a 45° angle) a short distance to a primitive campground on Mills Creek known as Hickey Gap Camping Area. Park at the camping area.

If the "Crandall" sign is missing, ask for directions to F.S. 630 in the Dewberry Baptist Church–Gallman's Grocery area.

Cohutta Ranger District
Gilmer and Fannin Counties

MOUNTAINTOWN CREEK TRAIL (5.6 miles one way to its end at a primitive campground). Moderate.

In previous editions, Mountaintown Creek Trail started at F.S. 214 and traveled northward, uphill, to its other end at F.S. 64. Recent activities by private landowners near its lower F.S. 214 access point have made it necessary to change the orientation of this trail. Mountaintown Creek now will have only one trailhead, on F.S. 64, and it will travel from north to south, high to low.

This trail is ideal for a two-day backpacking trip. The first day you can walk downhill to the level campsites along Mountaintown Creek, and on the second day, after eating a few pounds of your load, you can take your time heading back up the mountain.

Occasionally blazed with orange, this little-used, primitive trail begins on an old roadbed near Rich Knob at approximately 3,120 feet. Mountaintown Creek follows one old road or another for most of its length. For the first 0.5 mile, until it turns sharply to the left, the trail descends steadily and often steeply. Beyond the turn, it continues on an easy downgrade through a young forest recovering from a cut made around 1977. The trail rockhops a tributary of Crenshaw Branch, the first of many crossings to come, at mile 1.2.

At mile 1.7 the trail passes by a sliding cascade, 25 to 30 feet wide, enough to let the sun in, and perhaps 15 feet high. Two-tenths of a mile farther, Mountaintown Creek makes its steepest descent through its most scenic section. Above and to the right, a rock outcrop lines the path. Below and to the left, a continuous cascade a hundred yards or more in length races down the water-carved notch of a miniature, V-shaped gorge. Pinched into narrow, tilted chutes, parts of this entrenched sluiceway resemble the fast, straight runs of commercial waterslides. There is a diverse forest of mature trees on the slope below the trail. Among them are unusually large red maples, tall and shaggy-barked, seemingly different trees from the small, smooth-barked red maples so often found in the understory.

Where the downsloping grade ends at mile 2.3, the trail turns left, crosses a side stream, then switches to the main stem of Crenshaw Branch. The path remains level or gradually downhill for the next 1.3 miles as it follows the turbulent branch downstream. Tall basswoods — easily distinguished by their large, sharply pointed, heart-shaped leaves — are common beside this section of trail.

At mile 3.6 the trail reaches a cleared camping area at the junction of two old roads. Here, where Mountaintown Creek and Crenshaw Branch flow together, the path changes streams again. Continue straight ahead from the campsite and cross Mountaintown Creek. The final 2.0 miles, nearly level and easily walked, follow this shallow, unusually calm creek, crossing it three more times. The trail ends at a primitive campground (1,660 ft.).

At normal water levels, you will probably get your feet wet on several of the stream crossings.

For those interested in wildflowers, mid-May is a good time to walk this trail.

Directions: Take Georgia 52 West 9.5 miles from the Ellijay square. At the Lake Conasauga Recreation Area sign, turn right onto F.S. 18 and continue 3.5 miles on that road before turning right onto F.S. 68. Once on F.S. 68, proceed straight ahead, uphill. After traveling approximately 6.0 miles on F.S. 68, you will reach the three-way F.S. 68-64 junction near Potatopatch Mountain. Turn right onto F.S. 64 and drive approximately 6.9 miles to the trailhead sign on the right side of the road. You can park at a primitive camping area to the left of the road less than 100 yards before the trailhead.

Tallulah Ranger District
Rabun County

RAVEN ROCK TRAIL (0.8 mile one way to Raven Rock Cliff on the Chattooga River). Easy to Moderate.

Forest Service 511B should not be attempted in a low-slung, conventional car. If you don't have a pickup or a jeep, but still want to see Raven Rock, you will have to hike this road, only a mile long and easily walked, to the trailhead.

Blazed with white metal diamonds, Raven Rock Trail follows the old roadbed, now closed, but still used occasionally, that continues from the back right corner of the turnaround area for F.S. 511B. After 0.4 mile, where the old road is blocked with felled logs, the trail angles down and to the left on wooden steps and descends, sometimes steeply, 400 feet to the river. Along the way the trail approaches Daniel Creek, then turns left and leads to a level area with a fire ring. Here the trail turns 90° to the right, dropping downhill to the Georgia bank of the Chattooga National Wild and Scenic River.

The path ends beneath a hemlock rooted at the top of a tiny white-sand beach. Upstream and down, the banks are jumbled with boulders; between them are more pockets of sand. Directly across a deep, eddying pool, just downstream from a shoal, Raven Rock arches upward from either side, coming to a point perhaps as high as 150 feet, perhaps higher; it is difficult to judge. The cliff face is striated gneiss, vertically streaked with black mineral stains. Stunted, improbably rooted red cedars are growing on ledges and out of cracks in the cliff.

The beauty of the river is easily marred by inconsiderate sightseers. Please do not build fires along the shoreline, and remember to leave this small, special place cleaner, if possible, than you found it.

Directions: From the post office (to the right of U.S. 441 North just before the bridge over the dam on the Tallulah River) in the city of Tallulah Falls, travel northward for approximately 3.0 miles on U.S. 441, then turn right onto Camp Creek Road, a wide dirt road with a small sign for Camp Creek Baptist

Church set back from the highway. After driving approximately 1.5 miles on Camp Creek Road, turn left onto Forest Service 511 just up the hill from a small concrete culvert bridge and immediately beyond a large house on the left. Continue on F.S. 511 for approximately 2.3 miles, then begin looking for F.S. 511B — Daniel Creek Road, a narrow, unmarked road with two entrances, the first dropping down and to the left at less than a 90° angle. Seventy-five yards farther on F.S. 511, you will find the second entrance, seldom used, angling toward the first. Beyond the second entrance there is a pulloff place to the left of the road. You should find this road after approximately 2.4 to 2.7 miles on F.S. 511.

Once on F.S. 511B, stay on the main road at all forks; it ends at a turnaround area after approximately 1.0 mile. The trail begins at the lower right corner of the turnaround area, where the road once continued.

Each dirt road is narrower and rougher than the one before. I strongly recommend that you not attempt F.S. 511B in a conventional vehicle.

Toccoa Ranger District
Gilmer and Fannin Counties

RICH MOUNTAIN TRAIL (8.8 miles one way between trailheads). Moderate.

White blazed but still somewhat primitive, Rich Mountain Trail begins at the entrance of a rutted jeep road at Stanley Gap (2,317 ft.). After an easy to moderate upgrade of slightly less than 0.2 mile, the road ends and narrows to an easily followed path. The path continues its easy to moderate climb until it first reaches ridgetop at 0.6 mile. Here the Benton MacKaye Trail, blazed with white metallic diamonds, approaches from the east (right) and joins the Rich Mountain Trail. The trails share the same treadway for the next 2.1 miles.

Instead of following the ridgetop up and over each crest, the trail works its way up gradually, alternating between ridgetop and mountainside. Where the ridge rises sharply, the trail drops off it and ascends more slowly along the eastern slopes of Rocky Mountain, reaching the ridgetop again at the next gap. The trail is still gaining elevation as it passes well below the peak of Rocky Mountain (3,442 ft.) at mile 1.7. It is not until mile 2.2, on a ridge north of Rocky Mountain's crown, that the path reaches its highest point, probably no more than 3,200 feet. The grades on this first ascending section remain easy to moderate.

The trails split immediately beyond the double metal diamonds at mile 2.7. Rich Mountain Trail turns right and heads downhill; Benton MacKaye continues straight ahead, uphill with the ridge.

On its own again, Rich Mountain descends to Deep Gap at Aska Road. Several times along the way the path approaches but does not cross a new forest service road. A short distance before it reaches the gap, the trail turns right onto an old road, which continues to a parking area beside Aska Road at mile 5.1. The trail angles to the right across the pavement toward the stickperson hiker sign on the other side. Deep Gap, at 2,243 feet, is the lowest point on the trail until it nears Lake Blue Ridge.

Immediately after crossing the road, the trail ascends for the second time, again alternating between ridge and slope as it works its way up. This climb is shorter and steeper than the first. The initial 0.1 mile is strenuous; the rest, though progressively easier, is still at least moderate until it levels out on top of Green Mountain (2,520 ft.) at mile 5.9. One tenth of a mile farther, the path turns right, drops off the ridge and begins its downgrade to the lake.

The section of trail from Green Mountain to the lake, often an old road, is easier to follow than it used to be, but you still need to be observant. The trail first ventures beside a narrow cove of the lake (elevation 1,690 ft. when full) at mile 7.6. A tenth of a mile farther, it makes a right turn in front of a gated road. A few yards beyond this junction, the trail turns back to the left and soon closely parallels the lake's shoreline. Unless you intend to search for rocks or lost fishing lures, you will probably enjoy Lake Blue Ridge more during spring and early summer before the T.V.A. begins to lower it to provide flood storage.

Much of Rich Mountain's last mile remains near the lake. At mile 7.8 the trail turns right at a double-blazed junction. After crossing a rivulet, the rest of the trail winds through or beside a recent timber cut, then gradually rises to the hillsides above the lake before veering off to its end at a blazed post.

Potable water is scarce along the Rich Mountain Trail. Beyond Deep Gap, the only branch that might survive dry weather flows past homes upstream from the trail.

Directions: Rich Mountain Trail is accessible to motorized vehicles at three points: its beginning at Stanley Gap on Rock Creek Road, its ending point at Lake Blue Ridge and its near midpoint at Deep Gap on Aska Road. All three points can be reached from Aska Road.

To reach Rich Mountain's southern trailhead at Stanley Gap, take U.S. 76 from Ellijay or Blue Ridge. From the U.S. 76-Georgia 52 junction in East Ellijay, travel U.S. 76 East for approximately 8.2 miles, then turn right onto Rock Creek Road at the signs for Rich

200

Mountain Wildlife Management Area and Camp Patoka. Just before the turn you will cross over Rock Creek and notice Rock Creek Baptist Church to the right. From the U.S. 76-Georgia 5 intersection just north of Blue Ridge, travel U.S. 76 West for approximately 8.0 miles, then turn left onto Rock Creek Road. This turn is shortly after the Cherry Log Post Office.

After driving approximately 5.3 miles (the pavement ends after 2.2 miles) on Rock Creek Road, you will come to a pulloff on the right side of the road immediately past the entrance to F.S. 338, also on the right. Less than 100 yards farther on Rock Creek Road, there is a deeply entrenched jeep road to the left at the crest of a hill. This jeep road is the first 0.2 mile of the trail.

To reach Rich Mountain's near midpoint where it crosses Aska Road at Deep Gap, travel approximately 4.3 miles on Aska Road from Blue Ridge. There is a parking area to the right of the road just before the stickperson hiker sign to the left.

To reach Rich Mountain's southern trailhead at Stanley Gap from Aska Road at Deep Gap, continue approximately 3.8 miles farther on Aska Road, then turn right onto Stanley Creek Road at the Toccoa River Outpost. This turn is also marked with a Rich Mountain W.M.A. sign. Stanley Creek and Rock Creek are different names for opposite ends of the same road. After driving approximately 4.0 miles on Stanley Creek Road, you will reach the jeep-road trailhead to the right at the crest of a hill. Less than 100 yards farther on Stanley Creek/Rock Creek Road, there is a pulloff to the left immediately before the entrance to F.S. 338, also on the left.

To reach Rich Mountain's northern trailhead, travel approximately 3.0 miles on Aska Road to the paved entrance and large sign for Ozion Baptist

Church. At the church, turn around and head back the way you came (back toward Blue Ridge) on Aska Road, then turn right onto the second gravel road (the first is a driveway) from the church. This road forks after 0.3 mile; turn left and proceed through a farm. Approximately 1.0 mile beyond the first fork, you will come to another in an area of new homes (new home in the middle of the fork). Take the right fork — F.S. 711 — and continue (staying to the right at the next fork) approximately 1.5 miles to a one-lane road that leads to the left in the middle of a sharp curve to the right. The trailhead, marked by a white-blazed post, is to the right of the one-lane road less than 50 yards from F.S. 711.

The entrance to Aska Road is located 0.3 mile to the east of the Valley Village Shopping Center in Blue Ridge. The road that passes by the shopping center and continues to Aska Road is known locally as "Old 76." To reach this road, turn onto Georgia 5 Bus. South at the U.S. 76-Georgia 5 intersection (at McDonald's) just north of Blue Ridge. Continue on Georgia 5 Bus. South to a hilltop stoplight in Blue Ridge, where Bus. 5 turns right at the three-way intersection. If you turn left at this intersection, you will be on Old 76; the shopping center is less than 1.0 mile away to the east.

————

Tallulah Ranger District
Rabun County

SUTTON HOLE TRAIL (0.3 mile one way to the Chattooga River). Easy.

The road behind the dirt mounds at the turnaround area for F.S. 290A is the trail. Beyond the vehicle blocks, which mark the boundary of the Chattooga National Wild and Scenic River, travel is by foot only.

The trail quickly descends through a mixed pine-hardwood forest to Sutton Hole, where the river is deep and slow enough for swimming. To the right, downstream, you can see and hear the beginning of the Chattooga's only lawfully canoed Class 6 rapid — Woodall Shoals, a long pitch of whitewater famous for its whale-sized rock and its boat-holding hydraulic. Depending upon the time of year and level of the river, you can bushwhack, rock-hop or river-wade the 300 yards down to the shoals. Woodall's fast water has scoured a beautiful pool, wide and deep and green, with a white sand beach on its Georgia side.

Directions: Take U.S. 76 East from Clayton toward Westminster, South Carolina. If you are traveling northward on U.S. 441, the turn will be to your right. After driving approximately 7.5 miles on U.S. 76 East, turn right onto unpaved F.S. 290, Woodall Shoals Road, and continue on this road for slightly less than 0.3 mile. In the middle of a sharp curve to the right, you will see a narrow road, unmarked and blocked with a dirt mound, to the left. F.S. 290A, which leads to the trailhead, is inside and to the right of this blocked road.

F.S. 290A (Woodall Shoals Spur Road) should not be attempted in a conventional vehicle. If you don't have a pickup or a jeep but want to see the Chattooga River at Sutton Hole, you will have to hike this road, only 0.5 mile long and easily walked, to the trailhead. There is a pulloff near the entrance of 290A. The trail begins at the turnaround area where further vehicular travel is blocked by dirt mounds.

THREE FORKS TRAIL (1.2 miles one way to the end of the designated trail at Holcomb Creek). Easy to Moderate.

Three Forks Trail, as it was originally designed, starts at the summit of Rabun Bald and ends beside the West Fork Chattooga River near Three Forks. With this design, however, vehicular access can be gained only in the middle sections of the trail, and several miles of the trail are routed on F.S. 7 (Hale Ridge Road) and an old road that runs from F.S. 7 to F.S. 86 (Overflow Road). In an effort to provide vehicular access and eliminate confusing, unblazed roads from the middle of the trail, I have made the beginning and ending sections of the Three Forks Trail from Rabun Bald into two separate trails — Rabun Bald Trail from Hale Ridge Road and a much shorter Three Forks Trail from Overflow Road. This change takes advantage of trail signs (provided they are replaced), eliminates walking on roads and helps avoid confusion. At least that is my hope. (See Rabun Bald Trail, Chapter 4.)

This much shorter version of the Three Forks Trail, starting at John Teague Gap (2,360 ft.), leads hikers through a mixed pine-deciduous forest often dominated by white pine and several species of oak. After traversing 0.7 mile of predominantly level or gently descending terrain, the trail crosses the blue-blazed boundary of the Chattooga National Wild and Scenic River. The immediate Three Forks area and a narrow corridor along both banks of the entire West Fork Chattooga River are protected as part of the National Wild and Scenic River.

The trail remains level or slightly downhill until it dips to its three-way intersection with an old jeep road at mile 1.0. Follow the road to the left as it drops sharply for nearly 0.2 mile to a flat, rocky area overlooking a swirlhole-carved cascade on Holcomb Creek. This is the end of the blazed trail. Three Forks — where Holcomb, Overflow and Big Creeks run together at right angles to create West Fork Chattooga River — is to the right, downstream, approximately 0.2 mile from the cascade.

There is an easy, direct way down to the forks — easy compared to bushwhacking at least. To get there, walk upstream beneath the overhanging bluff until, after 25 to 30 yards, the banks narrow to a jump's width. Cross Holcomb there. Straight ahead from the crossing, a path leads away from the creek. Don't take that one. That one soon forks to the right and left, becomes dimmer and slimmer, deteriorates to a deer run, peters out to a possum track, then snake wiggles up a tree and ends in a knot hole. And leaves you to bushwhack the slide-on-your-butt, steep lower slopes of High Top.

A few yards to the right of the wrong route, another path enters the woods through a duck-your-head hole in the rhododendron. That's the one you want. That one will lead you downstream, above the long, tilted chutes on Holcomb Creek to Three Forks (1,840 ft.). The path becomes progressively steeper toward its bottom end at a firering beside Overflow Creek.

Note: The Easy to Moderate difficulty rating applies only to the designated 1.2-mile trail. The path from Holcomb Creek to Three Forks is potentially dangerous (you could slide off the path and fall into the steep-sided creek) when it's muddy from rain.

Directions: In Clayton, where U.S. 76 turns west, turn east onto Warwoman Road. If you are traveling north on U.S. 441, the turn will be to your right near the Hardee's, which is the second building to the right on Warwoman Road. Once on Warwoman Road, turn right at the stop sign and proceed on Warwoman Road past the Georgia Power building.

After traveling 14.0 miles on Warwoman Road, turn left onto F.S. 86 (Overflow Road) immediately after crossing West Fork Chattooga River. Continue 3.9 to 4.0 miles on F.S. 86 to the cleared pulloff area on the right side of the road at John Teague Gap. Begin looking for the pulloff after cresting a hill.

There may or may not be a sign to mark the trail. Behind the oak closest to the road in the parking area, the trail enters the forest through the gap between two trees. The first white metal blaze is 70 feet in from the parking area.

6
STATE PARK TRAILS

Introduction

State parks now offer a wide range of hiking opportunities. In addition to short footpaths, several parks now have longer, more difficult backpacking trails.

From mid-fall to early spring, the trails are nearly deserted. And surprisingly, even during the summer crowds, weekdays and weekend mornings (the earlier the better) are still good times to hike state park trails. Park naturalists, environmental programs and self-guiding nature trails help interested visitors identify and learn about the plants and animals indigenous to North Georgia.

State parks in this chapter are arranged in alphabetical order. When a state park has more than one trail, the trails are listed according to length, shortest to longest.

Note: Acreages in state parks are subject to change from time to time. Those given in this book were the official figures at the time of printing.

AMICALOLA FALLS
STATE PARK

Dawson County
Two Trails

Nestled along the southernmost edge of the Blue
Ridge Mountain chain, this 701-acre park is primarily
known for two features: its waterfall and its trail.
Sliding and falling in stages, Amicalola Falls, a 729-
foot drop, is the highest in Georgia. The 8.1-mile
approach to the southern terminus of the Appalachian Trail at Springer Mountain begins behind the
visitor center. One and one-half miles of the approach
trail are within park boundaries. (See Chapter 4 for
the complete description of the Southern Terminus
Approach.)

Plentiful wildflowers and the usual high volume of
"Amicalola" — the Cherokee's tumbling waters —
make April and May ideal times to enjoy the park.

**TRAIL TO BASE OF AMICALOLA FALLS (0.3
mile one way to the observation deck). Easy to
Moderate.**

The signed trail begins on a flagstone walkway to the
outside of the lower road's turnaround loop. Following red blazes, the rocky path heads uphill to an
observation deck, where you can view the lower portion of Amicalola Falls. Rock stairs and handrails help
you negotiate the few short, steep spots on the trail.

The path, winding through a cove hardwood forest
along cascading Little Amicalola Creek, is the most

scenic in the park. Several large yellow poplars tower over the trail.

WEST RIDGE LOOP TRAIL (0.8 mile for the entire loop). Easy; access from Visitor Center: Easy to Moderate.

This trail now has four access points: at the turn-around loop of the main (lower) park road, across the road and field from the visitor center, to the right of the upper park road (the one that turns to the left before the visitor center) and farther along that upper road, at the picnic tables to the right. These access points are marked with "Nature Trail" signs. The visitor center has a pamphlet that maps and describes the park's trails.

This description begins at the access point across the road and field from the visitor center. Here the yellow-blazed, 0.2-mile approach path snakes up the hillside above Little Amicalola Creek, then ties into the loop near a concrete structure. Because the loop is a flattened circle, direction of travel is not important. Bearing to the left, however, seems to be easier. Confusing side trails have been created by people who have made their own shortcuts either to or away from the loop. Park maps don't show these side trails, nor would they want to — downhill trails and those cutting across switchbacks cause erosion. When traveling to the left (clockwise), take the fork to the right at branching trails to avoid confusion.

Walked in a clockwise direction, the yellow-blazed loop arrives at a junction at 0.5 mile. The orange-blazed trail to the left — the West Ridge Spring Trail — leads 0.3 mile to the picnic tables on the upper level road. This path is one of the four access trails to the loop. Slightly more than 0.1 mile farther the West

210

Ridge Loop Trail reaches another junction. The yellow-blazed path to the left, below the set of wooden steps, is the approach from the lower road's turn-around. The main trail turns right and finishes its loop.

Virginia pine and black gum are common along much of the trail.

Directions: Amicalola Falls State Park can be reached from many different directions; the three easiest routes, however, are from Dahlonega, Dawsonville and Ellijay. Travel Georgia 52 East from Ellijay, Georgia 52 West from Dahlonega or Georgia 53 West from Dawsonville and follow signs to the park.

BLACK ROCK MOUNTAIN STATE PARK

Rabun County
Three Trails

Black Rock received its name from the dark granite cliff faces, boulders and outcroppings scattered throughout the park. On the park's narrow ridges these rock outcrops make splendid natural overlooks that provide panoramic vistas of the nearby valleys and mountains. Black Rock is large — 1,502 acres — and the elevation, highest of Georgia's state parks, is 3,460 feet at park headquarters.

With over 65 inches of rainfall per year, the park's luxuriant vegetation supports a varied wildlife population. Thick patches of evergreen rhododendron provide concealment for turkey, deer, bobcat and an occasional bear.

ADA-HI FALLS NATURE TRAIL (0.2 mile one way to the observation deck at falls). Moderate.

I wish that all trails, even those down the worst of dirt roads, were as well marked as Ada-Hi Falls. Once inside the park, turn left at the signs for the Tent and Trailer Camping Area. Across the road from the Information Cabin, next to the Concession Area, a sign denotes the trail's location, and a wooden doorway frames its entrance. During the glaring drought days of summer, this formal trailhead heightens the perception of entering, intensifies the difference between the oppressiveness of the pavement and the cool richness of the forest.

This short path immediately descends into a moist cove where ferns and wildflowers grow in lush abundance. Vasey's trillium, bloodroot and Jack-in-the-pulpit bloom here in spring; touch-me-not (spotted jewelweed), mountain mint, rattlesnake plaintain and black cohosh in summer. Continuing downhill through a diverse hardwood forest, the trail ducks into a dense arbor-like thatching of rhododendron before dropping to its end at the observation deck beside Ada-Hi Falls.

The end of the trail is as botanically rich as the beginning. The umbrella leaf, an aptly named plant infrequently found on rocky seepage slopes, grows below the left side of the deck. (See Sosebee Cove Trail, Chapter 1, for a description of this unusual plant.)

Calling Ada-Hi a falls, especially in Rabun County, is charitable to say the least. Depending upon the season and recent rainfall, Ada-Hi varies from glistening rockface to thin veneer of sliding water. Most often, this Taylor Creek headwater fall is a dripping trickle.

TENNESSEE ROCK LOOP TRAIL (2.2 miles one way for the entire loop). Moderate.

Tennessee Rock is one of the most varied and scenic state park trails. Easily walked in an hour or two, its loop traverses the botanically rich slopes and ridgecrest of Black Rock Mountain. Flame azalea, mountain laurel and numerous species of wildflowers bloom beside the path from April 15 through May.

The wide, yellow-blazed walkway begins with a short, moderate climb up wooden steps. After less than 100 yards, the trail reaches the place where its loop begins and ends. A sign states that the loop is easier to walk to the right, counterclockwise. This description follows its advice.

After turning right, the trail continues on an easy upgrade through a hardwood forest dominated by oaks. Beyond 0.2 mile the path becomes level or slightly descending as it winds along a slope that is alternately moist, then dry. The loop turns left onto an old road at 0.7 mile. This road soon enters an extensive planting of white pine where pinesaps — saprophytic wildflowers — are abundant. These unusual plants do not produce chlorophyll and obtain their nourishment, with the aid of fungi, from organic matter. Most of the pinesaps in this colony were pale yellowish-orange rather than their more common coloration of reddish-orange. They bloom during the second half of July and early August.

A short distance after the road leaves the pine forest, the treadway turns left and becomes path again at mile 1.2. Here the trail makes a moderate to strenuous climb to the ridge of Black Rock Mountain. Once on the ridge, the footpath continues slightly uphill through an open deciduous forest. Several patches of starry campions — wildflowers identified by their five fringed, white petals and four whorled leaves — bloom along this section of the loop in late July and early August.

At mile 1.7 the trail climbs wooden steps over the first mound of the granite outcrop known as Tennessee Rock. This narrow backbone crest of the mountain affords surprisingly scenic views of valleys, towns and mountains to either side. Beyond the lookoffs, the path drops to a road, then curls downhill and to the left away from the pavement. The trail's ending segment passes above a colony of Vasey's trillium. They flower from mid- to late May.

JAMES E. EDMONDS BACKCOUNTRY TRAIL (6.5 miles for the entire loop). Moderate to Strenuous.

Park officials hope to have this trail ready for back-country camping by the spring of 1988. Until then, only dayhiking is allowed.

The beginning of this path makes an easy, then moderate, descent through a hardwood forest along the lower slopes of Black Rock Mountain. At 0.7 mile the orange-blazed treadway reaches the junction where its loop begins and ends. This description takes the advice of the sign and follows the loop to the right, counterclockwise. The trail continues easily uphill on an old road. At mile 1.1, where the road turns to the right, the loop turns left onto path. After this change in direction, it drops sharply until it crosses a paved park road at mile 1.4. (There is orange paint on the road and a "Trail" sign on its other side.)

Across the pavement, the trail proceeds steadily downhill, passing through a hardwood cove before swinging parallel to Taylor Creek at mile 2.1. The loop ascends beside this lively, sliding stream before crossing it and a gravel road near Taylor Gap at mile 2.4. Here the path rises moderately by switchback for 0.5 mile to the top of Scrugg Knob. It then rides the ridge down the Knob's other side to mile 3.2, where it turns left onto an old road at Scrugg Gap. After following this nearly level walkway for 0.2 mile, the trail comes to an important junction. A sign marks the loop's turn downhill and to the left onto another old road.

The road you were on before this junction continues straight ahead to an excellent view. Its moderate, upridge climb leads to a rock slab outcropping atop Lookoff Mountain. The Little Tennessee River

Valley is below; Smokehouse Knob is across the valley. Dillard and the U.S. 441 corridor are to the right. (This blazed sidetrail to the overlook, 0.7 mile round-trip, is not included in the 6.5 mileage given for this trail.)

After its left turn at the junction, the loop descends sharply, turns right onto another old road, then continues its descent along the lower slopes of Lookoff Mountain. At mile 4.5 the path crosses the gravel road again; 100 yards farther it crosses Taylor Creek again. Here the trail begins the ascent to the end of its loop at mile 5.8. The upgrade becomes progressively steeper after the Greasy Creek crossing at mile 5.4. The final 0.7 mile back up to the parking lot is the trail's toughest climb.

Spring-blooming wildflowers are abundant along the backcountry trail. One of the wildflowers people most want to see—the pink lady's-slipper, or pink moccasin flower — is fairly common in Black Rock Mountain State Park. Look for colonies of these native, perennial orchids where the trailside forest is predominantly pine. These colonies should have individual plants in bloom from May 10 through May 25.

The pink lady's-slipper, which occurs occasionally on public land throughout the state's mountain region, has been designated as "threatened" in Georgia. The plant received this listing because of exploitation — people picking them or digging them up. Please do not harm them; to do so is extremely selfish and against the law. These plants have a symbiotic relationship with mycorrhizal fungi. If you dig them up and take them home, they will die. Fungi-independent varieties are commercially available. End of lecture. Enjoy their beauty.

Directions: Take U.S. 441 North through Clayton to Mountain City. In Mountain City, turn left onto Tal-

216

madge Trail, the paved road that leads from U.S. 441 to the park's entrance. A prominent sign marks the turn.

The two longer trails — Tennessee Rock and Edmonds Backcountry — begin along the road that leads to the cottages. Two-tenths mile beyond the fork in the main park road (camping to the left, cottages to the right), turn right into the large Day Use Play Area Parking Lot. Both trails start behind their signs at the back of the gravel lot.

CLOUDLAND CANYON STATE PARK

Dade County
Three Trails

Located in the extreme northwestern corner of the state, 2,217-acre Cloudland Canyon is, to the eyes of many, the most scenic state park in the North Georgia region. Nature has combined the best features of many parks into one: waterfalls and sparkling streams, overlooks and picturesque vistas, boulders and canyon cliffs make the park a photographer's paradise.

The canyons are shaped like a "Y" tilted 90° to the right. Situated in the narrow point of the wedge, the main overlook provides magnificent views of the gulches and their long horizontal bands of exposed sandstone. To the left, Daniel Creek has sculpted the West Canyon and its waterfalls. To the right, the East Canyon is Bear Creek's masterpiece; together the canyons merge to form the long part of the "Y" — Sitton Gulch. Far below, Sitton Gulch Creek flows 900 feet beneath the highest point on the canyon rim.

WATERFALL TRAIL (0.3 mile one way to where the stairways fork; the left fork is 0.1 mile one way to the upper falls; the right fork is 0.3 mile one way to the lower falls). Moderate to Strenuous.

Wooden walkways now lead down into the canyon to both waterfalls on Daniel Creek. Starting at the large trailhead sign, the path follows its yellow blazes behind the cabins, past a lookout, then down to the first fork. As the signs indicate, the Waterfall Trail continues to the right, the West Rim Loop Trail to the left. A short distance beyond the turn, a log bench offers a shady but slightly disconcerting "what if" rest spot beneath overhanging rock. The boardwalks split after slightly more than 0.3 mile. To the left it is 0.1 mile further to the upper falls; to the right it is 0.3 mile to the lower falls.

Near the end of the trail to the upper waterfall, huge boulders, packed one behind the other, are slowly slipping toward the opposite bank of Daniel Creek. Hemlock and rhododendron — vegetation associated with Southern Appalachian trout streams — flourish in the cool, moist soil of the canyon floor. At trail's end, Daniel Creek dives over its amphitheater wall, plunging into a dark green catch pool 50 feet below.

The walkway to the lower falls skirts a cliff face, then descends sharply to the bottom of the canyon, which has deepened to nearly 400 feet. The entrenched area at the end of the steps is one of the most beautiful spots in Georgia. Gracefully tapering hemlocks and large yellow poplars grow between streamside rocks. Spring-blooming hepaticas, also known as liverleaf, are abundant. Their distinctively patterned three-lobed leaves, supported by underground stems, make them easy to identify even when not in bloom. When they do blossom, usually in late March or early April, their flowers range from white to shades of pastel purple and blue. With the exception of the 20-foot-high, spray-catching rock that sits in its plunge pool, the lower waterfall is a double-scale replica of the one above. At trail's end, Daniel Creek again leaps over an amphitheater wall, this time plummeting to a dark green catch basin 100 feet below.

Note: The area downstream from the upper falls is potentially dangerous. Immediately downstream from the large boulders, Daniel Creek begins its shallow slide to the top of the lower falls.

WEST RIM LOOP TRAIL (4.9 miles one way for the entire loop). Easy to Moderate.

The first 1.6 miles of the West Rim Loop were formerly signposted as the Bridge Trail, which ended at a lookout on the canyon rim. That section of trail was extended into a loop and renamed.

The yellow-blazed loop starts at the trailhead sign beside the railing near the overlook parking lot. From this point the trail gently descends along the rim, past where the Waterfall Trail turns to the right, into the upper reaches of the canyon, where it crosses Daniel Creek at near water level. Across the creek the path curves to the right and climbs steadily for the first and only time. On their way up careless hikers have made their own shortcuts across the switchbacks. To avoid confusion and prevent erosion, please stay on the marked path.

The trail gains the opposite rim from where it started at 0.6 mile. From here, it closely follows the top of the chasm, often across bare rock only a step or two away from cliff's edge. Looking cross-canyon you can see, below the timbered cap of the plateau, the alternating layers of cliff face and forest that stretch the length of Sitton Gulch. Looking down into the gorge in winter, you can see the gray-boulder talus — debris from section after section of fallen cliff— wedged on the slopes below. Almost at your feet, you can see where the most recent section of cliff top has split apart and has slumped a few feet toward its eventual fall. For now, the boulders still lie there like crooked lines of puzzle pieces separated by fissurelike clefts on three and sometimes four sides.

After 1.1 miles the trail begins to curl around a hanging side canyon carved by a small, unnamed stream. This creek soon becomes the thin waterfall visible from the opposite rim. At mile 1.3 the loop portion of the trail begins and ends where it crosses the spring-fed stream. A loop, of course, can be traveled in either direction; the quicker way to the succession of railed overlooks, however, is straight ahead across the creek and back out to the main canyon.

These overlooks provide views into all three of the park's gorges. Down and to the right, Daniel and Bear Creeks have cut a double-sided cliff at the wedge point where their canyons meet. Below and to the left, Sitton Gulch Creek deepens its trough to nearly 900 feet before it flows into Lookout Valley. Cloudland looks like a region strayed eastward from across the Mississippi. Adding to this somewhere-out-west image of rock-wall chasm and talus slope, photogenic Virginia pines grow stunted and wind-twisted where nothing else can exist on the cliff-edge rock.

The loop continues to parallel the West Rim, past blazed sidetrails leading to the cabins, to a second set of lookouts at mile 2.1. These two overlooks afford vistas of Sitton Gulch as it widens toward its mouth and, in the valley beyond its entrance, the city of Trenton with its surrounding patchwork of fields and woodlots. The trail reaches its last railed overlook a half-mile farther along the canyon. A short distance from this final view of Sitton Gulch and Lookout Valley, it turns away from the cliffs and enters the forest of the plateau. At mile 2.9 the trail crosses a road, then completes its loop portion at the creek where it began.

CLOUDLAND BACKCOUNTRY TRAIL (5.4 miles for the entire loop). Moderate.

The Backcountry Trail was constructed to provide primitive camping opportunities in a remote section of the park. If you wish to backpack this trail, which makes a loop on the plateau to the east of Bear Creek Canyon and Sitton Gulch, you must stop by the park office to obtain a permit and pay $2 per night per person in your party. There are two specified camping sites along the loop portion of the trail. Park officials will give you a map and discuss regulations for these sites. You don't need a permit or money to dayhike the backcountry trail, but you do need to inform park personnel of your plans. Since you must stop at the park office anyway, I will let them give you directions to the trailhead.

The backcountry trail does not remain level for long. Most of its grades, however, are easy or moderate. You will encounter only one strenuous upgrade longer than 0.1 mile. That will be at the end of your hike, after you cross Bear Creek for the second time.

Starting at the "Primitive Camping" sign that points to the first orange blaze, the trail descends through a mixed deciduous-evergreen forest to Bear Creek at 0.7 mile. The last 0.2 mile is a steep, rocky, switchbacking downgrade. Once it reaches the creek, the trail continues beneath the undercut bluff for a few yards, then rock-hops across the stream at the guiding blaze. The backcountry trail rises from the creek until its loop begins beside a rivulet at 0.9 mile. The loop was built to be walked to the right, counterclockwise. The path continues to follow the small watercourse upstream, crossing it seven times in 0.2 mile. This rivulet, which may be dry during periods of little rain, is the last water source before the two campsites.

At mile 1.3 the treadway turns away from the streamlet and ascends for 0.2 mile to the plateau-like area above the gorges. Once on top, the loop undulates up and over a series of low hardwood ridges for the next 1.5 miles. It then descends through a cove and swings parallel to Bear Creek Canyon. Here the trail follows an old road through Virginia pine, occasionally approaching within 20 or 30 feet of the cliffs. At mile 3.9 the path curls down and away from the rim. The long, easy downslope leads to the end of the loop across the small stream.

Directions: Take U.S. 27 North through La Fayette. Approximately 4.0 miles north of La Fayette, turn left onto Georgia 136 and follow the signs to the park.

The Waterfall and West Rim Loop trails begin at the same sign near the picnic area parking lot adjacent to Campground No. 1 and cottages 1–5. The trail sign is along the railed canyon rim to the left of the parking lot and below the line of cottages.

FORT MOUNTAIN
STATE PARK

Murray County
Five Trails

Fort Mountain, situated in the Cohutta Mountains within the Chattahoochee National Forest Purchase Corridor, is the second-largest state park in Georgia's mountain region. According to rangers, the park preserves 1,913 acres, enough room for an occasional bear or two.

The name Fort Mountain stems from the intriguing ancient rock wall of piled stones which stretches snakelike for 885 feet. The park's name implies one of the explanations for the wall's existence — fortification. But there are other fascinating theories for this mysterious structure. Read the park signs by the wall and decide for yourself.

BIG ROCK NATURE TRAIL (0.5 mile for the entire loop). Easy to Moderate.

To reach the trailhead, travel approximately 0.5 mile into the park from its entrance, then turn left at the sign for camping, swimming and picnicking. Continue approximately 1.3 miles on this road before turning left into a small parking area across the road from the trail's large sign. This parking area is past the dam.

The Big Rock Nature Trail traverses an area that is both botanically rich and scenic. The pathside forest includes upland trees — Virginia pine, chestnut oak, sassafras — as well as moisture-requiring species such

224

as sweet birch, witch hazel and rhododendron. Although its "Big Rock" name is singular, there are thousands of rocks along the loop, both large and small. This jumbled boulder field provides pockets of shade and moisture for several species of ferns. The small ones that grow on the boulders are rock cap ferns.

The orange-blazed trail quickly descends to a small unnamed stream. This stream is not only unnamed, but it is also unmapped on the U.S.G.S. Crandall Quadrangle. After slightly less than 0.2 mile, the Gahuti Backcountry Trail crosses the stream and joins the Big Rock Nature Trail. The two trails share the same rocky treadway for the next 0.2 mile.

At the loop's midpoint, a cliff-edge outcrop provides a view of the forested valleys and mountains of the Cohuttas. Beyond a wooden walkway, the path curls to the right, then parallels Goldmine Branch as it gently cascades down a run of stair-step ledges. A bluff line across the branch delineates the stream's beginning gorge. The remainder of the loop leads back uphill, past another flight of stair-step ledges. The path ends at the road downhill from the trailhead.

GOLDMINE BRANCH TRAIL (0.7 mile one way). Easy.

To reach the beginning of this trail, you must first walk slightly more than 0.3 mile on the Lake Trail. (See the next trail for further directions.) Goldmine Branch is the white-blazed trail that leads to the right, up and away from the lake. Its initial segment follows an old roadbed through a predominantly hardwood forest. Flowering dogwoods are abundant.

225

At 0.2 mile the treadway turns left where a red-blazed access path ends. Two-tenths of a mile farther, the trail swings alongside Goldmine Branch — shallow, four to five feet wide and beautiful like all mountain streams. The footpath follows the rhododendron-lined brook upstream, crossing it four times. After the fourth crossing, the trail turns away from the branch and climbs 130 yards to its end at the orange-blazed Gahuti Backcountry Trail. This short upgrade is moderate.

There is a colony of grass-of-Parnassus 100 yards past the trail's first crossing of Goldmine Branch. Contrary to its name, grass-of-Parnassus is a wildflower — a beautiful one with a circle of orange-tipped stamens above fluted, creamy white petals that are veined light green. The flowering plant has a conspicuous simplicity: one stem, one leaf, one blossom. The 1- to 1½-inch flower, which blooms in late September and early October, is held 4 to 8 inches above the rounded leaf.

LAKE TRAIL (1.2 miles for the entire loop). Easy.

To reach the Lake Trail, travel approximately 0.5 mile into the park from its entrance, then turn left at the sign for camping, swimming and picnicking. Continue approximately 1.3 miles on this road before turning left into a large parking area next to a pavilion. This parking area is past the dam and immediately past the large sign for Big Rock Nature Trail, which is on the right side of the road. The blue-blazed trail is down at the lakeshore.

This description follows the treadway to the right, counterclockwise, around the long, narrow lake. Its initial segment closely parallels the forested and relatively undisturbed southern shoreline. After slightly more than 0.3 mile, the white-blazed Goldmine Branch Trail begins to the right.

By 0.5 mile the trail has looped to Fort Mountain Lake's northern shoreline and its activity areas: camping, swimming, paddle boats, miniature golf. The beach is fenced. To continue the trail, walk around the beach house, then work your way back to the lake. The trail finishes its loop by crossing the grassy dam on a pathway below the road.

OLD FORT TRAILS (1.8 miles of interconnected trails). Easy to Moderate.

To reach the Old Fort Trails, travel the park's entrance road straight ahead to its turnaround loop. The trail system begins on the right side of the loop; signs, plaques and a wooden entryway mark its location. Trail maps are available at the park office along the way.

A color-coded system of interconnected pathways leads walkers to the rocky mountaintop's three main attractions: the fascinating stone wall, the lookout tower and the overlook deck. All the trails are marked with signs. The yellow-blazed trail, which begins and ends at the pavement, makes a 1.3-mile loop around the top of Fort Mountain. This loop leads to the attractions and the other three trails. After less than 100 yards, the yellow-blazed walkway splits into its loop. This description follows the loop to the right, counterclockwise.

As you start your walk through this scenic area, you quickly realize that this is a good place to find building materials for a rock wall. Thousands of rocks, from small stones to room-sized boulders, lay strewn about the mountaintop. After walking slightly less than 0.5 mile along the loop, you will reach the spot where the red-blazed trail leads to the left. The red trail, a little more than 0.2 mile long, cuts across the wide top third of the yellow loop, meeting it again at the tower. Leading away from the red trail's midpoint, the blue-blazed trail heads toward the rock wall. Two-tenths of a mile long, the blue trail parallels the serpentine line of piled rocks before it ends at the yellow loop.

Continuing from its junction with the red trail, the loop skirts the mountain's craggy northern rim, then curls back toward its beginning. At 0.8 mile the side-trail to the right sharply descends 140 yards to an observation platform, which provides splendid vistas of valleys and the mountains beyond. The yellow loop turns left, away from the sidetrail's entrance, and continues 80 yards to the tower. Sitting on the mountain's highpoint (2,840 ft.), the rock and wood tower has been rebuilt since the late 1970's. You are welcome to walk to its top, which is slightly below treeline. An imaginative worker placed a heart-shaped stone in one of its sides.

The loop turns to the right at the tower and begins its easy downgrade back to the parking lot. At mile 1.0 the blue trail leads to the left, toward the lichen-splotched rocks and sunken pits of the wall.

GAHUTI BACKCOUNTRY TRAIL (8.2 miles for the entire loop). Moderate to Strenuous.

Gahuti Backcountry was constructed to provide primitive camping opportunities in remote areas of the park. If you want to backpack this trail, you must stop by the park office to obtain a permit and pay $2 per night per person in your party. Three designated campsites are spaced along the loop. Park officials will give you a map and discuss regulations for these sites.

You don't need a permit or money to dayhike the backcountry trail.

To reach the Gahuti trailhead, travel straight ahead past the information office toward the "Old Fort" section of the park. A short distance before the road curls into its turnaround loop, turn right at the sign for Cool Spring Overlook. The trail starts behind its prominent sign in the gravel parking lot.

Gahuti Backcountry's loop often skirts the isolated border the park shares with the Chattahoochee National Forest. Away from the busy activity areas, the trail winds along the ravines, spur ridges and slopes of Fort and Cohutta Mountains. It follows the contours of this terrain up and down numerous grades, most easy or moderate. There are a few long, steep descents and a few short, very sharp climbs. But there are no steady, strenuous ascents.

The first 2.6-mile section of the loop follows a tortuous, undulating route. Pay close attention to the frequent orange blazes. If you stop seeing them, you have probably walked past a turn.

The path roller-coasters down through a mixed pine-hardwood forest to a Mill Creek tributary at mile 1.4. Here it turns left and parallels the branch before crossing Mill Creek below where the streams flow together. The loop continues beside Mill Creek, crossing it again at mile 1.8. After turning away from the stream, the treadway proceeds up and over spur ridges and in and out of ravines until it reaches the park's entrance road at mile 2.6. The trail crosses the pavement at a sharp angle to the left, then climbs a short distance to an old road on top of a ridge.

The wide walkway of the road descends gradually through a maturing forest. After a full mile of this easy hiking, the trail ascends moderately for 0.2 mile. Eighty-five yards before reaching a paved road, the loop turns left off the road onto path. At mile 4.2 it crosses another paved park road. Once across, the trail quickly settles into a pattern of alternating ups and downs similar to its beginning. On this side of the loop, however, the grades are generally longer and more strenuous. Following a long, often steep descent, the footpath crosses an unnamed stream and turns left onto the Big Rock Nature Trail at mile 5.5. Gahuti Backcountry shares the treadway with the nature trail through this scenic area for 0.2 mile, then turns left and crosses Goldmine Branch.

The footpath climbs away from the branch along a line of bluffs. It then rises to near the top of a ridge before dropping back down to the slopes of Fort Mountain. Here the treadway, which was cut into the mountainside, continues nearly level as it half-circles around ravines. At mile 7.2 it crosses the beginning spring flow of Rock Creek. Beyond this rivulet, which may be dry in summer, the trail ascends moderately through a dense stand of Virginia pine. This long upgrade ends where Gahuti Backcountry crosses the park road above the turn to Cool Spring Overlook.

The loop's final 0.3 mile dips to an old road, then rises back up to a view of the Cohutta Mountains to the northeast. This crumpled mass of sharp ridges is my favorite view in Georgia. Up high across the valley, the Cohutta Wilderness preserves the pure wildness of an unbroken mountain forest. The tallest peak in sight, Big Frog at 4,200 feet, straddles the northern boundary of the wilderness, across the state line in Tennessee.

Directions: Fort Mountain State Park is located 7.0 miles east of Chatsworth on Georgia 52. From Atlanta, take I-75 North to U.S. 411 North, then continue on U.S. 411 to Chatsworth.

RED TOP MOUNTAIN
STATE PARK

Bartow County
Two Trails

This park preserves 1,427 acres of a peninsula that juts nearly 2 miles into Allatoona Reservoir. The Homestead Loop, which was originally constructed as a horse-riding trail, is now restricted to foot travel only.

Most conspicuous of the park's wildlife, the white-tail deer prospers within the park's protective boundaries. Walking the longer loop trail one November morning, I saw 14 deer. They were often in groups of three — a doe and her two fawns.

SWEETGUM NATURE TRAIL (0.6 mile for the entire loop). Easy.

This orange-blazed footpath dips from its beginning sign to another at slightly more than 0.1 mile. Along the way, sapling pines have reclaimed the opening created by a tornado in the late 1970's. The second sign marks the beginning of the yellow-blazed Homestead Loop and the loop portion of the nature trail. The nature walk, which is blazed to be followed to the right, counterclockwise, gradually descends to the first observation deck above an unnamed rivulet. The path parallels this tiny stream and its miniature flood plain to the beech tree below the second deck, then curves to the left and rises to its end.

Two species of pine and five species of oak dominate the dry slopes traversed by the nature trail. The

231

larger of the pines, the loblolly, occurs much more commonly in the upper Piedmont than in the higher mountains to the north. In general, as you travel northward from foothills to mountains, you stop seeing the loblolly where you start seeing the white pine. One of the oaks, the post oak, is also much more common in the hilly upper Piedmont than in the mountains. The post oak's leaf has a cross-like appearance.

HOMESTEAD LOOP (5.8 miles for the entire loop). Moderate.

The Homestead Loop undulates through an area of hills and stream-carved ravines in the northeastern quarter of the park. Most of its grades are easy; the others are moderate. There are no long, strenuous climbs.

This trail features a diverse upper Piedmont forest. Eight species of oaks and two pines — loblolly and shortleaf — are numerically predominant. Other common trees include pignut and mockernut hickories, red maple, yellow poplar, sweetgum and beech. The effect of moisture, or the lack of it, on the distribution of plant communities is especially noticeable along the loop.

The first 0.1 mile of the orange-blazed Sweetgum Nature Trail serves as an access path to the beginning of the Homestead Loop. (This access is included in the 5.8 mileage figure.) Leading to the left from the second set of signs, the yellow-blazed trail is predominantly level or downhill until it crosses a bridge over the first stream. At 0.5 mile a sign marks the beginning of the loop. This description follows the arrow to the right, counterclockwise.

Much of the loop's first half roughly follows the Allatoona shoreline. At 0.9 mile the trail leads into a timber cut where a stand of beetle-infested pines has been removed. Park officials plan to reroute the trail around the cut. The treadway comes to a sign that marks a blue-blazed path at mile 1.6. This path is the first of several early-exit shortcuts across the loop. After winding in and out of a series of ravines that open toward shoreline, the trail rises higher above the lake near the end of the peninsula. Here the loop curls back toward its beginning.

The last half of the trail returns through a predominantly hardwood forest along the center of the peninsula, not far from the park's highest ridge — Red Top Mountain. This side of the loop has longer, somewhat more strenuous grades. At mile 4.6 the trail crosses a dirt road, then parallels the main park road before turning toward the end of its loop.

Directions: Travel I-75 North toward Cartersville, then take the Red Top Mountain Road Exit and follow signs to the park. This road leads directly into the park. Seven-tenths mile beyond Red Top's entrance sign, turn left into the trading post's large parking lot. The trailhead signs are in the back of the lot near the tennis courts.

UNICOI
STATE PARK

White County
Two Trails

Adjacent to the Chattahoochee National Forest's
Anna Ruby Falls Scenic Area, Unicoi State Park, formerly an outdoor recreation experiment station,
embraces 1,023 acres of forest, field and lake. Perhaps
better known to many for its restaurant, conference
lodge and barrel-shaped cottages, Unicoi also has hiking trails that allow visitors to savor the park's wildlife
and wildflowers apart from the crowds. Smith Creek
Trail stretches from the scenic area to the park. This
trail is described in Chapter 1. A trail system map is
available at the information center.

**UNICOI LAKE TRAIL (2.4 miles for the entire
loop). Easy.**

The yellow-blazed trail begins through the two posts
at the far end of the picnic area behind the park's
information cabin. This A-frame cabin is to the left of
Georgia 356, after the left turn to Anna Ruby Falls
and before the dam. The trail's official ending point is
the back end of the restaurant parking lot. For the
purpose of this guide, however, I chose to end the
Unicoi Lake Trail where it begins, at the information
center. Thus the 2.4 mileage figure represents the
total distance of a complete loop — around the lake,
across the dam and back to the information cabin.
  The wide pathway closely follows the western
shoreline of Lake Unicoi through a mixed deciduous-

evergreen forest. On this side of the 43-acre lake, the treadway is often at or near water level. The loop meanders near or through many of the park's activity areas. At the first such area the path crosses the beach, climbs onto the wooden deck, then continues to skirt the lakeshore.

The trail crosses successive bridges over an unnamed Smith Creek tributary and Smith Creek, the lake's source, at 0.8 mile. Across the second bridge, the path turns right and follows Smith Creek downstream through a picnic area shaded by tall white pine. Look for trout where the stream first slackens.

The loop turns away from the lake for the first time at mile 1.3. Near the trading post, where it approaches a paved road, the trail turns right onto a graveled treadway. After it passes in front of the trading post and crosses another bridge, the path turns 90° to the right onto an old road. The remainder of the loop follows this wide walkway beneath a row of cottages set back from the lake. The Unicoi Lake Trail reaches the junction of two paved roads — Georgia 356 and the road that leads to the park's campgrounds — at mile 2.0. The official ending segment of the trail crosses the camping approach road, crosses Georgia 356, and then continues a short distance to the restaurant parking lot.

BOTTOMS LOOP TRAIL (2.1 miles for the entire loop). Easy to Moderate.

To reach the Bottoms Loop Trail, travel Georgia 356 across the dam from the A-frame information center, then turn right onto the paved road that leads to the park's conference lodge and restaurant. Continue through the gap in the buildings. Just before you turn left to park, look straight ahead. The archway through the gray fence in the loading/unloading area is the trailhead.

The yellow-blazed trail drops steadily through pines until it crosses a paved park road at 0.2 mile. On the other side of the pavement, the trail continues on a gravel road that quickly leads to the loop's beginning across a wooden bridge. Here the path angles to the left (following the directional arrow) and enters a forest with a canopy of pine and an understory of mountain laurel. After paralleling a small, unnamed stream through hardwoods, the loop comes to an early-exit junction at 0.7 mile. The shortcut back to the restaurant is straight ahead. The trail turns 90° to the left and crosses the stream.

For the next 0.8 mile the treadway winds through an area of small streams, rhododendron thickets and low ridges. The path twice crosses bridges over Smith Creek at mile 1.5. After a short walk through lush flood-plain vegetation, the trail enters a large field that provides good views of mountains to the north. In addition to vistas and sunshine, this field offers a chance to see wildflowers that don't grow in the heavily shaded forest. One such flower is the blue-eyed grass. This member of the Iris family has grass-like stems and small blue or violet-blue blossoms with yellow centers. Large clumps of these flowers bloom in early June.

The loop continues across the field to the gravel road where it began.

Directions: Take Georgia 75 North through Helen to the nearby Robertstown Community. At Robertstown Community, turn right onto Georgia 356 and follow the sign to the park.

VICTORIA BRYANT
STATE PARK

Franklin County
Two Trails

Encompassing 382 acres of hilly upper Piedmont, just
20 miles south of the Appalachians, Victoria Bryant
possesses a flora that reflects its location in a zone of
transition between physiographic provinces. This
intermingling of plant species from both provinces —
the Blue Ridge and the Piedmont — has two obvious
results: diversity and unusual plant associations, such
as dog-hobble growing beneath river birch, not found
much farther north or south.

VICTORIA PATH NATURE TRAIL (0.5 mile for the entire loop). Easy.

Victoria Path Nature Trail has been changed. While
its length and starting point have remained the same,
the pathway has been rerouted so that its loop turns
in the opposite direction. Now, instead of turning to
the left and crossing the road twice, the trail turns to
the right and crosses Rice Creek twice. When I
walked Victoria Path for the second time, it no longer
had the numbered posts and corresponding pamphlets that had identified and described many of the
trailside plants. Park officials, however, intend to
install numbered posts soon. They have already
printed an excellent new pamphlet.

The initial section of the loop angles downward to
an observation deck above Rice Creek, a shoaling
tributary of the Broad River. From the overlook, the

237

trail closely follows the creek downstream to a road. Here the path, which is guided by arrowed markers, turns right onto the road, crosses the bridge over the creek, then heads back upstream. With 0.1 mile remaining, the loop reaches the road above the vehicular ford across Rice Creek. The trail crosses the creek on a footbridge farther upstream.

Victoria Path Nature Trail features an unusually diverse forest. There are at least 25 tree species, 7 of them oaks, in the small area traversed by the loop. Three of the trees — water oak, post oak and river birch — are not found along most of the trails included in this guide.

Trailing arbutus, galax, wild ginger, dog-hobble, mountain laurel and sweet shrub are also found along this nature trail.

VICTORIA BRYANT PERIMETER TRAIL (1.3 miles one way to its end). Easy to Moderate.

The Perimeter Trail is a pleasant woodland path that winds through a variety of habitats. Its trailside forest, with species such as sweetgum, persimmon, loblolly pine, post oak and southern red oak, is typical of the upper Piedmont. Near the watercourses, however, the smaller plants are often a mixture of mountain and Piedmont.

The wide yellow-blazed trail starts out on an easy upgrade through a predominantly pine forest. After it turns away from the fenced park boundary at 0.2 mile, the path makes a moderate, 100-yard climb to a low ridge, where it turns to the right onto an old road. The trail follows this road as it gently undulates through a pine-oak forest. Loblolly saplings are reclaiming several areas that were open a few years ago.

The path swings alongside Rice Creek at 0.7 mile. Lousewort and rattlesnake plantain — wildflowers most often found in the mountains — are common in the creek's flood plain. After paralleling the stream for 0.1 mile, the trail turns left and crosses the creek. Look for this blazed turn where the stream becomes plainly visible through a gap in the vegetation.

The remainder of the trail traverses an area of low hills timbered with hardwoods. Most often, the path angles up or down a slope, staying below the ridgetop and above the hollows and their small streams. The Perimeter Trail ends at unpaved Hickman Road. Look for bracken ferns along its edge. Their characteristic three branches and long, tapering tips make them easy to identify.

Directions: Travel northward on Georgia 327 from Franklin Springs and follow the signs to the park. The city of Franklin Springs is located 4.0 miles west of Royston on U.S. 29.

Once inside the park, proceed straight ahead past the park office and swimming pool (uphill and to the left of the road), turn right at the "Nature Trail" sign, then turn right again at the downhill stop sign. Beyond the stop sign, ford the creek, turn right and park where the road ends at the picnic area lot. The nature trail starts next to its large sign.

The Perimeter Trail starts on the same road as the Victoria Bryant Nature Path. After you ford Rice Creek, turn left and drive until you see the grass hill of a dam to the right of the road. There is a gravel pulloff next to a picnic table just before the dam. The Perimeter Trail begins at the far side of the fishpond dam (there are two fishponds in the park). Park officials hope to have a trailhead sign posted soon.

VOGEL
STATE PARK

Union County
Three Trails

Vogel's size (238 acres) is not nearly as important as its location. Federally owned national forest land offering a wide range of additional recreational opportunities surrounds the park. The Appalachian Trail, Blood Mountain and several National Forest Scenic Areas and National Forest Recreation Areas are nearby. Vogel has three trails of its own — all of them loop trails and all of them beginning and ending at the same place within the park. The two longer trails, Bear Hair Gap and Coosa Backcountry, traverse National Forest land for much of their lengths.

BYRON REECE NATURE TRAIL (0.4 mile for the entire loop). Easy.

Follow the green-blazed access trail 0.1 mile from the first trail sign, past a wooden overlook, to the second sign. All the park's trails begin and end here. Continue straight ahead on the white-blazed trail and follow the loop around to the right. Along the way a sign points to an overlook above a cove.

Byron Reece Nature Trail features a diverse forest. Along this short trail an observant walker can identify over 20 tree species. The richness of the Southern Appalachian forest is unequaled over most of the world's temperate zone. The most diverse Southern Appalachian forest, that in Great Smoky Mountains National Park, has more tree species than all of

Europe. More types of trees grow within Vogel's 238 acres than within Yellowstone National Park's 2.2 million acres. This diversity deserves appreciation and protection.

BEAR HAIR GAP TRAIL (3.6 miles for the entire loop). Moderate.

To reach Bear Hair Gap, as well as Vogel's other two trails, walk the green-blazed access path that begins at the steps and trailhead sign to the right of the road that leads to the camping area. The access path travels 0.1 mile to another sign, which marks the beginning of all trails in the park. Both Coosa Backcountry (yellow blaze) and Bear Hair Gap (orange blaze) turn left at the sign and follow Burnett Branch. The trails soon cross the branch and arrive at the third sign next to a road. Here — at 0.3 mile — the loops of both trails begin and end.

The Bear Hair Gap Trail was blazed so that it could be followed in either direction. If you want to follow the signs, turn right onto the road and hike the loop in a counterclockwise direction. If you wish to walk in the opposite direction, continue on the blazed path straight across the road. To the right, counterclockwise, is the easier way to walk the trail. Traveled in that direction it is uphill for 1.4 miles, then predominantly level or downhill the rest of the way. Hiked clockwise, the trail has several steep ascents between miles 1.0 and 2.0.

Although Bear Hair Gap Trail alternates between road and path, there is no need for a turn-by-turn description. The trail is well blazed, well signed and easily followed. If a road doesn't have orange blazes, you probably missed a turn onto path. As always, a double blaze means watch out for a sudden turn.

At mile 1.3 (hiked counterclockwise) the loop comes to a sign that points to a green-blazed trail to the left. This sidepath, which forms a loop after slightly less than 0.2 mile, climbs gradually to an overlook. Its round-trip distance is 0.5 mile.

The first time I hiked this trail, I found this "Overlook" sign and followed its sidepath. I didn't find an overlook on my first walk through, so I doubled back and searched the outside edge of the path's loop again. I still didn't find anything that could be considered an overlook. The sign was still there the second time I hiked this trail, so I tried once again. And found an obvious overlook — a big, beautiful, unobstructed view of Vogel's Lake Trahlyta and high mountain ridges in the distance. Between the times I had walked this trail, workmen had made the overlook: they had removed the trees from a narrow corridor down the uppermost slope of the mountain.

Bear Hair Gap is an excellent trail for beginning hikers of all ages. It is short enough to be walked leisurely in a morning or afternoon, yet long and difficult enough, especially hiked clockwise, to be challenging. All trails are nature trails, this one especially so. Bear Hair Gap encompasses as great a variety of habitats — dry ridges, moist hillsides, moister coves, damp streamsides — as its 3.6-mile length will allow.

Near the end of the loop, hiked counterclockwise, there are several large stumps and bleached gray boles lying on the forest floor. These are slow-rotting monuments, grave markers for the magnificent stands of mature American chestnuts that once dominated many areas of North Georgia. Before the blight, they grew best and reached their largest dimensions — often 15 to over 20 feet in circumference — in sheltered coves throughout the Southern Appalachians. Today, chestnut saplings still survive along the trail; occasionally they grow large enough to bear a few of their cocklebur-like seeds before dying.

The largest Fraser magnolia that grows along the trails described in this book stands a few feet to the right of this trail. Look for the tree's large whorled leaves and light gray bark at 0.8 mile on the trail walked counterclockwise.

COOSA BACKCOUNTRY TRAIL (12.4 miles for the entire yellow-blazed trail). Strenuous.

Coosa Backcountry is a challenging dayhike for experienced walkers. But beginning hikers, especially hikers unaccustomed to the roller-coaster elevation changes of the mountains, should follow the advice of the rangers at Vogel State Park, who strongly recommend this trail as a backpacking trip, not as a dayhike. A further recommendation: Beginning backpackers who have not developed the strength to lug packs up long, steep grades should not attempt this trail. Both backpackers and dayhikers need a permit, available at park headquarters, to walk the Coosa Backcountry.

Like the shorter Bear Hair Gap Trail, Coosa Backcountry is a loop that is blazed so it can be walked in either direction. And because it is a loop, the trail gains and loses exactly the same amount of elevation — 3,480 feet up, 3,480 feet down — hiked in either direction. Thus the location and steepness of the ascents and descents become the most important consideration when choosing your direction of travel. Following the loop in a counterclockwise direction gives you a chance to warm up and make a few easy miles before the long climb to Coosa Bald begins. Following the loop in a clockwise direction, however, forces you to climb 1,820 feet to near the top of

Slaughter Mountain, drop 860 feet to Wolfpen Gap, then climb another 880 feet to near the top of Coosa Bald — all within the first 5.4 miles.

The loop section of Coosa Backcountry begins at the third trail sign. (See Bear Hair Gap Trail in this section for a description of the first 0.3 mile of Coosa Backcountry.) If you want to walk the trail in the easier, designated direction, turn right onto the road. If you want to go against the flow — do it the hard way — continue straight across the road. This description follows the easier, counterclockwise route.

Less than 0.1 mile after turning onto the road, the yellow-blazed trail bears to the right at the sign, quickly crosses Burnett Branch, then follows an easy to moderate upgrade through a largely deciduous forest to Highway 180 (Burnett Gap) at 0.9 mile. Coosa Backcountry, which began at an elevation of 2,320 feet, crosses Highway 180 at 2,800 feet and continues, after a turn to the right, on an old logging road. The loop descends gradually along slopes dominated by yellow poplar to 2,020 feet, where it crosses West Fork Wolf Creek on a log bridge at mile 3.2. The level area to the right of the ford is one of two designated campsites marked on the trail maps available at park headquarters.

After crossing the creek, the trail turns right onto F.S. 107, Wolf Creek Road, then turns immediately back left into the woods. Here, as it ascends a slope recovering from a timber cut, the path climbs steeply for the first time. Once atop the hill at mile 3.5, the trail winds along the steep slopes of Ben Knob, gradually gaining elevation to where it crosses Locust Stake Gap (2,540 ft.) at mile 4.5. From Locust Stake Gap the trail continues level or upward to another gap, Calf Stomp (3,100 ft.), at mile 5.8. The steady and often strenuous 1,060-foot climb to near the top of Coosa Bald (4,160 ft.) begins here across Calf

Stomp Road. Along the way, a rivulet to the right and below the trail is the last source of water on the way to Coosa Bald (mile 6.9) and beyond.

After the loop crosses a nearly level section of Coosa Bald's broad crown, it ties into the blue-blazed Duncan Ridge National Recreation Trail at an old road. If you want to finish the walk to the mountain's highest point (4,271 ft.), turn right onto the road and follow Duncan Ridge Trail for 0.2 mile. The "Coosa" bench mark embedded in a knot of protruding rock pinpoints the exact spot.

Coosa Backcountry turns left onto the old road and joins Duncan Ridge. Together they descend sharply, first by rocky road, then by rocky, switchbacking path. At mile 7.4 the trail turns left onto Duncan Ridge Road (F.S. 39), follows it for 30 yards, then returns to the woods on the left side of the road. Here the treadway ascends a moderate, 0.3-mile grade to the top of Wildcat Knob (another designated camping area) before continuing its rugged descent to Wolfpen Gap (3,260 ft.) at mile 8.3.

At Wolfpen Gap the trail crosses Highway 180 onto a dirt road, then immediately turns left onto the yellow-blazed path. The loop's next 0.9 mile rises to the upper slopes (approximately 4,140 ft.) of Slaughter Mountain. The first 0.5 mile of this climb is the trail's steepest grade. After 0.7 mile of easy walking on the moist mountainside, Coosa Backcountry turns 90° to the left and begins its 1,820-foot descent to Vogel State Park. This turn is marked by a sign and double yellow blaze at mile 9.9. (Duncan Ridge continues straight ahead to Slaughter Gap.) The trail's final segment switchbacks through an area of lush ferns, small streams and big boulders. At mile 11.0 the path turns to the right and finishes its loop on a treadway shared with Bear Hair Gap Trail.

Coosa Backcountry traverses areas — moist, rocky slopes, hardwood coves, the Coosa Bald mountaintop — that are botanically rich. The section of the loop from Calf Stomp Gap across Coosa Bald is a wild garden. The U.S. Forest Service has designated Coosa Bald Cove as a Botanical Natural Area. This 244-acre tract preserves and protects the cove's unique plant communities. A short segment of the backcountry trail wanders through the southeastern corner of the botanical area.

North Georgia's most beautiful spring-blossoming wildflowers can be found along the Coosa Backcountry Trail. The showy orchis is fairly common, and it usually blooms from early to mid-May.

Directions: To reach Vogel State Park, travel U.S. 19 North from Dahlonega or U.S. 129 North from Cleveland toward Blairsville and follow signs to the park's entrance, which is on the left side of U.S. 19-129 North.

Once inside the park, turn left immediately beyond the information center and continue over the speed breaks toward the camping area. Just before the road forks, look for a set of stone steps and the Nature Trail sign to the right. The green-blazed access trail leads 0.1 mile to where all of Vogel's trails begin and end.

7

MISCELLANEOUS TRAILS

CARTERS LAKE
TRAILS

Gilmer and Murray Counties
Three Trails

Constructed and managed by the U.S. Army Corps of
Engineers, Carters Lake is located in the Blue Ridge
Mountains southwest of Ellijay. The Corps has developed public use areas for camping, picnicking, hiking
and water-related activities at six sites around the
3,220-acre lake.

All the public use areas have trails; however, much
of their mileage serves as short sightseeing trails from
the main roads to the lakeshore or as circulation
between campsites, comfort stations and picnic tables.
Three of the public use areas — Damsite, Reregulation Dam and Ridgeway — have longer, designated
trails guided by signs or arrowed posts.

BIG ACORN NATURE WALK–BURNT OAK
NATURE WALK, Damsite Public Use Area (0.5 mile
for the entire loop). Easy.

These two trails form a loop that begins and ends at
the Carters Lake Visitor Center. The first half of the
loop is the Big Acorn Nature Walk, which starts
through the backdoors of the visitor center. A sign
marks the exact entrance point. The wide, wood-
chip-cushioned path traverses a mixed pine-hardwood forest near the top of a dry slope above the lake.
Along the way, signposts identify and describe many
of the tree and shrub species growing beside the trail.
Several signposts provide additional information con-

cerning their former uses. The bark of the chestnut oak, for instance, was used by settlers to tan leather and treat burns. Black gum twigs were used by Indians and settlers as toothbrushes.

At the halfway point, the nature walk reaches a concrete overlook of Carters Lake. The loop continues directly across the road from the overlook, at the sign for Burnt Oak Nature Walk. The second half of the loop dips, then rises back up to the road across from the visitor center. This trail does not have signposts.

Directions: From the Georgia 52-U.S. 411 junction in Chatsworth, travel U.S. 411 South for slightly more than 13.0 miles, then turn left onto Georgia 136 East. Continue approximately 2.5 miles on Georgia 136 before turning left at the sign for Carters Lake Dam. Proceed straight ahead for approximately 2.3 miles (take the right fork where the road divides) to the parking area next to the Visitor Center.

HIDDEN POND TRAIL, Reregulation Dam Public Use Area (0.6 mile for the entire loop). Easy.

Hidden Pond's large sign and wide graveled entrance leave no doubt where it begins and ends. And its posts with directional arrows leave no doubt where it goes. After less than 40 yards, the loop turns to the right and crosses a bridge over an unnamed tributary of the nearby Coosawattee River, then slants up and over a low, forested hill. At 0.2 mile the trail crosses a long boardwalk bridge over the marshy end of a beaver pond. This shallow pond is old — the dead snags have almost all fallen — and may soon be abandoned for a site with more food. At the end of the bridge, the graveled walkway to the right leads 160 yards to an overlook. The wooden deck affords a good view of the beaver pond, large by mountain standards.

The belted kingfisher, often sounding its loud ratchet-rattle call on the wing, is commonly seen along the pond's edge. In addition to its distinctive call, the belted kingfisher's blue-gray back and breast-band, bushy crest, large dagger-like bill and 13-inch length make it one of the easiest birds to identify. The female's rusty belly band makes her more brightly colored than the male, a rare exception among birds.

After doubling back to the bridge, the remainder of the loop follows the creek back to the trailhead. This final section of trail also closely parallels the reregulation dam.

Directions: From the Georgia 52-U.S. 411 junction in Chatsworth, travel U.S. 411 South for slightly more than 13.0 miles, then turn left onto Georgia 136 East. Continue 0.4 mile on Georgia 136 before turning left onto the first paved road beyond the railroad tracks. After driving 0.7 mile on this road, turn right into the public use area at the "Downstream Fishing Area" sign. Proceed 0.2 mile to the parking area on the right side of the road next to the large trailhead sign.

TUMBLING WATERS NATURE TRAIL, Ridgeway Public Use Area (1.2 miles for the total two-way distance). Easy to Moderate.

The 1.2 mileage figure represents the complete round-trip distance — back and forth on both side-trails, then back to the beginning of the trail.

The pamphlets and numbered posts that once made Tumbling Waters an excellent nature trail are gone, victims of frequent and long-standing vandalism. The Corps of Engineers does not plan to replace them.

Tumbling Waters Nature Trail has numerous rises and dips, but none are long or difficult. Guided by posts with arrows and instructions, the first segment of this scenic walk winds through a mixed evergreen-deciduous forest on a hillside above Carters Lake. At 0.4 mile the trail forks near the bridge spanning Tails Creek. If you follow the posted instructions, you will take the right fork first. It leads 120 yards to an overlook perched above the creek. Here, below the deck, a long shoaling run over ledges culminates in a 15-foot high cascading slide.

After backtracking from the overlook, the trail continues across the footbridge high above Tails Creek. Once across, it again follows arrows as it angles to the right before quickly turning 90° to the right. Tumbling Waters soon reaches another posted fork. A second observation deck, this one near bank level upstream from the cascade, is straight ahead. This platform provides a close view of the creek's ledges, which come to rounded downstream points, forming an overlapping feather pattern of rock.

The trail continues down the wooden steps for a second look at the cascade and its pool. This section of the trail forms a short loop; it follows the creek downstream nearly to the bridge before bending back uphill to the right. From here, the footpath backtracks to the trailhead.

Directions: Ridgeway Public Use Area is located off U.S. 76 between Chatsworth and Ellijay. From the U.S. 411-Georgia 52 junction in Chatsworth, travel approximately 5.3 miles on U.S. 411 South before turning left onto U.S. 76-Georgia 282 East. Stay on this highway (it turns several times) for slightly more than 11.0 miles, then turn right onto the dirt road at the "Ridgeway" sign. From the Ellijay square, travel U.S. 76-Georgia 282 West approximately 8.5 miles, then turn left at the sign. U.S. 76 turns right 1 mile south of the Ellijay square.

Proceed slightly more than 3.0 miles (bearing left at the fork) on the Ridgeway approach road to the large Carters Lake sign and entrance gate. The rough dirt road becomes paved after 2.0 miles. Immediately past the gate, turn right and continue to the parking area above the boat ramp. The trailhead, framed and signed, is on the right-hand edge of the parking area.

CROCKFORD-PIGEON MOUNTAIN WILDLIFE MANAGEMENT AREA

Walker County
Two Trails

Located in the Ridge and Valley Province of Northwest Georgia, this 18,793-acre wildlife management area was named, in part, for its mountain, which was named for the now extinct passenger pigeon. Although you won't see the pigeon, chances are good that you will see one of the mountain's larger animals: deer, coyote, bobcat, turkey, gray and red fox.

Two special places, Rocktown and the Pocket, are now preserved as natural areas. Rocktown protects approximately 200 acres, the Pocket approximately 800 acres. Hikers and backpackers are welcome any time of the year except during management area hunts.

POCKET TRAIL (6.2 miles for the entire loop). Moderate to Strenuous.

Pocket Trail can be walked in either direction. But no matter which way you go, you must climb to the plateau-like top of Pigeon Mountain. Walked in a counterclockwise direction — as it is designed to be walked and is described in the following narrative — the trail makes the ascent in 2.4 miles. Walked in a clockwise direction, the trail climbs from the edge of a field to ridgetop in 1.2 miles. Several of the grades along this ascent rank among the steepest in North Georgia.

Starting in "The Pocket" at an elevation of approximately 1,040 feet, the trail immediately crosses spring-fed Pocket Branch, then begins its winding climb above the valley. The loop passes through a diverse hardwood forest along the way. Sugar maple, eastern redbud, pawpaw, black locust, white oak, flowering dogwood and red mulberry are common on the lower slopes of Pigeon Mountain. Like the sassafras, leaves of the red mulberry can have three different shapes — three-lobed, two-lobed or, most often, entire (not lobed at all) — on the same tree or even the same branch. The entire leaves are large and broadly oval with long pointed tips and toothed margins. Red mulberries are rarely seen beside most trails in North Georgia.

Although the initial section of the loop ascends to ridgetop, it takes its time getting there, rarely holding a moderate or strenuous upgrade for long before switching to easier grades, including a few downhills. At mile 2.4, where it reaches the broad top of the mountain, the trail takes the road to the left at the fork. After this turn, which is marked with sign and blaze, the trail remains nearly level for 0.2 mile, then continues gently uphill to the "High Point" sign at mile 3.2. High Point is Pigeon Mountain's highest spot — elevation 2,330 feet.

The forest on Pigeon Mountain's crest, in contrast with the one on its moist slopes, is often open, sunny and dominated by short, low-branching chestnut oaks. The other common trees — red maple, sourwood, black gum, Virginia pine and several species of oak and hickory — are typical of ridgeline forests across North Georgia.

The trail remains atop Pigeon Mountain for 2.3 miles, most of that length closely paralleling its rim — a perimeter of bluff-like rock outcrops that ring the steep outside edges of the mountain's crest. Before

High Point, a rugged jumble of large, eroded boulders provides a panoptic view to the left. The rural valley of fields and low, forested ridges is McLemore Cove; the long, high ridge across the cove is Lookout Mountain. Beyond High Point, the rim becomes a well-defined line of jagged, flat-topped cliffs, jutting over sheer drops of 50 to 75 feet.

From High Point, where a clearing is slowly returning to forest, the trail turns right and follows an old road away from the rim. Soon beside the rim again, the loop continues level or gently downhill to a vehicle-blocking gate at mile 4.2. Turn left at the gate onto a management area road, and follow it for 0.5 mile before turning left at the "North Pocket" sign. Look for this turn onto path where the easy upgrade of the road becomes noticeably sharper.

The loop quickly works its way down the mountainside for the next mile. With numerous steep downslope pitches, this often rocky section of trail is rough going, especially when muddy. At mile 5.9 the loop reaches an open field that affords views of the surrounding ridges. It travels straight across the field, to the left of the few trees out in the middle, then continues on the gravel road between the spring and small pond. The loop ends where it began, straight ahead beyond the gate.

Except for Pocket Branch, there is no water along this trail. All roads that are not permanently closed are open to vehicles only during management area hunts.

Directions: From the city of La Fayette, travel approximately 8.1 miles on Georgia 193 North to its junction with Georgia 341 at Davis Crossroads. At this intersection, where Georgia 341 heads to the right, turn left onto paved Hog Jowl Road. Continue approximately 2.7 miles on Hog Jowl Road to the top of a hill past Mt. Herman Baptist Church, then turn left onto paved Pocket Road. Proceed approximately 1.6 miles (after 0.5 mile it turns to gravel) on this road to the clearing before the gate. The trail begins to the right of the road, next to the stream which it crosses, approximately 90 yards back from the gate. If there isn't a trailhead sign, look for the initial blue blaze and orange "Foot Travel Only" sign.

Georgia 193 begins at its junction with U.S. 27 in La Fayette. If you are driving north on U.S. 27, the turn, additionally marked with a sign for Davis Crossroads, is to your left.

ROCKTOWN TRAIL (1.1 miles one way to the trail sign in Rocktown). Easy.

This easily walked, white-blazed trail immediately crosses a headwater branch of Allen Creek, then slants uphill to the old road it follows for the rest of its length. The trail continues on nearly level grades through a predominantly hardwood forest dominated by oaks. At 0.4 mile the road turns right, then quickly back left at successive forks. Two-tenths of a mile farther, the trail reaches the first group of boulders, a small-scale version of what is to come, on the outskirts of Rocktown.

As you walk toward its center, Rocktown's boulders become progressively larger and more fascinating. Before long the old road winds through rock formations 20 to 35 feet high, occasionally passing beside upward-jutting overhangs. At mile 1.1 the white-blazed trail comes to its end at a sign in the heart of Rocktown, where the tallest of these strangely eroded boulders has grown to 70 feet. Another trail ends at the sign in Rocktown. This one is unblazed and starts at Rape Gap.

Rocktown, which ranges from 1,740 to 1,800 feet in elevation, is a maze of oddly shaped, sandstone-conglomerate boulders scattered throughout a plateau-like area atop Pigeon Mountain. Portions of these boulders are often striated, pitted, pocked or honeycombed. Many are eroding faster on their sides than their tops, leaving overhanging caps with no support. The weathering patterns and the unusual profiles they produce — mushroom, parapet, fish fin, upside-down bowling pin — remind me of sections of several national parks in southern Utah. So do the narrow passageways between broken boulders.

The only way to see the boulders of Rocktown, which cover approximately 140 acres, is to leave the trail and wander from jumble to jumble. But after you have finished exploring, you may find yourself spatially disoriented, turned around a bit, worse yet — lost. To prevent this, you may want to carry a compass.

If you intend to walk through the tight passageways and scramble among the rocks, I recommend that you do so in cold weather — when you don't have to worry about wasps and snakes.

See Rocktown.

Directions: From the city of La Fayette, travel approximately 2.8 miles on Georgia 193 North, then turn left onto paved Chamberlain Road. Proceed approximately 3.5 miles on this road before turning right onto a wide gravel road at a large Crockford-Pigeon Mountain Wildlife Management Area sign. Continue on this gravel road for approximately 4.8 miles as it ascends to the top of Pigeon Mountain, then turn left onto an unmarked one-lane dirt road. This road is approximately 0.2 mile beyond the upper end of a large wildlife opening to the left, and before another wildlife opening to the right.

The Rocktown approach road is narrow and rough, but most conventional vehicles can negotiate it — if driven carefully. After 0.7 mile the road ends at a turnaround area, where the white-blazed trail begins behind its sign.

Georgia 193 begins at its junction with U.S. 27 in La Fayette. If you are driving north on U.S. 27, the turn, additionally marked with a sign for Davis Crossroads, is to the left.

TIPS FOR BEGINNING HIKERS

The following information and suggestions represent only a few of the topics discussed by books about hiking and backpacking. I highly recommend that inexperienced hikers read several of these books — the more recent the better.

Perhaps the best suggestion that this book, or any book for that matter, could give beginning walkers is the advice to start with the shorter and less strenuous trails first, then gradually progress to the longer, more difficult ones. Starting with a trail that is beyond your level of fitness and experience makes for an unpleasant introduction to hiking, especially if each step is on blistered feet.

Footcare

Blisters are frequently the beginning hiker's most persistent problem. To help prevent this discomfort, wear two pairs of socks — a heavy outer pair and a lighter inner pair. Wool is generally considered to be the best material; however, wool-nylon and wool-acrylic blends are also quite good.

Although it is sometimes impossible to do so, try to keep your feet dry. Carry extra socks and use foot powder to absorb some of the dampness. If excess moisture makes your feet uncomfortable, you may want to use a pair of very thin "dry-wick" socks; they draw perspiration through to the heavier socks, thereby keeping your skin drier.

Break in new hiking shoes gradually. Never wear stiff, unbroken boots on a long hike, and until your boots become flexible, tape sterile gauze pads or place moleskin on the spots that are likely to blister. Even after you think your boots are broken in, continue to take gauze pads or moleskin so that you can prevent blisters should you feel painful chafing. Insert thin pads in your hiking boots for extra cushioning and added protection against blisters on the bottoms of your feet. If your arches hurt after a few miles of walking, try arch supports, available at most drug stores.

Hiking Pants

Many beginning hikers wear pants, especially jeans, that are too tight for comfortable walking. Fighting a steep uphill grade and tight-fitting jeans at the same time has made many first-time hikers wish they had stayed at home. Even on relatively easy trails, tight jeans needlessly shorten your stride, slow your pace and increase your fatigue.

Practicality, not style or fashion, should be the primary consideration when choosing hiking pants. Ideal pants for summer hiking should be loose-fitting, fast-drying and light in weight and color. Lightweight khaki work pants are excellent.

Shorts are suitable for hiking wide trails such as the Appalachian, but on the narrower, more primitive trails, where vegetation (such as blackberry briers) occasionally crowds the path, shorts do not provide adequate protection.

Hiking Sticks

Hiking sticks are useful in a number of situations, especially on the longer, more primitive trails. A hiking stick will help you maintain your balance when you traverse rough terrain or ford slippery-bottomed rivers and creeks. On strenuous ascents you can use the stick to allow your arms to do some of the work, and conversely, on steep downgrades you can use a stick to brace your descent, which becomes more difficult with the additional weight of a pack. While hiking the Appalachian Trail in Georgia, I saw two backpackers take bad spills: both were carrying heavy packs, and both were descending steep, muddy slopes without the aid of a hiking stick.

Some of North Georgia's trails pass through small areas that have been recently logged. The vegetation in these cuts, responding to full sunlight, quickly crowds the trail. Blackberry briers are especially troublesome. A hiking stick will help you clear the path and avoid scratches and torn clothing.

A hiking stick can also be used to knock down spider webs that stretch across the path, usually about face high. These webs often become a nuisance on many of the narrow, infrequently used trails during late summer and early fall.

Items to Take

In addition to the obvious items you should take on a long dayhike, you may want to include the following:

compass
matches (in a waterproof case)
whistle
extra food (high energy)
small flashlight
raincoat
heavyweight shirt
maps (topographical if possible)
first-aid kit (including snakebite kit, sterile gauze pads and adhesive tape or moleskin for the prevention or treatment of blisters).

To sound a distress signal, blow a whistle three times, ten seconds apart; wait one minute and start again.

Pace

Beginning hikers often make a twofold misjudgment: they overestimate the distance they can comfortably travel in a day, and they underestimate the difficulty of the trail. The authors of many hiking books state that three miles an hour or even four miles an hour for experienced hikers is an easily attainable pace on level or nearly level trail. However, because of the mountainous terrain, most hikers walk the longer trails in North Georgia at a much slower pace. Anticipate an average of only one to two miles an hour on trails with a difficulty rating of Moderate to Strenuous or Strenuous.

When planning a hike, allow yourself plenty of time to stop and enjoy the wildflowers, waterfalls and scenic views along the way.

SAFETY TIPS

Cold Weather Hiking
and Hypothermia*

Many hikers consider winter, with its solitude and snow and unobstructed views, the best time of the year to hike. For the unprepared and inexperienced, however, winter hiking can be as dangerous as it is beautiful.

Do not underestimate the severity of the weather conditions you will be likely to encounter. Especially at the higher elevations, be prepared for temperatures near or below zero and unexpectedly fierce winds on the unprotected ridges. Even in mid-March, when temperatures in the 50s are predicted for areas south of the mountains, you may have to contend with freezing temperatures and snow at the higher elevations.

All cold-weather hikers should be aware of hypothermia, its symptoms and its treatment.

What Is It? Hypothermia is a lowering of body temperature. A drop of only 5° is very serious. Few people whose body temperature drops more than 10° survive. Hypothermia can occur in air temperatures as high as 41°F (5°C).

How Does It Happen? Wetness and exhaustion are contributing factors. Many people have died of hypothermia because they thought they could keep warm by moving and not stopping to take the necessary precautions, such as adding a sweater or putting on rain gear. Wet clothes can lead to heat loss and increase your chances of hypothermia. Remember,

---

*Hypothermia information courtesy United States Forest Service.

wool retains its insulating qualities when it is wet; cotton does not.

What Are the Symptoms? The first symptom is shivering. Continued shivering means continued seriousness. Shivering may be followed by slurred speech, impaired judgment, weakness, loss of coordination. The final symptom is unconsciousness.

What Can You Do? Get the victim into warm clothes. Make him rest. Give him hot drinks and food. If the condition is very serious, put the victim in a sleeping bag with another person. Make a fire. Put up a tent or make a shelter for the victim. As soon as he is able, get him to a hospital for further treatment. Do not continue your trip after one of your party has had hypothermia.

Drinking Water

After the water they have taken runs out, many hikers drink from the small spring-fed streams along the trails of North Georgia without experiencing any ill effects. There are, however, no guarantees that the water is pure.

If you wish to purify your drinking water, you can use water purification tablets, available at most canoe and backpacking shops. If you don't want to use the tablets, chlorine bleach (Clorox) will also work quite well. Use only one or two drops of chlorine bleach to a quart of water. When using water purification tablets or chlorine bleach, shake your canteen several times and wait 15 to 20 minutes before drinking the water.

Another way to purify water is to boil it. Although time-consuming and most impractical, boiling is the most effective method of water purification. There is now a solution to the drinking water problem: a water purification device commonly known as a filter. A good filter will protect you against giardia. Before buying one, make sure it will remove all particles larger than 0.4 micron.

If you are unable to purify your water, remember:

- Drink only flowing water.

- The higher and smaller the stream, the better. Water flowing from springs is usually pure. Low-lying streams and rivers, or their tributaries, may have passed through agricultural lands.

- Where a stream crosses a trail, especially a heavily used trail such as the Appalachian, where people wash their dishes in the stream, the water downstream from the trail may be contaminated. Fill your canteen upstream from the trail.

Poisonous Snakes

While it is likely that you will see nonpoisonous snakes along the trails of North Georgia, your chances of seeing a poisonous snake are slim. Your chances of being bitten by a poisonous snake are even slimmer — in fact, they are remote. I have now hiked well over 1,500 miles in North Georgia and have had only one close call with a venomous snake — a copperhead. I have yet to see my first rattlesnake while hiking on a trail in this region. There are records of hikers who have walked the entire Appalachian Trail, from Georgia to Maine, without seeing a single poisonous snake.

Only 12 deaths from snakebite have been reported in any recent year for the entire United States. More people are killed each year by lightning and by wasp and bee stings than by venomous snakes. By far the most dangerous part of your hiking trip is spent traveling to and from the trail.

The copperhead, Carolina pigmy rattlesnake and timber rattlesnake are indigenous to the North Georgia region. The sluggish, unaggressive copperhead is more common than either of the two more aggressive rattlesnake species. Forest Service work crews usually find and kill two to three times more copperheads than rattlesnakes.

The eastern cottonmouth (water moccasin) does not exist in the Blue Ridge Mountains or in the counties included in the North Georgia region directly south of the Blue Ridge Mountains. There are, however, occasional reports of eastern cottonmouths along the larger streams in the Ridge and Valley and Cumberland Plateau Physiographic Provinces of northwestern Georgia. Most of the large snakes seen in and along the streams of the North Georgia mountains are nonpoisonous banded water snakes, not cottonmouths as is often assumed.

Snakebite Prevention: Wear long trousers and thick hiking boots. The higher the boots, the more protection you will have against snakebite.

Look before you sit or lie down.

Be careful where you put your hands. Do not reach blindly into holes or crevices. (Do not stick your face close to look, either.)

When crossing logs, step up on the log and take a long stride or look on the other side of the log before crossing.

If you are camping, wear shoes and use a flashlight when walking around the campsite after dark.

Where vegetation crowds the trail, slow your pace and use a stick to rustle the vegetation ahead of you.

Be extra observant when walking through or near rocky areas and clear cuts. These two areas provide prime habitat for poisonous snakes.

Learn the color patterns and other distinctive characteristics of the poisonous snakes.

First Aid for Snakebite: There is considerable difference of opinion, even among doctors, concerning the proper first aid and treatment of venomous snakebite. Because of this controversy, the National Academy of Sciences, National Research Council (NAS/NRC) has recently made recommendations updating the treatment of venomous snakebite. The American Red Cross has prepared a "First Aid for Snakebite" pamphlet based upon these recommendations.

Your snakebite or first-aid kit should contain a constricting band, antiseptic, lance and suction device. Wipe or rinse the bite with antiseptic before making the incisions.

Have someone call ahead so that a doctor can be ready to give immediate attention.

If possible, have more than one person accompany the victim so that if resuscitation is necessary it can be accomplished without stopping the transporting vehicle.

Safety Reminders

The biggest threat to safety is poor judgment. Because hikers are often hours away from the nearest hospital, the potential consequences of poor judgment become doubly serious.

It is not advisable to hike alone; however, if you choose to do so, always leave a written trip plan with family or friends detailing where you are going and when you expect to return.

Do not rock climb without proper safety equipment.

Exercise extreme caution around waterfalls. Do not climb the waterfall or its sides, and do not cross the

267

stream directly above the waterfall. Supervise children closely at all times.

Carry a first-aid kit.

If someone in your party is thinking of or attempting something foolish, take the responsibility of trying to stop that person. Saying "I knew he or she shouldn't have tried it" won't do much good after an accident has occurred.

WILDLIFE, BIRDWATCHING AND ENVIRONMENTAL PROTECTION

Wildlife

Seeing a wild animal, even if only for an instant, always adds to the enjoyment and excitement of a hike in the mountains. However, because of its relatively harsh environment, the Blue Ridge Mountain region has the lowest density of wildlife per square mile in Georgia. Spotting wildlife along the trails of North Georgia is a bonus and cannot be expected or guaranteed on any given day or trail. One day you may walk 15 miles and see only a turtle; the next day you may see two or three deer and several grouse within the first 3 miles. There is only one guarantee: the more miles you hike, the more wildlife you are likely to see.

If you hike many of the trails described in this guide, the chances are good that you will see, sooner or later, ruffed grouse, gray squirrel, striped skunk, whitetail deer, turkey, woodchuck, and European wild boar. However, your chances of catching a glimpse of some of North Georgia's wary predators — black bear and bobcat, red and gray fox, raccoon and mink — while walking along a trail are slim. Because these animals are generally most active at night, the best time of day to see them is in the morning shortly after sunrise or in the evening shortly before sunset.

Although the results will not be spectacular, there are a few common-sense things you can do to improve your chances of seeing wildlife along the trail:
 • Walk alone or in small groups.
 • Leave your dog at home.

• Choose trails that traverse a variety of habitats — ridges, coves, clearings, streams and so on.

• Learn more about the habits and habitats of the animals you are trying to see.

• Begin your hike early in the morning (the earlier the better). Although you can see wildlife throughout the day, you will see more wildlife, especially deer, in the early morning and near dusk than at other times. For dayhikers, early morning is the best and most practical time to see wildlife.

Birds and Birdwatching

If you look and listen carefully, have patience and would rather count birds instead of miles, you will discover that many of the trails described in this guide offer good birdwatching opportunities. Almost 200 species of birds have been identified in the Chattahoochee National Forest and its adjacent lakes and fields. Nearly 70 percent of all summer breeding birds in Georgia — approximately 110 species — nest in the mountain region. The permanent or breeding range of at least 20 species, including the raven, rose-breasted grosbeak, winter wren and seven kinds of warblers, extends southward only as far as North Georgia. Some of these birds can be seen nowhere else in Georgia; others can be seen south of the mountains only during migration.

Small, highly migratory perching birds — wrens, warblers, vireos, flycatchers, thrushes, tanagers, grosbeaks and others — are particularly common in the forests of the mountain region. The best time of year to see and identify the greatest number of these small perching birds is during their spring migration. Each year from late April through early May millions of these birds pass through the Blue Ridge Mountains of North Georgia. Their migration normally reaches its numerical peak from May 1 through May 15. It is during this time that the hiker has the greatest opportunity to identify the many birds which are neither summer nor winter residents to the North Georgia region.

Although some are rare and not likely to be seen, approximately 35 species of warblers, summer residents plus those heading for nesting grounds farther north, flit through the mountains during this period. Male warblers wear their distinctive, brightly colored breeding plumage in spring and summer. During the fall migration, immature warblers wearing dull plumages usually outnumber the adults, and most adults are less gaudily colored than in spring.

Timber cuts and wildlife openings, north-slope cove forests near streams, and moist evergreen and hardwood forests from 2,000 to 4,000 feet are especially productive birding areas. Because of their length, habitat variety and wide range of elevation, the Appalachian and Bartram trails offer excellent opportunities to see many species of birds. Bird-watching is also good on the trails in and around the Cohutta Wilderness.

Environmental Protection

Environmental deterioration along any given trail is almost invariably proportionate to the number of people using the trail. The inherent problems of overuse — erosion, sanitation, litter, trampled and cut vegetation — are difficult to prevent. Portions of the popular Appalachian Trail and the Beech Bottom area in the Cohutta Wilderness are sad examples of what overuse can do to the trailside environment.

Fortunately, most of the trails described in this guide do not yet suffer from overuse. But as our population continues to expand and as hiking and backpacking become increasingly popular, it will become more and more important for individual hikers to minimize their impact upon the trail corridor. Be aware that your detrimental actions, multiplied by the similar actions of others, can seriously mar the trail. Follow these environmental protection guidelines:

• Do not litter. Do not bury trash; wild animals often dig up cans and other items that smell of food. If you have a campfire, burn only the trash your fire will completely consume. Do not leave litter on top of your extinguished fire thinking the next person using the campsite will burn it. Pack out all unburned trash!

Today's hiker should go one step beyond the "Take only pictures — leave only footprints" and "Pack it in . . . Pack it out" slogans. Whenever possible, carry out trailside litter. Leave the trail cleaner than you found it.

• Do not operate motorized vehicles in wilderness areas or other areas where they are unlawful.

• Do not wash yourself, your clothes or your cooking utensils in streams.

• Bury human waste at least 100 feet from streams and campsites.

• Do not deface rocks or trees. Carving or spray painting initials on rocks or trees, no matter how artistically done, most certainly falls under the category of defacement.

• Do not injure, kill, pick or dig up vegetation.

• Use only wood that is "dead and down" for fires. Standing dead trees are more valuable for wildlife habitat than for firewood. Use a backpack stove to lessen the need for firewood.

• Completely extinguish all fires.

• Leave a clean campsite, preferably so no one else can tell you were there. If you are planning to have a fire, make an effort to use an existing fire ring. If you make your own, scatter the rocks and ashes and do the best you can to repair the burned area. Fire rings and scorched spots every few hundred yards greatly detract from the beauty of a trail. If possible, camp 50 or more feet away from trails and streams.

• Do not take shortcuts or cut across switchbacks. The winding loops — switchbacks — that help hikers ascend or descend steep slopes have been carefully planned to reduce erosion and leg strain. When you cut across the switchbacks, you needlessly trample vegetation and cause erosion.

• Keep hiking parties small.

The practice of picking and eating wild plants comes in direct conflict with environmental guidelines. If you must do this, please use some discretion. The effects of this practice have become particularly noticeable along the Appalachian Trail in recent years. Remember, most people want to see the ferns and other plants, not eat them.

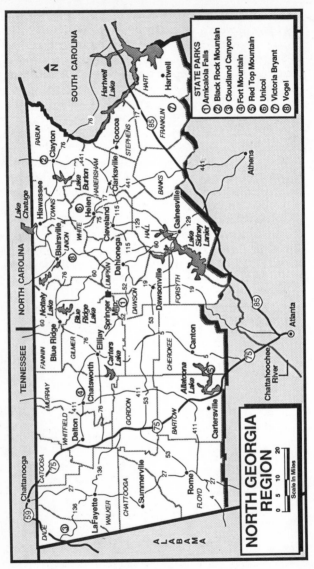

NORTH GEORGIA
REGION

STATE PARKS
1 Amicalola Falls
2 Black Rock Mountain
3 Cloudland Canyon
4 Fort Mountain
5 Red Top Mountain
6 Unicoi
7 Victoria Bryant
8 Vogel

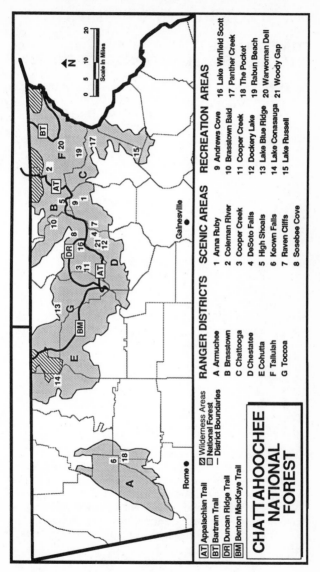

CHATTAHOOCHEE NATIONAL FOREST

AT Appalachian Trail
BT Bartram Trail
DR Duncan Ridge Trail
BM Benton MacKaye Trail

Wilderness Areas
National Forest
— District Boundaries

RANGER DISTRICTS

A Armuchee
B Brasstown
C Chattooga
D Chestatee
E Cohutta
F Tallulah
G Toccoa

SCENIC AREAS

1 Anna Ruby
2 Coleman River
3 Cooper Creek
4 DeSoto Falls
5 High Shoals
6 Keown Falls
7 Raven Cliffs
8 Sosebee Cove

RECREATION AREAS

9 Andrews Cove
10 Brasstown Bald
11 Cooper Creek
12 Dockery Lake
13 Lake Blue Ridge
14 Lake Conasauga
15 Lake Russell
16 Lake Winfield Scott
17 Panther Creek
18 The Pocket
19 Rabun Beach
20 Warwoman Dell
21 Woody Gap

N

Scale in Miles
0 5 10 20

Rome ●

Gainesville ●

275

ADDRESSES AND MAPS

CHAPTERS 1-5:
CHATTAHOOCHEE NATIONAL FOREST

USDA Forest Service
Supervisor's Office
508 Oak Street
Gainesville, GA 30501
(404) 536-0541

Armuchee Ranger
   District
P.O. Box 465
706 Foster Boulevard
La Fayette, GA 30728
(404) 638-1085

Brasstown Ranger
   District
Hwy. 19/129 South
Box 216
Blairsville, GA 30512
(404) 745-6928

Chattooga Ranger
   District
P.O. Box 196
Burton Road
Clarkesville, GA 30523
(404) 754-6221

Chestatee Ranger District
P.O. Box 2080
200 West Main
Bank of Dahlonega Bldg.
Dahlonega, GA 30533
(404) 864-6173

Cohutta Ranger District
401 Old Ellijay Road
Chatsworth, GA 30705
(404) 695-6736

Tallulah Ranger District
P.O. Box 438
Chechero/Savannah St.
Clayton, GA 30525
(404) 782-3320

Toccoa Ranger District
E. Main St., Box 1839
Blue Ridge, GA 30513
(404) 632-3031

Maps of the Chattahoochee National Forest
The Chattahoochee National Forest Administrative Map, a detailed map of the forest excluding the Armuchee Ranger District, is available from the Forest Supervisor's Office in Gainesville. The Chattahoochee National Forest Recreation Map, a general map of the entire forest featuring scenic and recreation areas, is also available from the Forest Supervisor's Office.

Chapters 1 and 2: National Forest Scenic Area Trails, National Forest Recreation Area Trails

A free directory of scenic and recreation areas is available from the Forest Supervisor's Office.

Only a few of the recreation areas having campgrounds are open year-round. Write the Forest Supervisor's Office or appropriate ranger district for opening and closing dates.

Anna Ruby Falls, Coleman River, Cooper Creek, DeSoto Falls and Keown Falls Scenic Areas are located adjoining or adjacent to recreation areas.

Chapter 3: Cohutta Wilderness Trails

A large waterproof trail map of the Cohutta Wilderness is available from the Cohutta Ranger District and Forest Supervisor's Office.

Chapter 4: Long Trails and Their Approaches

Appalachian Trail Information:
  Georgia Appalachian Trail Club, Inc.
  P.O. Box 654
  Atlanta, GA 30301

Guide to The Appalachian Trail in North Carolina and Georgia.

This book is available at most hiking supply stores. If you cannot find the book, write:
  The Appalachian Trail Conference
  P.O. Box 807
  Harpers Ferry, WV 25425-0807

A detailed map of the Appalachian Trail in Georgia is available from the Forest Supervisor's Office.

The Tallulah Ranger District has a brochure on the Bartram Trail.

Chattooga River Trail Information:
A detailed map of the Chattooga Wild and Scenic River is available from the Forest Supervisor's Office.

Chapter 6: State Park Trails

Parks and Historic Sites
Floyd Towers East
Suite 1352
205 Butler St., S.E.
Atlanta, GA 30334

Amicalola Falls State Park
Star Route, Box 213
Dawsonville, GA 30534
(404) 265-2885

Black Rock Mountain State
    Park
Mountain City, GA 30562
(404) 746-2141

Cloudland Canyon State
    Park
Route 2
Rising Fawn, GA 30738
(404) 657-4050

Fort Mountain State Park
Route 7, Box 1-K
Chatsworth, GA 30705
(404) 695-2621

Red Top Mountain State
    Park
781 Red Top Mtn. Rd., S.E.
Cartersville, GA 30120
(404) 974-5182

Unicoi State Park
P.O. Box 849
Helen, GA 30545
(404) 878-2201

Victoria Bryant State Park
Route 1, Box 257
Royston, GA 30662
(404) 245-6270

Vogel State Park
Route 1, Box 1230
Blairsville, GA 30512
(404) 745-2628

Chapter 7: Miscellaneous Trails

Carters Lake Information:
U.S. Army Corps of
    Engineers
Resource Manager
Carters Lake
P.O. Box 86
Oakman, GA 30732-9999
(404) 334-2248

Crockford-Pigeon Mtn.
    Wildlife Management
    Area Information:
Georgia Dept. of Natural
    Resources
Game and Fish, Game
    Management
Route 1, Floyd Springs
    Rd.
Armuchee, GA 30105
(404) 295-6041

278

TRAIL FACT TABLE

Chapter 1: National Forest Scenic Area Trails

Trail	Difficulty Rating	Miles One Way	Features	Nearest City	Map(s)
Anna Ruby Falls Scenic Area				Helen	
Anna Ruby Falls	1 to 2	0.4	stream, waterfalls, rock outcrops		Tray Mtn.
Smith Creek	1 to 2, SD	4.5	forest, stream		Helen, Tray Mountain
Coleman River Scenic Area				Clayton	
Coleman River	1	0.9	cascades, outstanding forest, huge boulders, Coleman R.		Hightower Bald
DeSoto Falls Scenic Area				Cleveland (S) Blairsville (N)	
DeSoto Falls	1 to 3, SD	1.8, SD	streams, waterfalls		Neels Gap

Difficulty Rating: 1 = easy
2 = moderate
3 = strenuous
SD = See Description

Miles One Way: Lp = Loop
SD = See Description

Nearest City: N = north of trailhead
S = south of trailhead
NW = northwest of trailhead
SE = southeast of trailhead

Maps: 1:24,000 topographical quadrangles

280

High Shoals Scenic Area

Trail	Difficulty Rating	Miles One Way	Features	Nearest City	Map(s)
High Shoals	2	1.2	stream, waterfalls	Helen (S) Hiawassee (N)	Tray Mtn.

Keown Falls Scenic Area

Trail	Difficulty Rating	Miles One Way	Features	Nearest City	Map(s)
Johns Mountain	1 to 2, SD	3.1 Lp	bluffs, waterfall	La Fayette	Sugar Valley
Keown Falls	1 to 2	1.7 Lp	bluffs, waterfall	La Fayette	Sugar Valley

Raven Cliffs Scenic Area

Trail	Difficulty Rating	Miles One Way	Features	Nearest City	Map(s)
Raven Cliffs	1 to 2	2.5	stream, scenic view, waterfalls, rock outcrops, cliffs	Helen	Cowrock

Sosebee Cove Scenic Area

Trail	Difficulty Rating	Miles One Way	Features	Nearest City	Map(s)
Sosebee Cove	1 to 2	0.6	outstanding forest, outstanding wildflower display	Blairsville (N) Cleveland (S)	Coosa Bald

Chapter 2: National Forest Recreation Area Trails

Trail	Difficulty Rating	Miles One Way	Features	Nearest City	Map(s)

Andrews Cove Rec. Area

Trail	Difficulty Rating	Miles One Way	Features	Nearest City	Map(s)
Andrews Cove	2 to 3	1.8	cove forest, Appalachian Tr. approach	Helen	Tray Mtn.

Brasstown Bald Visitor Info. Center

				Helen (S) Hiawassee (N) Young Harris (N) Blairsville (W)	
Arkaquah	2 to 3, SD	5.4	Georgia's highest mtn., diverse flora, wilderness		Blairsville, Hiawassee, Jacks Gap
Jack's Knob	2 to 3, SD	4.5	Georgia's highest mtn., Appalachian Tr. approach		Jacks Gap
Trail to Summit	2	0.5	Georgia's highest mtn., scenic views, visitor center		Jacks Gap
Cooper Creek Rec. Area				Dahlonega (S) Blairsville (N)	
Mill Shoals	2	2.4	forest		Mulky Gap
Yellow Mountain	2	3.6, SD	forest		Mulky Gap
Dockery Lake Rec. Area				Dahlonega	
Dockery Lake	2 to 3	3.4	Appalachian Tr. approach, small streams		Neels Gap
Lakeshore	1	0.5 Lp	Dockery Lake		Neels Gap
Dukes Creek Rec. Area				Helen	
Dukes Creek Falls	1 to 2	0.8	streams, waterfalls		Cowrock

Lake Blue Ridge Rec. Area				Blue Ridge	
Lake Blue Ridge	1	0.6 Lp	lakeshore		Blue Ridge
Lake Conasauga Rec. Area				Ellijay Chatsworth	
Grassy Mountain	2	2.0	scenic view		Crandall
Songbird	1	0.6	Songbird Management Area, beaver ponds		Crandall
Lake Russell Rec. Area				Cornelia	
Lake Russell	1	3.3, SD	Lake Russell		Lake Russell, Baldwin
Lake Winfield Scott Rec. Area				Blairsville (N) Dahlonega (S)	
Jarrard Gap	1 to 2	1.2	Appalachian Tr. approach		Neels Gap
Slaughter Creek	1 to 2	2.7	Appalachian Tr. approach, small streams		Neels Gap
Panther Creek Rec. Area				Clarkesville (S) Tallulah Falls (N)	

Trail	Difficulty Rating	Miles One Way	Features	Nearest City	Map(s)
Panther Creek	1 to 2, SD	5.5	stream, waterfalls, bluffs		Tallulah Falls, Tugaloo Lake
Pocket Rec. Area				La Fayette	
Pocket	1	2.6 Lp	small streams, springs		Sugar Valley
Rabun Beach Rec. Area				Tallulah Falls	
Rabun Beach	1 to 2	0.9	stream, waterfalls		Tiger
Fall Branch	1	0.2	stream, waterfall		Tallulah Falls, Tiger
Warwoman Dell Picnic Area				Clayton	
Warwoman Dell	1	0.4 Lp	nature trail, small waterfall		Rabun Bald

Chapter 3: Cohutta Wilderness Area Trails

Trail	Difficulty Rating	Miles One Way	Features	Nearest City	Map(s)
Conasauga River Drainage: *These trails lead to or follow the Conasauga River*					
Conasauga River	1 to 2, SD	13.1	record trees, Conasauga R., bluffs, numerous shoals	Chatsworth Ellijay	Dyer Gap, Hemp Top, Tennga

Chestnut Lead	1 to 2, SD	1.8	outstanding forest, stream	Ellijay	Dyer Gap
Panther Creek	2 to 3, SD	3.4	waterfall, stream, bluff, scenic view	Chatsworth Ellijay	Hemp Top
Tearbritches	2 to 3, SD	3.4	ridge trail	Ellijay	Crandall, Hemp Top
Hickory Creek	1 to 2	8.6	stream, Conasauga R.	Chatsworth	Hemp Top, Tennga

East Cowpen: *This trail leads indirectly to both the Jacks and Conasauga Rivers and all of their lead-in trails.*

East Cowpen	SD	7.0	isolated forest	Chatsworth Ellijay	Hemp Top

Jacks River Drainage: *These trails lead to or follow the Jacks River*

Jacks River	1 to 2, SD	16.7	Jacks R. Falls, bluffs, follows Jacks R., shoals	Blue Ridge Chatsworth	Hemp Top, Tennga
Sugar Cove	2 to 3, SD	2.2	unusual forest, stream	Ellijay	Hemp Top
Penitentiary Branch	1 to 2, SD	3.5	stream	Blue Ridge	Hemp Top
Rough Ridge	2 to 3, SD	7.0	ridge trail, stream	Ellijay	Hemp Top
Hickory Ridge	2 to 3, SD	3.5	ridge trail	Chatsworth	Hemp Top
Beech Bottom	1 to 2	4.0	stream, Jacks R. Falls	Chatsworth	Hemp Top

Trail	Difficulty Rating	Miles One Way	Features	Nearest City	Map(s)
Rice Camp	1 to 2	3.9	streams	Chatsworth	Hemp Top
Horseshoe Bend	2, SD	3.0	scenic view	Chatsworth	Hemp Top

Hemp Top: *This trail leads to Big Frog Mountain and trails in the Big Frog Wilderness.*

Hemp Top	3	2.1	highest mountain in Cohutta Wilderness	Blue Ridge	Hemp Top

Chapter 4: Long Trails and Their Approaches

Trail	Difficulty Rating	Miles One Way	Features	Nearest City	Map(s)

Note: The trails in this chapter are divided into sections. The city given for a section is nearest its starting point.

Appalachian Approach Trails

Blood Mountain Spur	1 to 2	0.7	forest	Blairsville (N) Cleveland (S)	Neels Gap
Logan Turnpike	2 to 3	1.9	stream, historic turnpike, wilderness	Cleveland	Cowrock
From Amicalola Falls State Park	3	8.1	southern terminus of the Appalachian Tr., view	Dahlonega (E) Dawsonville (SE) Ellijay (NW)	Nimblewill

Appalachian National Scenic Trail (South to North)

Section	Rating	Miles	Features	Towns	Landmarks
Springer Mountain to Woody Gap (GA 60)	2 to 3	20.8	waterfall, scenic views	Dahlonega (E) Ellijay (W)	Noontootla Suches
Woody Gap (GA 60) to Neels Gap (U.S. 19-129)	2	11.5	scenic views, Blood Mtn.	Dahlonega	Neels Gap
Neels Gap (U.S. 19-129) to Hogpen Gap (Richard B. Russell Scenic Hwy.)	2 to 3	6.8	scenic views, wilderness	Blairsville (N) Cleveland (S)	Neels Gap Cowrock
Hogpen Gap (Richard B. Russell Scenic Hwy.) to Unicoi Gap (GA 75)	2	14.0	isolated forest	Helen	Cowrock Jacks Gap Tray Mountain
Unicoi Gap (GA 75) to Dicks Creek Gap (U.S. 76)	2 to 3	16.6	scenic views, isolated forest, Tray Mtn., wilderness	Hiawassee (N) Helen (S)	Tray Mtn. Macedonia Hightower Bald
Dicks Creek Gap (U.S. 76) to Bly Gap at the Georgia-North Carolina border	2 to 3	9.0	scenic views, isolated forest, wilderness	Hiawassee (W) Clayton (E)	Hightower Bald

Bartram Approach Trails

Section	Rating	Miles	Features	Towns	Landmarks
Chattooga River	2	10.7	Chattooga R. (SD)	Clayton	Rainy Mountain

Rabun Bald	3	2.9	Georgia's second highest mountain, scenic view	Clayton	Rabun Bald

Bartram National Recreation Trail *(North to South)*

Hale Ridge Road (F.S.7) to Warwoman Road	2 to 3	17.6	Georgia's second highest mountain, views, streams, waterfalls	Clayton	Rabun Bald
Warwoman Road to Hwy. 28	2	19.2	large streams, Chattooga R., waterfall (SD)	Clayton	Rainy Mtn. Whetstone Satolah

Benton MacKaye Trail

Springer Mountain to GA 60	2	17.5	streams, waterfall, Toccoa River, scenic view	Ellijay (W) Dahlonega (E)	Noontootla Wilscot

Duncan Ridge National Recreation Trail *(Section 1—south to north, Section 2—west to east)*

Near Three Forks to GA 60	2	10.5	waterfall, isolated forest, Toccoa River	Ellijay (W) Dahlonega (E)	Noontootla Wilscot
GA 60 to Slaughter Gap	3	20.4	scenic view, isolated ridge trail, Coosa Bald	Blue Ridge (NW) Dahlonega (SE)	Wilscot Mulky Gap Coosa Bald Neels Gap

Chapter 5: More National Forest Trails

Trail	Difficulty Rating	Miles One Way	Features	Nearest City	Map(s)
Bear Creek	1	0.8	stream, huge tree	Ellijay	Dyer Gap
Broad River	1 to 2	4.1	streams, forest	Cornelia	Ayersville
Emery Creek	1 to 2	3.2	streams, waterfalls	Chatsworth	Crandall
Helton Creek Falls	1	0.1	waterfall, outstanding forest	Blairsville (N) Cleveland (S)	Coosa Bald
Holcomb Creek	2	SD	waterfalls, outstanding forest	Clayton	Rabun Bald
Horse Trough Falls	1	0.3	small waterfall	Hiawassee (N) Helen (S)	Jacks Gap
Mills Creek Falls	1 to 2	0.5	stream, waterfall	Chatsworth	Tennga
Mountaintown Creek	2	5.6	streams, cascades	Ellijay	Dyer Gap
Raven Rock	1 to 2	0.8	Chattooga R., cliff	Tallulah Falls	Rainy Mountain
Rich Mountain	2	8.8	forest, Lake Blue Ridge	Blue Ridge	Blue Ridge
Sutton Hole	1	0.3	Chattooga River	Clayton	Rainy Mountain

289

Trail	Difficulty Rating	Miles One Way	Features	Nearest City	Map(s)
Three Forks	1 to 2	1.2	cascade, streams	Clayton	Satolah

Chapter 6: State Park Trails

Trail	Difficulty Rating	Miles One Way	Features	Nearest City	Map(s)
Amicalola Falls S.P.				Dahlonega (E) Ellijay (W) Dawsonville (S)	Nimblewill, Amicalola
Trail to Base of Amicalola Falls	1 to 2	0.3	highest waterfall in GA, stream		
West Ridge Loop	1	0.8 Lp			
Black Rock Mountain S.P.				Clayton	Dillard
Ada—Hi Nature	2	0.2	diverse flora, very small waterfall		
James E. Edmonds Backcountry	2 to 3	6.5 Lp	primitive camping, view, diverse flora		
Tennessee Rock Loop	2	2.2 Lp	view, diverse flora		
Cloudland Canyon S.P.				La Fayette, Trenton	Durham
Cloudland Backcountry	2	5.4 Lp	primitive camping, bluff, canyon view		

Waterfall	2 to 3	0.7	cliffs, stream, waterfalls	
West Rim Loop	1 to 2	4.9 Lp	canyon rim, canyon views	
Fort Mountain S.P.				Chatsworth (W) Crandall Ellijay (E)
Big Rock Nature	1 to 2	0.5 Lp	view, boulder field, cascade	
Gahuti Backcountry	2 to 3	8.2 Lp	primitive camping, cascade, view	
Goldmine Branch	1	0.7	small stream	
Lake	1	1.2 Lp	lakeshore	
Old Fort	1 to 2	1.8, SD	mysterious rock wall, view, lookout tower, boulder field	
Red Top Mountain S.P.				Cartersville Allatoona Dam
Homestead Loop	2	5.8 Lp	wildlife, forest, lakeshore	
Sweetgum Nature	1	0.6 Lp	forest, wildlife	
Unicoi S.P.				Helen
Bottoms Loop	1 to 2	2.1 Lp	field, view	Helen
Unicoi Lake	1	2.4 Lp	lakeshore	
Victoria Bryant S.P.				Royston Carnesville

291

Trail	Difficulty Rating	Miles One Way	Features	Nearest City	Map(s)
Victoria Bryant Perimeter	1 to 2	1.3	forest		
Victoria Path Nature	1	0.5 Lp	posted nature trail, stream		
Vogel S.P.				Blairsville (N) Cleveland (S)	Coosa Bald
Bear Hair Gap	2	3.6 Lp	small streams, view		
Byron Reece Nature	1	0.4 Lp	diverse forest		
Coosa Backcountry	3	12.4 Lp	primitive camping, diverse flora, Coosa Bald		

Chapter 7: Miscellaneous Trails

Trail	Difficulty Rating	Miles One Way	Features	Nearest City	Map(s)
Carters Lake Damsite Pub. Use Area					
Big Acorn—Burnt Oak Nature Walk	1	0.5 Lp	scenic view, posted nature trail	Chatsworth	Oakman
Reregulation Dam Pub. Use Area					
Hidden Pond	1	0.6 Lp	beaver pond	Chatsworth	Oakman
Ridgeway Pub. Use Area					

	Difficulty Rating	Miles One Way	Features	Nearest City	Maps
Tumbling Waters	1 to 2	1.2 SD	stream, small waterfall	Chatsworth (W) Ellijay (E)	Webb
Crockford—Pigeon Mountain Wildlife Management Area					
Pocket	2 to 3	6.2 Lp	scenic views, bluffs	La Fayette	La Fayette, Cedar Grove
Rocktown	1	1.1	unique rock formations	La Fayette	Cedar Grove

Difficulty Rating:
1 = easy
2 = moderate
3 = strenuous
SD = See Description

Miles One Way:
Lp = Loop
SD = See Description

Nearest City:
N = north of trailhead
S = south of trailhead
NW = northwest of trailhead
SE = southeast of trailhead

Maps:
1:24,000 topographical quadrangles

TRAIL NOTES

TRAIL NOTES

TRAIL NOTES

TRAIL NOTES

TRAIL NOTES

TRAIL NOTES

TRAIL NOTES

TRAIL NOTES

TRAIL NOTES

TRAIL NOTES

TRAIL NOTES